2/13

H. Smith

Barrios to Burbs

Barrios to Burbs

The Making of the Mexican American Middle Class

Jody Agius Vallejo

Stanford University Press
Stanford, California

Stanford University Press
Stanford, California

Printed in the United States of America on acid-free, archival-quality paper.

Library of Congress Cataloging-in-Publication Data

Agius Vallejo, Jody, author.
   Barrios to burbs : the making of the Mexican-American middle class / Jody Agius Vallejo.
     pages cm
   Includes bibliographical references and index.
   ISBN 978-0-8047-8139-8 (cloth : alk. paper)
  1. Middle class Mexican Americans.   2. Mexican Americans—Social conditions.
3. Social mobility—United States.   I. Title.
   E184.M5A64 2012
   973'.046872—dc23   2012004369

Typeset by Westchester Book Group in 10/14 Minion

For Johnny, with love and gratitude

Contents

Tables

Acknowledgments

I FIRST WISH TO THANK JENNIFER LEE, my intellectual mentor, for the many opportunities she has provided me with and for her constant stream of insightful comments, support, and inspiration that have shaped this project. The knowledge I continue to gain from Jennifer's tutelage has proved invaluable in both my professional and personal life. Jennifer is not only a brilliant scholar, she is also an amazingly kind and generous person. The earliest manifestation of this research was produced in collaboration with her and was subsequently published in the journal, *Ethnicities*. She is thus a coauthor of the fourth chapter of this volume.

I also owe tremendous thanks to Frank Bean, Min Zhou, Susan Brown, Cynthia Feliciano, Cal Morrill, and Dave Snow, all of whom helped to greatly shape the theoretical and empirical questions examined in this book. Others who gave sage advice on various aspects of this project include Rubén Rumbaut, Lisa García Bedolla, Joy Pixley, Jen'nan Ghazal Read, Cecilia Menjívar, Wendy Roth, Jim Bachmeier, Mark Leach, and Jeanne Batalova. I also wish to extend a special thank you to Wang Feng, Judy Treas, Philip Cohen, Nancy Foner, Carolynn Bramlett, Lisa Keister, and George Wilson for their support. Others shared wisdom and tips about the publishing process, including Zulema Valdez and Jessica Vasquez. Goldie Komaie and Frances Benjamin provided invaluable research assistance.

I am very fortunate to have the support of the editorial staff at Stanford University Press, especially Kate Wahl, who has shown unwavering enthusiasm for this project and whose astute suggestions greatly improved the manuscript. I am also extremely indebted to Tomás Jiménez and one additional anonymous reviewer for their thoughtful and critical comments that strengthened this book.

This project was completed in part at the University of California–San Diego (UC San Diego), where I held a joint fellowship at the Center for Comparative Immigrant Studies (CCIS) and the Center for U.S.-Mexican Studies (US-MEX). I am indebted to Wayne Cornelius, David S. Fitzgerald, John Skrentny, Alberto Díaz-Cayeros, Ana Minvielle, Graciela Portelo, and Greg Mallinger. The manuscript was completed at the University of Southern California. I thank my colleagues for their thoughtful comments and support, particularly Tim Biblarz, Lynne Casper, Amon Emeka, Macarena Gómez-Barris, Ange-Marie Hancock, Sharon Hayes, Leland Saito, Pierrette Hondagneu-Sotelo, Roberto Suro, Jane Junn, Mike Messner, Dowell Myers, Manuel Pastor, Ed Ransford, George Sanchez, and Veronica Terriquez. Thanks are also owed to the faculty and staff at the University of Southern California's (USC) Center for the Study of Immigrant Integration (CSII), especially Rhonda Ortiz and Jackie Agnello, and The Tomás Rivera Policy Institute. I also thank the staff of USC's Department of Sociology, Lisa Rayburn-Parks, Melissa Hernandez, Amber Thomas, and Stachelle Overland, who miraculously manage the fort and who always make sure there is a vegetarian option for me to devour at our events. Thanks are also due to Terry Feiertag who gave generously of his time to discuss his role in the landmark 1978 *Silva v. Levi* court case (see Chapter 2). Finally, I am grateful to Gustavo Arellano, Leslie Berestein-Rojas, James J. Green, Héctor Tobar, and Jesse Torres, who helped bring this research into the public sphere.

I also benefited greatly when I presented this work to participants at workshops and colloquia at Harvard University, UC San Diego, UC Irvine, Cal Poly Pomona, USC, Pepperdine University, and Nanzan University in Japan. Moreover, the larger research benefited when I presented this work to nonacademics at the California Hispanic Chamber of Commerce Annual Convention and the East Los Angeles Rotary Club.

Finally, I have been very fortunate to receive numerous grants and fellowships that have supported this study. Early and continuous support came from the Department of Sociology at UC Irvine. I also thank UC Irvine's School of Social Sciences for an Early Career Fellowship, which allowed me to concentrate on collecting data during the early years of the project. I am indebted to UC Irvine's Chancellor's Club for selecting me as a recipient of the Chancellor's Fellowship for Research, Excellence and Leadership. This research was also supported by a National Science Foundation Grant, a UC Mexus Grant, the University of California Office of the President's Miguel Contreras Labor and Employment Research Fund, and the Center for Research on Latinos in a Global Society at UC Irvine. An American Publication Fellowship from the American Association of University Women helped to support the final writing and editing of the manuscript. Finally, this research received generous support from the John and Dora Haynes Foundation, where I am particularly indebted to Bill Burke.

I also wish to acknowledge the special friendships I made with the Latino professionals, entrepreneurs, and community leaders I studied, without whom this research would not be possible. They work tirelessly on behalf of the Latino community and have made invaluable contributions that promote the socioeconomic integration of Latinos. I truly hope that I do the remarkable people I studied justice and that I represent them accurately.

I am fortunate that I was able to live close to my family the entire time I worked on this project and I thank them greatly for their support. I am deeply thankful for my parents, Pam and Keith Offel and Walt and Grace Agius, whose support and encouragement have never wavered. I thank my sisters, Brenda Beasley and Jamie Agius, and my brother, Brian Behnke. I also owe my gratitude to Ray Beasley, Bailey Beasley, Jack Martin, Nicole Mayo, Kris Effertz, Kevin and Heidi Offel, and the Barkshire-Mallory-Williams family, who kept my stomach full and a smile on my face during this endeavor. I also owe thanks to the Rivera family, Yachcik family, and Melissa Grace. I am deeply grateful for the friendships of Kelly Luther, Willie LaGraffe, Mercedes Ugalde, and Goldie Komaie. I am forever indebted to the Vallejo and Moreno families, whom I have known for more than half of my life and who have adopted me into their clans. The support of Juan and Martha Vallejo, Ezra Vallejo, Wiwi Gonzalez, Diego Vallejo, Nichol and Victor Mejia, Esperanza Maria Moreno, and the late Maria Moreno and Francisco Moreno was important to this work. I am especially appreciative for the friendships of Christina Quintero, Adrian Quintero, Alex Vallejo, and Maleni Hernandez and to all my other cousins, tíos, and tías who have encouraged this endeavor and waited patiently for this book to be complete so that I could join them at family events once again.

I dedicate this book to my husband, Johnny, who possesses a genuine interest in my research and this study in particular. Johnny has devoted a prodigious amount of time and energy supporting this enterprise by attending research-related events with me, constantly discussing my research, reading my papers, and shouldering much of the domestic burden so I could focus on writing. Johnny, thank you for your steadfast support, optimism, and hilarious sense of humor and for being my emotional and social rock for the last thirteen years.

Barrios to Burbs

1 Class, Assimilation, and Mexican Americans

BRIAN REYES IS "LIVING THE DREAM" with his wife and two children in a charming middle-class neighborhood in Southern California. The exterior of Brian's sprawling, ranch-style home on Maple Circle was recently refreshed with a coat of light brown paint. Unfurled ferns and blooming begonias line the walkway and the lawn is a sea of emerald green. Brian's shiny new car is parked next to the family's minivan. Enter Brian's front door and step into a home that is tastefully decorated, with leather furniture, plush neutral carpet, a flat-screen television, and two large picture windows that look out onto an expansive back-yard. Brian and his family exhibit all of the stereotypical symbols of middle-class life: the house in the suburbs, a fancy car, white-collar jobs, vacations, and weekends spent cruising in the minivan shuttling between Little League games and swimming lessons.

By all socioeconomic indicators, Brian is a member of the American middle class; however, his childhood was nothing like *Leave It to Beaver*, the iconic midcentury television show depicting middle-class suburban life. Brian used to visit Maple Circle as a young boy every week, but not as the playmate of the middle-class children who rode their bikes up and down the cul-de-sac. Brian would accompany his mother, who was employed as a domestic by several of Maple Circle's homeowners. As he explained, "My mom cleaned houses. She used to clean up and down the street here." Brian was raised in a *colonia*, a poor agricultural workers' community in sharp contrast to the sprawling ranch homes and well-manicured lawns of Maple Circle, by uneducated parents who toiled in low-wage, low-status jobs. Today, Brian Reyes holds a college degree, works as a midlevel manager, and owns a home on the very street where he once watched his mother scrub floors and clean toilets.

Latinos are the country's largest minority group, comprising 16 percent of the population—of which the Mexican-origin population constitutes nearly two thirds. Latinos' proportion of the population is expected to double by midcentury, a demographic change that is pushing the United States toward a society where whites will no longer be a numerical majority (Passel and Cohn 2008).[1] Immigrants have traditionally represented the prospect of success in America, but many scholars, political commentators, and laypersons fear that the growing Mexican American population will never achieve the rapid upward mobility and American middle-class dream that Brian Reyes exemplifies. These fears are rooted in the marginalized context of Mexican migration to the United States. Mexican immigrants typically migrate with low levels of human capital, they live in poor and working-class communities on arrival, many are unauthorized, and they face a society that is hostile to them (Bean and Stevens 2003; Portes and Rumbaut 2001; Telles and Ortiz 2008). By adopting such labels as "illegal aliens," "government drains," and "unassimilable," the media has greatly contributed to common assumptions and widespread panic that Mexican immigrants' native-born descendants will remain poor and uneducated, becoming a permanent drain on America's coffers (Chavez 2008; Hayes-Bautista 2004; Santa Ana 2002). The majority of research on the Mexican-origin population in the United States unintentionally contributes to the idea that Mexican Americans will never assimilate into the middle class, by focusing primarily on poor and unauthorized workers and their similarly low-income children who remain in disadvantaged or working-class ethnic communities.

Brian Reyes contradicts worries, research, and pervasive stereotypes about Mexican Americans, and provides a more optimistic glimpse into the future, by demonstrating that the children of low-wage, poor, and uneducated Mexican immigrants can rise up from the barrio and achieve the American dream, yet we know little about the experiences of people like him. This is a book about middle-class Mexican Americans, a population that has been disregarded and left out of the pessimistic public, political, and scholarly debates surrounding Mexican Americans and their prospects for social mobility. The objective of this book is to examine the mobility paths, lived experiences, and incorporation outcomes of today's Mexican American middle class in order to provide a more comprehensive understanding of this population and a more promising outlook for the future.

Traditional and contemporary models of assimilation generally apply racialized or linear assimilation frameworks as group-specific models to explain immigrant incorporation and adaptation. Drawing on the experiences of African Americans, proponents of the racialization perspective assert that the Mexican-origin population faces limited prospects for successful socioeconomic incorporation into the middle class. Their concern is that the Mexican second and third generations, many of whom are visibly nonwhite and most who are the children and grandchildren of low-skilled migrants, will be viewed as racialized minorities and face the added challenge of obtaining jobs in a restructured economy that ultimately leads to downward mobility or economic stagnation over the generations (Portes, Fernández-Kelly, and Haller 2005; Portes and Rumbaut 2001; Telles and Ortiz 2008). On the opposite end of the spectrum, the traditional assimilation perspective argues that immigrants who achieve upward mobility will follow a pattern of linear incorporation into the white middle class (Gordon 1964). The burning question is, are the descendants of Mexican immigrants experiencing a pathway of downward assimilation or stagnation that is akin to the blocked economic progress of African Americans, or will the children of Mexican immigrants become upwardly mobile and incorporate into the white middle class? Of these two possible pathways, Mexican Americans who have entered the middle class are clearly not experiencing downward or stagnated mobility as the racialization framework predicts, but does this mean that middle-class Mexican Americans incorporate in a straight line into the white middle class? I show that neither the racialization or linear perspectives fully explains Mexican American incorporation because these group-based models overlook variations in incorporation pathways within immigrant national origin groups (Bean and Stevens 2003; Telles and Ortiz 2008; Jiménez 2010). In other words, incorporation might not be an either-or proposition of downward assimilation as a minority or upward assimilation into the white middle class. In this vein, scholars have recently proposed that the mainstream middle class is composed of more than just white ethnics (Alba and Nee 2003) and that there might be an additional pathway into the middle class—incorporation into a minority middle class through a minority culture of mobility (Neckerman, Carter, and Lee 1999). The central questions of this volume are, how do middle-class Mexican Americans experience life in the American middle class? Do middle-class Mexican Americans follow a linear assimilation trajectory where they disappear into the white middle class, or are they incorporating into a minority middle-class culture and community?

This book details the variations in experiences and incorporation pathways among middle-class Mexican Americans, variations that are largely structured by class background. A consistent problem in research on Mexican Americans is a lack of attention to issues of class and the ways in which class background affects different spheres of social life and mobility pathways.[2] Recent innovative studies of structurally incorporated Mexican Americans primarily focus on one dimension of assimilation, ethnic identification (Jiménez 2010; Vasquez 2011), and do not examine the experiences of those who, like Brian Reyes, have achieved rapid social mobility. This book examines middle-class Mexican Americans who hail from varying class backgrounds and generations and who are at different points on the mobility journey, from 1.5- (born in Mexico and migrated before the age of 12) and second-generation (the native-born children of immigrants) middle-class pioneers to the second generation who were raised in middle-class households to later-generation (the grandchildren and great-grandchildren of immigrants) Mexican Americans who hail from both low-income and middle-class families. To elucidate mobility experiences and incorporation pathways, this book details the mechanisms that foster upward mobility into the middle class and examines different measures of assimilation, including giving back and family obligations, racial and ethnic identity, and civic participation.

As will become clear throughout the book, the different experiences, dilemmas, and opportunities associated with growing up in poverty or middle-class privilege shape incorporation pathways and also how Mexican Americans experience American middle-class life. I demonstrate that Mexican Americans who grow up poor face challenges stemming from their social mobility, which leads to the adoption of a class-based minority identity and a minority pathway into the middle class. I also show that those who are raised in middle-class households and neighborhoods closely approximate the linear assimilation model as they are more likely to view themselves, and are viewed by others, as closer to whites. By using class background as a comparative analytical tool, this book refines assimilation theory by delving into the middle-class Mexican American category to demonstrate that there are multiple pathways into the middle class, that assimilation into the middle class does not always entail becoming white, and that assimilating as a minority is not necessarily a liability.

While the book makes important contributions by applying an underutilized theoretical paradigm, the minority culture of mobility, to an understudied group, examining the incorporation experiences of the Mexican American middle class also has considerable public-policy implications. The relatively young age structure of the Mexican American population[3] combined with the graying of the white population and the impending mass retirement of the baby boomers means that the growing second and third Mexican American generations will make up a significant proportion of the working-age population, with demographers estimating that Latinos will constitute nearly one quarter of the labor force by 2050 (Suro and Passel 2003). Minorities, especially the growing population of Mexicans Americans, are poised to fill the white-collar positions vacated by the baby boomers if they can close the education gap, making it critical to examine the mobility paths and educational and workplace experiences of those who succeed (Myers 2007; Alba 2009).

Defining the Mexican American Middle Class

Scholars disagree about the most comprehensive way to define and measure social class. Traditional indicators of class status are income, occupation, and education (Blau and Duncan 1967; Pattillo-McCoy 2000), and most studies examining the immigrant middle class define middle-class status by investigating only one or two of these economic gauges (Clark 2003; Schleef and Cavalcanti 2009). In this book, I define middle-class status as a combination of the following four attributes: a college education; a total household income over the national median, which was $50,221 in 2009; employment in a white-collar occupation or business ownership; and homeownership. Income is an important indicator because it affords access to material goods and middle-class patterns of consumption (Levy 1998). However, income alone is only one gauge of middle-class status, which is why additional measures of middle-class status are included. Income fluctuates with age, and when defining social class among minorities, occupation or the type of business one owns offers a measure of prestige and the job's promise as a career that affords a particular set of opportunities, middle-class social networks, and connections. For example, a well-paid Mexican American plumber may engage in middle-class patterns of consumption, but he is not going to run in the same social circles as a similarly paid Mexican American financial adviser (Alba 2009). Indeed, scholars have demonstrated that the combination of earning a higher-than-average income, having a college education, and being employed in a white-collar job correlates to subjective perceptions of being a member of the middle or upper class (Hout 2008). Homeownership is also an important measure of middle-class status because it is the single asset in which middle-class families hold the majority of their wealth (Conley 1999). And in America, homeownership indicates a higher social standing and has traditionally been revered as the cornerstone of middle-class life (Clark 2003; Halle 1984).

The Mexican American respondents in this book are all employed in white-collar occupations or own businesses, and all make incomes well over the national median. Nearly three quarters of the respondents hold a combination of three middle-class indicators, and a quarter hold all four. Before I discuss the characteristics of my sample in greater detail, it is important to contextualize the middle-class Mexican American populations in the United States and in Los Angeles, California, the metropolitan region where this study is based. Table 1 details the nativity and generation, educational attainment, occupational status, and economic status (measured by homeownership, poverty rate, and total household income), by race and ethnicity for the United States using data from the 2008 Current Population Survey.[4] At the national level, the Mexican-origin population exhibits the lowest levels of education of any other racial or ethnic group. Only 7.3 percent of Mexican Americans hold a bachelor's degree or higher, compared to 28.8 percent of whites, 16.1 percent of blacks, and 45.8 percent of Asians. Mexican Americans are also the least likely of all groups to be employed in middle- (service and skilled blue-collar jobs) to high-status occupations (professional, technical, white-collar occupations) and are overly concentrated in low-wage labor, as measured by the Duncan Socioeconomic Index (SEI), which scores jobs according to occupational prestige. At 53.1 percent, Mexican Americans have rates of homeownership that are slightly higher than that of African Americans (50.8 percent), but much lower compared to those of Asians (64.6 percent) and whites (79.1 percent). The Mexican American poverty rate is slightly lower than that of African Americans, and Mexican Americans barely surpass African Americans in total household income. In the aggregate, Mexican Americans appear to be a poor and uneducated disadvantaged ethnic group. However, these larger trends are artifacts of high levels of unauthorized and low-wage Mexican migration to the United States during the last half of the twentieth century that mask the progress of the relatively small but nonetheless significant proportion of Mexican Americans who are achieving middle-class status.

A clearer snapshot of the Mexican American middle class emerges when the data is disaggregated by generation since immigration as shown in Table 2. First-generation Mexican Americans (the foreign born) exhibit extremely low levels of education; nearly two thirds of the population lack a high school diploma. However, the proportion of Mexican Americans lacking a high

Table 1. Socioeconomic characteristics by race and ethnicity, United States, 2008

| | Mexican | Non-Hispanic | | |
		White	Black	Asian
Total population	30,271,639	196,767,931	36,382,382	13,654,665
Nativity and generation (%)				
Foreign born, 13 or older at arrival (1.0 gen.)	28.5	3.0	5.8	51.9
Foreign born, under 13 at arrival (1.5 gen.)	10.1	1.4	2.1	14.4
U.S. born, foreign-born parent (2.0 gen.)	32.0	6.2	4.8	25.8
U.S. born, U.S.-born parent (3rd+ gen.)	29.4	89.3	87.3	7.9
Educational attainment (%)				
Less than high school	47.3	13.7	23.7	15.2
High school graduate	27.3	29.7	32.5	18.5
Some college	18.1	27.9	27.6	20.5
Bachelor's degree or higher	7.3	28.8	16.1	45.8
Occupational status index (%)*				
High	18.1	44.0	28.2	49.6
Middle	27.0	29.8	32.1	24.8
Low	54.9	26.2	39.8	25.6
Economic status				
Homeownership (%)	53.1	79.1	50.8	64.6
Poverty rate (%)**	23.1	8.2	24.5	10.4
Total household income ($)	53,428	85,091	52,989	94,893

SOURCE: Current Population Survey (2008).

*The high occupational status range consists of professional, technical, and white-collar occupations with Duncan Socioeconomic Index (SEI) scores above 51; the middle range consists of service and skilled blue-collar jobs with SEI scores between 25 and 50. The low range consists of jobs with SEI scores of 24 and below.

**In 2008 the poverty threshold for a family of four was $22,025 (U.S. Bureau of the Census 2008).

school diploma decreases steadily with each generation since immigration, declining from 65 percent in the first generation to 29.1 percent in the third. In the same vein, the proportion of Mexican Americans who have attained "some college" more than triples from the first to the second generation, from 7.1 percent in the first generation to 26.9 percent by the second generation, and increases 1 percent to 27.8 percent in the third generation. While college graduation rates double between the first and second generations, from 4.9 percent to 9.5 percent, the national data show an increase of only 1 percent between the second and third generation since immigration.

Relatively low levels of education over the generations have caused much alarm among scholars and policy makers, leading some to conclude that Mexican Americans are not assimilating as rapidly, and to the same extent, as their white ethnic predecessors. Scholars argue that the substantial increase in education between the first and second generations is attributable to a sense

Table 2. Socioeconomic characteristics of the Mexican-origin population by generation, United States, 2008

	Generation			
	1.0	1.5	2.0	3.0+
Total population	8,587,926	3,045,904	9,624,856	8,863,210
Median age	41	25	18	25
Educational attainment (%)				
Less than high school	65.0	45.5	36.1	29.1
High school graduate	23.0	29.9	27.5	32.7
Some college	7.1	19.9	26.9	27.8
Bachelor's degree or higher	4.9	4.8	9.5	10.5
Occupational status index (%)*				
High	7.8	17.6	27.8	28.3
Middle	17.2	28.1	36.8	35.5
Low	75.0	54.2	35.4	36.2
Economic status				
Homeownership (%)	43.2	45.3	55.4	62.4
Poverty rate (below poverty line; %)**	24.6	25.9	24.8	18.8
Total household income ($)	45,459	51,294	51,283	64,029

SOURCE: Current Population Survey (2008).

*The high occupational status range consists of professional, technical, and white-collar occupations with Duncan Socioeconomic Index (SEI) scores above 51; the middle range consists of service and skilled blue-collar jobs with SEI scores between 25 and 50. The low range consists of jobs with SEI scores of 24 and below.

**In 2008 the poverty threshold for a family of four was $22,025 (U.S. Bureau of the Census 2008).

of immigrant optimism that is inherited by the second generation, whose parents' striving for the American dream propels children to do well in school (Kao and Tienda 1995). Sociologists Eddie Telles and Vilma Ortiz (2008) assert that this sense of optimism fades over the generations and is not enough to buffer against the forces of institutional racism in education that stigmatizes Mexican Americans, leading to a reversal of educational mobility in the third generation. The data examined here are cross-sectional and detail educational attainment by generation since immigration and do not measure intergenerational educational attainment within families; however, a number of scholars have employed a birth cohort method or intergenerational analysis to demonstrate that each generation of Mexican Americans improves on the educational attainment of the last (Alba 2006; Jiménez 2010; Reed et al. 2005; J. Smith 2003; Zhou et al. 2008). Intergenerational analyses demonstrate that Mexican Americans' seemingly slow educational progress represents a delayed, rather than stagnated or reversed, assimilation trajectory (Bean and Stevens 2003; Bean et al. 2011; Perlmann 2005).

The national CPS data show that Mexican Americans in the United States, despite their relatively low levels of education, make significant progress on other important indicators of middle-class status by generation since immigration (although they do not approximate the patterns of whites, or Asians, whose levels of economic incorporation surpass those of all groups, including whites). For example, more than a quarter of the relatively young second and third generations work in high-status occupations. Total household income and homeownership rates increase with each generation since immigration and the poverty rate declines.

How do Mexican Americans in Southern California fare on these measures? Table 3 details the characteristics of Mexicans, whites, blacks, and Asians in the Los Angeles metropolitan region. In the aggregate, Mexican Americans in Los Angeles score significantly lower on all the variables of class status compared to whites, blacks, and Asians. Nearly 50 percent of the Mexican-origin population in Los Angeles have not graduated high school, as compared to only 10 percent of whites, 15.7 percent of African Americans, and 11.9 percent of Asians. On the other end of the educational spectrum, only 6.6 percent of Mexicans hold a bachelor's degree or higher as compared to 35 percent of whites, 19.5 percent of African Americans, and 49.8 percent of Asians, the most educated ethnic group in Los Angeles (note that whites, Asians, and blacks in Los Angeles are more highly educated on average than their counterparts nationally). When it comes to employment, more than half of Mexican Americans in Los Angeles toil in low-status, low-wage jobs. Barely one fifth of Mexican Americans overall work in high-status occupations, compared to more than half of whites, 42.2 percent of blacks, and more than 50 percent of Asians. Just more than 20 percent of Mexicans live in poverty, a rate higher than that of any other group. The only indicator on which a different ethnic group scores lower than Mexicans is homeownership. Forty-six percent of African Americans in Los Angeles own a home as compared to nearly half of Mexicans.[5]

At first glance, the portrait of Mexicans painted by these data is one that bolsters the argument that Mexicans in Los Angeles are an overwhelmingly poor group, reinforcing fears that Mexicans will never enter the middle class. However, despite the prevailing image that Mexican immigrants and their children are persistently poor, uneducated, and unlikely to achieve upward mobility, a more nuanced portrait of Mexican Americans in Los Angeles emerges when we examine educational attainment and occupational and economic status by generation since immigration.

Table 3. Socioeconomic characteristics by race and ethnicity, Los Angeles metropolitan region, 2008

		Non-Hispanic		
	Mexican	White	Black	Asian
Total population	6,456,763	6,522,310	1,299,513	1,920,181
Nativity/generation (%)				
Foreign born, 13 or older at arrival (1.0 gen.)	29.8	9.2	3.9	54.3
Foreign born, under 13 at arrival (1.5 gen.)	11.8	3.7	0.9	12.9
U.S. born, foreign-born parent (2.0 gen.)	38.7	14.5	5.2	25.8
U.S. born, U.S.-born parent (3rd+ gen.)	19.7	72.6	90.0	7.0
Educational attainment (%)				
Less than high school	49.9	10.0	15.7	11.9
High school graduate	25.2	23.3	28.3	13.6
Some college	18.3	31.8	36.6	24.7
Bachelor's degree or higher	6.6	35.0	19.5	49.8
Occupational status index (%)*				
High	18.8	57.0	42.2	53.8
Middle	28.6	26.9	31.1	29.0
Low	52.6	16.1	26.7	17.2
Economic status				
Homeownership (%)	49.6	68.3	46.0	66.1
Poverty rate (%)**	20.7	6.6	14.6	8.4
Total household income ($)	57,481	101,201	62,545	95,073

SOURCE: Current Population Survey (2008).

*The high occupational status range consists of professional, technical, and white-collar occupations with Duncan Socioeconomic Index (SEI) scores above 51; the middle range consists of service and skilled blue-collar jobs with SEI scores between 25 and 50. The low range consists of jobs with SEI scores of 24 and below.

**In 2008 the poverty threshold for a family of four was $22,025 (U.S. Bureau of the Census 2008).

Table 4 compares the Mexican-origin first, 1.5, second, and third-plus generations in Los Angeles. The cross-sectional data demonstrates that the proportion of Mexicans exhibiting traditional indicators of middle-class status (income, educational attainment, homeownership rates, and the percentage of Mexican Americans employed in white-collar occupations) increase with each generation since immigration. For example, nearly 70 percent of first-generation Mexicans in the Los Angeles region have not earned a high school degree. This is not surprising because Mexican migrants are generally low-wage labor migrants and the average number of years of education in Mexico is 7.9 (Santibañez, Vernez, and Razquin 2005), which is well below the twelve years of schooling needed to graduate high school in the United States. In sharp contrast to the low levels of high school completion among the first generation, the proportion of 1.5-generation Mexicans who have not graduated high school decreases by nearly half, to 36.1 percent. Among the second generation, the

Table 4. Socioeconomic characteristics of the Mexican-origin population by generation, Los Angeles metropolitan region, 2008

	Generation			
	1.0	1.5	2.0	3.0+
Total population	1,919,993	758,122	2,490,917	1,270,361
Median age	43	26	17	26
Educational attainment (%)				
Less than high school	69.8	36.1	16.9	15.8
High school graduate	19.1	33.8	33.0	37.4
Some college	7.7	22.1	31.7	32.6
Bachelor's degree or higher	3.5	8.1	18.4	14.2
Occupational status index (%)*				
High	7.9	21.8	27.0	31.2
Middle	18.5	28.9	40.3	37.3
Low-wage labor	73.6	49.3	32.7	31.5
Economic status				
Homeownership (%)	45.9	44.9	49.5	57.6
Poverty rate (%)**	22.8	23.5	23.6	10.5
Total household income ($)	49,104	53,916	55,587	75,820

SOURCE: Current Population Survey (2008).

*The high occupational status range consists of professional, technical, and white-collar occupations with Duncan Socioeconomic Index (SEI) scores above 51; the middle range consists of service and skilled blue-collar jobs with SEI scores between 25 and 50. The low range consists of jobs with SEI scores of 24 and below.

**In 2008 the poverty threshold for a family of four was $22,025 (U.S. Bureau of the Census 2008).

proportion not graduating with a high school degree decreases by half again, to 16.9 percent, and tapers off to 15.8 percent in the third generation.

At the other end of the educational continuum, only 3.5 percent of the first generation have earned a college degree as compared to 8.1 percent of the 1.5 generation. Consistent with previous research, the proportion earning a college degree more than doubles by the second generation, increasing to 18.4 percent (J. Smith 2003). However, third-generation Mexican Americans in Los Angeles are less likely to have graduated college than their second-generation counterparts, a fact that may lead some to argue that Mexican American gains in mobility reverse in the third generation. While persistently low levels of education are an important factor that constrains the large-scale mobility of the Mexican-origin population, a focus on educational attainment alone advances a myopic view of Mexican American assimilation and ignores notable advances in occupational and economic status with each generation since immigration. Mexican Americans make notable gains in employment in middle- and high-status occupations, homeownership, and income, the further they are from the immigrant generation. For example, only 7.9 percent of first-generation Mexicans in Los Angeles are employed in high-status occupations, as compared to 21.8 percent of the 1.5 generation, 27 percent of the second generation, and 31.2 percent of the third generation. Similarly, the total household income of the first generation on average is $49,104, just under the national median income of $50,221. The 1.5-generation Mexican households earn $53,916, just above the national median income. Total household income increases to $55,587 among second-generation Mexican Americans in Los Angeles, whereas the total household income of third-generation Mexican Americans in Los Angeles is $75,820, $20,000 more than the total household income of the second generation and well above both the national median and Los Angeles' median household income levels.[6] The data also reveal that homeownership increases steadily and poverty rates fall substantially with each generation since immigration.

In all, Mexican Americans have not achieved economic parity with whites or Asian immigrant groups, the majority of whom are highly educationally selected prior to arrival in Los Angeles (Feliciano 2005). While the majority of the Mexican American population is relatively low income, Mexican Americans are not on a pathway of straight downward mobility or stagnation. The CPS data illustrate that traditional indicators of middle-class status, such as income, employment in high-status occupations, and homeownership all increase with each generation since immigration, while poverty rates drastically decline.[7] And in the Los Angeles region, nearly a quarter of Mexican American households make more than Los Angeles' average household income of $74,686 (nearly $25,000 higher than the U.S. median household income). Of these 1.5 million Mexican Americans, over two thirds are native born, three quarters are homeowners, and 61 percent work in middle- to high-status occupations.[8] Overall, a noteworthy proportion of Southern California's Mexican American population live middle-class lives, like Brian Reyes, making the experiences and pathways of those who enter the middle class important to understand.

Theorizing Mexican American Incorporation

While many fear that Mexican Americans will become mired in poverty, the CPS data demonstrate that a small, but observable, middle-class Mexican American population exists, yet we know little about their experiences as they incorporate into the middle class. Mexican migration to the United

States is certainly not a new phenomenon, and Mexican American communities have historically always had a small middle-class population (Garcia 1991; Sanchez 1995), but the first studies of immigrant incorporation focused almost exclusively on Southern and Eastern European white ethnics. Researchers such as Robert Park, E. W. Burgess, and Roderick McKenzie (1925), and Louis Wirth (1928), at the University of Chicago, studied immigrant adaptation during the period of large-scale migration from Southern and Eastern Europe. Their theories of assimilation are joined by one common thread—the idea of Anglo conformity. In other words, assimilation in the classical sense is a unidirectional process typified by full convergence of newcomers from immigrant, living in ethnically concentrated areas, working in immigrant ethnic niches, and identifying as a distinct ethnic group, to middle-class white American. Park's (1950) "race relations cycle" is typical of the era, where assimilation was viewed as a series of stages that result in ever-increasing contact with whites and eventual assimilation into an Anglo-American middle class. The race relations cycle includes the phases of contact, competition, accommodation, and assimilation, which is finally achieved by the erosion of ethnic differences. Similarly, in their volume *The Social Systems of American Ethnic Groups* (1945), Lloyd Warner and Leo Srole analyzed second-generation white ethnics and documented their movement from working-class ethnic enclaves into better occupational positions and residential neighborhoods. They argued that assimilation was occurring for all ethnic groups (although they cautioned that different groups progress at different paces), that ethnic differences would eventually disappear, and that over time, class would become the critical element in determining one's life chances rather than race or ethnicity.

Building on these works, Milton S. Gordon introduced a typology of assimilation and advanced the idea that assimilation is a multidimensional concept in his volume *Assimilation in American Life* (1964). Gordon's canonical synthesis of assimilation, often referred to as linear, or straight-line assimilation, proposes that immigrants first acculturate by adopting the language, patterns of dress, and other cultural behaviors of the host society's core group. Gordon argued that the core culture that serves as a reference point for immigrants as they acculturate is the "middle-class cultural patterns of, largely, white Protestant, Anglo-Saxon origins" (Gordon 1964: 72). Gordon expected that immigrants would cut ties to coethnics and the ethnic community, acculturate and then achieve "structural assimilation," where immigrants integrate into the core education, occupation, and economic structures of America, after which all other types of assimilation would follow, including the decline of discrimination by the dominant group, identificational assimilation with Anglos, and widespread intermarriage, which he viewed as the endpoint of assimilation.

Although the canonical model of linear assimilation reigned supreme during the first half of the twentieth century, observers began to notice that structurally incorporated white ethnics were clinging to immigrant ethnic identities even though classical theorists had predicted that ethnic distinctions were a temporary phenomenon. In *Beyond the Melting Pot* (1963), sociologists Nathan Glazer and Daniel Moynihan noted that native-born Jews, Italians, Irish, Puerto Ricans, and blacks in New York City maintained strong ethnic affiliations and functioned as interest groups. Glazer and Moynihan rejected the idea that immigrants assimilate into a unified, white, Anglo-Protestant core. While Glazer and Moynihan acknowledged that white ethnics were far removed from the immigrant generation and thus have "been stripped of their original attributes," they maintained that white ethnics remain as "identifiable groups" (13). Sociologist Herbert Gans (1979) also observed that white ethnics, who were acculturated and structurally assimilated, continued to evoke ethnic attachments. However, Gans argued that these ethnic attachments are "symbolic" and inconsequential in everyday life. For example, a white ethnic with an Irish grandfather and Italian grandmother might feel Irish only on St. Patrick's Day and then make a claim to Italian ancestry when dining in an Italian restaurant. Sociologist Mary Waters (1990) later demonstrated that white ethnics, unlike racialized minorities, can choose when to be ethnic and that their ethnic identities are symbolic and do not structure their life chances.

More contemporary theories of incorporation consider the ethnic diversity of the post-1965 immigration flows, which are overwhelmingly nonwhite in origin, as well as the structural and societal constraints that potentially block migrants and their descendants from achieving upward mobility and incorporating into the middle class. For example, Herbert Gans (1992a) eventually argued that assimilation should not be conceived as occurring in a straight line but rather in a bumpy line with different groups experiencing bumps in the adaptation process that emerge from different circumstances. Reacting to the large number of Latin American, Asian, and Caribbean immigrants, who constitute over 80 percent of today's immigrant stream, Gans (1992b) also proposed that the children of today's immigrants might experience "second-generation decline" because they face a dearth of educational and economic opportunities, combined with continued racial discrimination, and therefore experience downward mobility relative to their parents. Because the second generation are American born and do not retain a dual frame of reference like their parents do, the second generation will refuse the low-wage jobs the immigrant generation evaluates positively, but will be unable to attain better positions themselves because of a postindustrial economy that has seen manufacturing jobs, once a stepping-stone to middle-class status, disappear.

Sociologists Alejandro Portes and Min Zhou (1993) and others have expanded Gans's argument into what is the most influential theory of incorporation today—segmented assimilation. Portes and Zhou maintain that today's immigrants face two divergent paths of incorporation: straight-line assimilation into the white middle class, as predicted by the canonical model, and downward assimilation into a minority underclass culture. They argue that a restructured hourglass economy lacking in mobility ladders, the nonwhite status of the majority of today's immigrants, and the second-generation's spatial proximity to inner-city youth culture make upward mobility uncertain for some immigrant groups. Alejandro Portes and Rubén Rumbaut (2001) further advanced this argument in their seminal study on the immigrant second generation. They examine how a welcoming or exclusionary context of reception and individual goals and aspirations can segment assimilation into these different pathways. While a positive context of reception and high parental capital can lead to linear assimilation, they argue that a negative context of reception, combined with low parental human capital and minimal economic resources will most likely result in the adoption of an oppositional culture, where norms, such as doing well in school, are devalued, resulting in a pattern of downward assimilation. In the case of Mexicans, Portes and Rumbaut (2001: 279) argue that "Mexican immigrants represent *the* [emphasis in original] textbook example of the theoretically anticipated effects of low immigrant human capital combined with a negative context of reception which cumulatively leads to downward mobility across the generations."

The segmented assimilation framework emphasizes that immigrant adolescents might also delay linear or downward assimilation by selectively acculturating. Selective acculturation occurs when immigrant parents actively work to prevent their children's full assimilation into American society by deliberately immersing them in a tight-knit ethnic community that supports educational attainment and reinforces parental authority. The ultimate objective is to prevent the adoption of an oppositional culture and downward mobility into the minority underclass. Selective acculturation thus "slows down the process of Americanization, promotes ethnic pride in ethnic identity and helps parents maintain authority while both they and their children accommodate to a new society" (S. Warner 2007: 108). Selective acculturation has been demonstrated among some Asian and black second-generation youths whose communities have strong ethnic institutions (Gibson 1988; Waters 1999; Zhou and Bankston 1998). However, Mexican ethnic communities are touted as lacking the community resources and institutions that can delay assimilation for the second generation and buffer against downward mobility (Baca Zinn and Wells 2001; Dohan 2003; D. Lopez and Stanton-Salazar 2001), leading some to conclude that the offspring of Mexican immigrants are most at risk for incorporation into a minority underclass culture.

The segmented assimilation framework helped to refocus the assimilation debate onto the children of today's new nonwhite immigrants, but the model depicts full incorporation as a choice between linear assimilation into the white middle class and downward assimilation into the minority underclass. The model oversimplifies the range of incorporation pathways, particularly those that lead to the middle class, discounting the possibility that some immigrants and their descendants assimilate into a minority middle-class community after they achieve upward mobility. To remedy this limitation, sociologists Kathryn Neckerman, Prudence Carter, and Jennifer Lee (1999) propose an additional pathway—incorporation into a minority middle class through a minority culture of mobility.

The minority culture of mobility paradigm is different from selective acculturation, which is practical for immigrant families in the early stages of incorporation when immigrant children are growing up in disadvantaged ethnic communities and at risk for downward assimilation. In contrast, the minority culture of mobility—which is not a separate culture but a set of cultural elements that emerge in response to distinct problems rooted in structural disadvantage and discrimination—becomes pronounced when socially mobile immigrants and their descendants leave ethnic communities and enter the economic mainstream. In other words, the minority culture of mobility becomes evident among *adults* after they have achieved structural incorporation. Drawing on the experiences of middle-class African Americans, Neckerman and colleagues (1999) contend that middle-class minorities face unique challenges as they enter the middle class. First, because they are upwardly mobile, they must manage relations with poorer coethnics who make repeated requests for financial and social support and who threaten to drain their resources. Second, they must navigate relationships with whites in middle-class social and professional settings who might view them as racial or ethnic minorities who are distinct from whites, despite their traditional indicators of middle-class status. It is the shared experiences and responses to these problems, such as identifying as a middle-class minority, participating in ethnic voluntary organizations, and seeking refuge in a supportive middle-class ethnic community, that constitute important elements of the minority culture of mobility. Contrary to the linear assimilation model, this framework also suggests that immigrants and their descendants might identify as a racial or ethnic minority rather than as white, even though they have incorporated into the middle class.

Another critique of the segmented assimilation model is that it is based on case studies of adolescents whose life-course trajectories are incomplete, which may therefore overestimate downward mobility (Waldinger and Feliciano 2004). Scholars have also critiqued segmented assimilation by arguing that the framework is based on a black–white model of race relations that places Mexican Americans as a group much closer to African Americans than to whites, which might lead some to overestimate Mexicans' likelihood of downward mobility, particularly because Mexican ethnicity may not hinder the incorporation of Mexican Americans in the same ways that race impedes the mobility of African Americans (Alba and Nee 2003; Bean and Stevens 2003; Kasinitz, Mollenkopf, and Waters 2006; Tienda and Mitchell 2006; Perlmann 2005). A boundary-oriented perspective, associated with sociologists Richard Alba and Victor Nee (2003), has emerged that views ethnicity as a social boundary embedded in differences between groups. Alba and Nee argue that ethnic boundaries with the majority group, whites, might not be as rigid for Mexican Americans as the segmented assimilation and racialization models propose and that assimilation, as a form of ethnic change, may occur through modifications taking place on both the Mexican and white sides of the boundary. As sociologist Philip Kasinitz and colleagues assert, the notion of segmented assimilation "accepts that American racial categories remain rigidly in place," even though many scholars "emphasize fluid identities, malleable boundaries, and situationally derived meanings of identities" (2006: 395). Boundaries have stretched in the past to enfold white ethnics, such as Irish and Italians, who were once viewed as nonwhite, and some argue that boundaries might stretch in the future to incorporate Mexican Americans (Alba and Nee 2003; Alba

2009; Bean and Stevens 2003; Perlmann 2005; J. Smith 2003, 2006; Yancey 2003) and that, unlike African Americans, Mexican Americans are more easily able to cross boundaries with whites, as evidenced by significantly high rates of intermarriage (Lee and Bean 2010).

In sum, contemporary assimilation theories question whether Mexican Americans live with the stigma of race and experience downward mobility where they incorporate as racialized minorities (closer to African Americans), whether they are experiencing linear assimilation into the middle class and incorporating closer to whites, or whether Mexican immigrants and their descendants follow a minority pathway into the middle class. In this book, I adjudicate between these views to demonstrate that not all Mexican Americans are headed for downward mobility and that there are multiple pathways into the middle class for today's Mexican immigrants and their descendants.

Research Strategy and Methodology

This study is based in the Los Angeles region (encompassing Los Angeles, Orange, San Bernardino, Ventura, and Riverside counties), which is home to the largest Mexican-origin population outside Mexico City, totaling more than six million persons as of 2008 (Current Population Survey 2008). The Mexican-origin population in Southern California includes both recent arrivals and their native-born children, as well as those whose ancestors made the journey from Mexico generations ago. Within this population, 42 percent of people with Mexican ancestry are foreign born (the first generation), 39 percent are U.S. born to Mexican-born parents (the second generation), and 20 percent are third generation or higher. In other words, more than half of the Mexican-origin population in Southern California were born on American soil (see Table 3). The combination of new arrivals and established second, third, and later generations makes Mexican Americans distinct among the diverse cadre of immigrant ethnic groups in Los Angeles, most of which are composed of a mix of recent immigrants and longer-settled natives (Sabah and Bozorgmehr 2001). This mix of established immigrant generations, and the presence of a Mexican American middle class, makes the region a natural social laboratory for studying patterns of incorporation among the Mexican American middle class.

To examine the mechanisms by which Mexican Americans achieve social mobility and their experiences as members of the American middle class, I immersed myself in the professional and personal lives of middle-class Mexican Americans for more than three years. This book draws on multiple qualitative methods, including in-depth interviews, observation, participant observation, and an ethnography of a middle-class Latina business association headquartered in a Latino community. First, I draw on the ethnographic interviews to examine the mechanisms, such as educational tracking and coethnic and Anglo middle-class mentors, that lead to educational and occupational attainment. Second, I study a new economic indicator of incorporation, which is a key component of the middle-class experience for socially mobile Mexican Americans who remain closely tied to poorer coethnics, the retention of family obligations, and patterns of social and financial support, or what I call "giving back." Third, I investigate the salience of middle-class Mexican Americans' ethnic identification and the nature of their relationships with poorer coethnics and middle-class whites as they move into traditionally white middle-class occupations. Fourth, I examine civic participation in ethnic professional associations embedded in ethnic communities, demonstrating the ways in which middle-class Mexican Americans develop and reinforce a middle-class minority identity and activate a minority culture of mobility.

To examine patterns of mobility, family obligations, giving back, ethnic identity, and civic participation, I conducted seventy-five in-depth structured interviews with a cross-section of the Mexican-origin middle class. I use pseudonyms to protect their identities and have changed certain identifying characteristics. The persons in this study represent a diverse group with respect to generation, class background, and their forebears' place of origin in Mexico. All of the respondents reside in Southern California. They were first selected from Santa Ana, a city in Orange County, where 76 percent of the population is Latino, 66 percent is of Mexican origin, and more than half of the residents are foreign born. The City of Santa Ana is divided into fifty-seven neighborhoods, each with a distinct name and neighborhood association. Using 2000 Census data, I attempted to draw my initial sample in the most systematic way possible by identifying three middle-class census tracts in Santa Ana that have household incomes above the national median, high rates of homeownership, and relatively low rates of poverty among Latinos (see Table 5). To recruit participants, I attended the summer neighborhood association meetings from the three middle-class tracts identified in Table 5. I informed the association members that I was conducting a study about people who were born in Mexico but came to the United States before the age of 13 (the 1.5 generation), who were born in the United States but whose parents were born in Mexico (the second generation), or whose grandparents or great-grandparents were born in Mexico (the third

Table 5. Characteristics of three middle-class census tracts in Santa Ana, California, 2000

Middle-class tracts	1	2	3	Total Santa Ana
Latino (%)	95	95	95	76
Latino median income ($)	53,900	50,933	42,104	41,558
Latino homeowners (%)	57	58	43	44
Latinos below poverty (%)	18	19	23	22
Foreign born (%)	61	59	60	53

SOURCE: U.S. Bureau of the Census (2000).

and later generations). I also recruited respondents in other neighborhoods in Santa Ana beyond the three census tracts by placing an announcement on the Santa Ana Citizens' Board—an active web log where members debate topics ranging from political issues affecting the city to the building of a new Starbucks coffeehouse. I obtained a third of the sample from these sampling methods and then used a snowball sampling technique to recruit additional participants, which resulted in the inclusion of middle-class Mexican Americans from the greater Los Angeles metropolitan area. A quarter of the respondents reside in Santa Ana, while the rest live in neighboring cities in the Los Angeles metropolitan region.

The respondents range in age from 25 to 51 with a median age of 32. Twenty-nine percent of the sample are 1.5 generation, 49 percent are second generation, and 22 percent are third and fourth generation. All of the respondents exhibit all, or a combination of, the traditional markers of middle-class status, which include employment in white-collar occupations, household incomes over the national median, and a college education (Blau and Duncan 1967; Oliver and Shapiro 1995; Pattillo-McCoy 2000). They are employed in a range of professional careers, such as lawyers, vice presidents of banks, teachers, financial planners, architects, public-sector professionals, or they are business owners. The majority have graduated from college, some from prestigious universities like the Massachusetts Institute of Technology, Harvard University, and the University of California. Their high level of educational attainment is especially remarkable considering that nearly two fifths of the respondents report that neither of their parents has gone beyond the sixth grade. The total household income for the respondents in the sample ranges from $100,000 to $125,999.[9] Many also own homes and are residentially assimilated, living in white, middle-class neighborhoods. The cities where many live also boast relatively higher median household incomes than the national average. For example, the median incomes for Newport Beach (a city in South Orange County) and Yorba Linda (a city in North Orange County) are $83,455 and $79,593, respectively.

Lasting between one and three hours, the in-depth interviews were conducted in English, structured, open-ended, tape recorded, and then transcribed verbatim. I took an inductive approach to interviewing and first asked respondents to give a history of themselves, their parents, and how and why their families migrated to the United States. I also delved into their educational backgrounds and charted their or their family's paths to the middle class. To ascertain whether my respondents retain strong or weak ties to poorer coethnics, I asked how often they speak with their parents and siblings, whether they have ever offered their family members and coethnics financial and/or social support, and whether they feel obligated to give back to kin. While I refer to family obligations, or "giving back," as providing financial and social support to kin and coethnics, I differentiate between these two types of assistance in this analysis. I define *giving back financially* as acts that involve monetary support, whereas I define *giving back socially* as acts that involve assistance in the form of extensive time devoted to particular tasks that respondents do on a regular basis for their family members and coethnics, such as acting as cultural brokers between foreign-born relatives and the English-speaking public. I also inquired whether they feel that giving back to poorer kin and coethnics impedes their ability to accumulate assets and wealth. I questioned the respondents about their civic participation and whether and to what extent they are involved in the community. Finally, I questioned the respondents about their racial/ethnic identification. The respondents were not paid for their participation in the study, and many viewed their willingness to be interviewed as a form of "giving back to the community" or "giving time for a good cause."

I asked the respondents to classify and describe in detail their socioeconomic status as children in order to examine intragenerational mobility and whether class background affects patterns of incorporation, family obligations, ethnic identification, and civic participation (see Table 6). Sixty-one percent of the respondents overall classified their economic status while growing up as "poor" or "extremely low income," with some describing their childhood neighborhoods as "Mexican ghettos." Note that 95 percent of the 1.5 generation respondents, and 55 percent of the second generation, grew up poor. Fewer than 10 percent overall categorized their class background as "lower middle class." Those raised in poor or lower-middle-class households are the adult children of landscapers, factory workers, domestics, and agricultural laborers. The

Table 6. Respondents' self-reported social class background

	Generation			
	1.5	2.0	3.0+	Total
Population	22	37	16	75
Class background (%)				
Poor	95	57	19	61
Lower middle class	5	5	25	9
Middle class	0	38	56*	30

SOURCE: Author's in-depth interviews.

*One third-generation respondent characterized her class background as upper middle class.

interviews examined here are not representative, but my research and the fact that the majority of first-generation Mexican immigrants are low-wage labor migrants suggest that a large segment of middle-class Mexican Americans who are 1.5 or second generation were raised in poor households, and thus have rapidly ascended into the American middle class. Their mobility trajectories are impressive considering that their parents have less than a sixth-grade education on average and are employed in low-wage jobs. Conversely, 38 percent of the second-generation respondents categorized their upbringing as "middle class" as do more than half of the third and later generations. Overall, the divergent class backgrounds of the Mexican American middle class are a critical within-group difference that is concealed in large-scale survey data. Notably, these differences also allow for a comparative framework that makes possible a nuanced analysis of how class background shapes experiences and incorporation pathways into the middle class.

I chose to augment the study with an ethnography of an ethnic professional association and the middle-class ethnic community because it demonstrates how middle-class Mexican American pioneers muster resources in the community to create a minority culture of mobility. One pattern that emerged early on from the in-depth interview data is that socially mobile Mexican Americans are much more civically active than those who grow up middle class and the majority are active in Latino business and professional associations. At first, I was surprised to discover that such organizations exist because scholars assert that Mexican ethnic communities, in an opposite pattern from many Asian communities, lack professional ethnic institutions and the social and cultural capital they generate that can promote mobility for Mexican Americans in general and business owners and professionals in particular (Baca Zinn and Wells 2001;

Lopez and Stanton-Salazar 2001; Portes and Zhou 1993). I wanted to understand why these organizations are created, who joins them, and the role they play in promoting incorporation into the middle class. I was provided entrée into the organization through a second-generation Mexican American woman whom I interviewed during my first round of research. She is a well-known member of the community and founding board member of the organization I studied.

To study ethnic associations and the ethnic community, I immersed myself into the lives of middle-class professional Latinos and conducted nearly three years of fieldwork and participant observations at a Latina professional association, the Association of Latinas in Business (ALB).[10] The ALB is based in Santa Ana, a city in Orange County, California. Members are Latino entrepreneurs or executives and the majority are of Mexican origin although some hail from Argentina, Colombia, and Ecuador. The majority are first-, 1.5-, or second-generation immigrants. The organization has nineteen board members, all of whom are women, and eight of the board members are entrepreneurs. The board members represent a variety of occupations; they own service-oriented businesses such as accounting or staffing agencies or are employed as bankers, lawyers, and high-ranking executives in large corporations.

I attended twenty-two 2- to 3-hour board meetings held once a month at the association's offices in Santa Ana. I also observed at the ALB's monthly breakfast meetings and quarterly mixers, which provide members with networking time and valuable business topics such as negotiating business deals and business etiquette. In addition, I attended two of the ALB's yearly strategizing retreats, a daylong event that is held at a luxury hotel located in coastal Orange County. It was at the first retreat, after I had spent a few months in the field, that the founding president and president-elect asked whether I would be interested in chairing one of the committees. My role went from passive observer to active participant in the organization. As I took on this role, my more visible participation and extensive duties gave me more credibility and a higher level of trust with the board members, members of the organization, and the middle-class Latino community in general. My participant observation also provides an insider's view of the challenges, dilemmas, and successes middle-class Mexican Americans face as they create group-specific strategies and processes for upward mobility in an effort to increase the power and resources of the middle-class Latino community.

In addition to the participant observation, I conducted five interviews with members of the board of directors (for a total of eighty in-depth interviews).

And without my tape recorder, I spoke more casually with a host of people involved in the middle-class community, including the ALB's members, those who have joined other Latino-focused business organizations, sponsors of community business events, Mexican American business leaders, and politicians. In all, I compiled over 1,000 hours of field notes (see Appendix A for a more detailed discussion).

In short, I employ multiple qualitative methods and data sources including in-depth, structured interviews with 1.5-, second-, and later-generation middle-class Mexican Americans from different class backgrounds, long-term participant and nonparticipant observation in the middle-class Latino business community, and interviews with middle-class persons of Mexican origin who belong to the organization. I deliberately employ these various qualitative methodologies in order to triangulate the data sources and increase the reliability of the results (Lofland and Lofland 1984; Morrill 1995). These different methods and the great deal of time I spent in the middle-class community ensure that this was not a superficial look at the Mexican American middle class but a systematic study of an emerging group that will be of increasing importance to the future of the United States.

While the study is anchored in Southern California, the region heralds the larger demographic transformations that are being replicated across the nation in traditional immigrant gateway cities, like Chicago and New York, and in new destination states, like Georgia, South Carolina, and Iowa. The future of the United States is one with an immigrant population and a native-born population in general and a growing Latino population in particular, and California is a window into that future (Alba 2009; Hayes-Bautista 2004; Myers 2007). California is a harbinger not only of national demographic trends but also of the nativism that is spreading across the country and the anti-immigrant Arizona-style and Proposition 187 copycat initiatives that are being enacted in places like Alabama and Georgia, and proposed in South Dakota, Tennessee, Virginia, and Mississippi, states that, like California in the 1990s, have recently experienced an influx of Latinos in a time of economic downtown (Marrow 2011; Singer 2008). Thus, the lived experiences of Mexican Americans in Southern California may provide insight into mobility processes in traditional settlement states where Mexican Americans also constitute a large proportion of the population, such as Texas, Arizona, and Illinois, and in new destination states in the South and Midwest where the Mexican American population is growing most rapidly.

The remaining chapters of the book illustrate the mechanisms by which the descendants of Mexican immigrants are able to join the middle class and detail their incorporation experiences and pathways. These experiences are embedded in the political, economic, and social history of Mexican migration to the United States and California, a topic to which I now turn.

2 Mexican Americans Yesterday and Today

THE ORIGINS OF the Mexican American population in the United States can be traced to the treaty of Guadalupe Hidalgo, which ended the Mexican American war when it was signed in 1848. The treaty forced Mexico to relinquish the present-day states of New Mexico and Nevada and parts of Arizona, Utah, Texas, and California to the United States. Fifty thousand Mexicans became colonized citizens overnight, but the majority of today's Mexican Americans trace their ancestral origins to those who migrated after 1848 (Griswold del Castillo 1990; Massey, Durand, and Malone 2003). At the time of annexation, Los Angeles was the largest city in Southern California and was organized around a semifeudal economic structure known as the "hacienda system." The haciendas were run by landholding Californios, an elite sociopolitical segment of the Spanish and Mexican populations. Californios and Anglos shared power in the first few years following annexation, but Anglos took calculated measures to shift the balance of power in their favor by disenfranchising Californios and divesting them of their property (García Bedolla 2005; Menchaca 2002; Zamora 1993). Political scientist Lisa García Bedolla (2005: 41) argues, "This social, economic, and political subordination was followed by the geographic segregation of the Mexican American population. Over time, two distinct societies developed in Los Angeles—one white and one Mexican."

In the 1880s, Mexicans became increasingly concentrated in the central plaza or southern section of Los Angeles, located in the Plaza District, or what is now Olvera Street (Monroy 1999). A housing shortage erupted and many fled across town to East Los Angeles (Griswold del Castillo 1990). According to historian Arnold Monroy, throughout their history in Southern California,

Mexican Americans would be "pushed to live 'across' something. A river or the tracks usually. Such positioning in the geographic fringes marked them in the eyes of American society, as would their distinct occupations, language, culture, and appearance" (1999: 18). As the Mexican-origin population became increasingly segregated in East Los Angeles, in part due to racially restrictive real estate covenants (Bender 2010), the area quickly became the center of Mexican American organizational and cultural life in the Los Angeles region.[1]

As the twentieth century dawned, Mexicans who did not live in East Los Angeles were segregated in suburbs in the Los Angeles metropolitan region, often referred to as "company towns" that revolved around industry and manufacturing or *colonias*, which, in Southern California, were typically segregated citrus-worker villages (Arellano 2008; García Bedolla 2005; G. González 1994). For example, Orange County was divided up into eighteen *colonias* in small towns organized around the citrus industry, like Placentia, La Habra, Fullerton, Anaheim, and Santa Ana, a city that is presently viewed as the center of Mexican American social and cultural life in Orange County (I elaborate on the cultural importance of Santa Ana in Chapter 6). In these company towns and *colonias*, Mexicans were isolated from the white population (often across railroad tracks or fenced in) in terms of housing, schools, entertainment, and even baseball teams (G. González 1994; Monroy 1999). The concerted segregation of Mexican workers in company towns and citrus-worker villages is the reason why suburbs and small towns in Orange County, Riverside, and the outer reaches of Los Angeles to this day have distinct multigenerational Mexican American–concentrated neighborhoods (such as Casa Blanca in Riverside, Atwood in Anaheim, and La Jolla in Placentia) that are working class and remain segregated, separated from affluent gated communities only blocks away (some middle-class Mexican Americans, like Brian Reyes, are raised in these very neighborhoods).

Thus, only fifty years after the signing of the Treaty of Guadalupe, Mexicans in California, and throughout the Southwest, had been divested of their land, disenfranchised, and herded into segregated neighborhoods, helping to construct them as a distinct and inferior population.

The First Great Wave of Mexican Migration to the United States

The first great wave of migration from Mexico did not begin until the early twentieth century, after social, political, and economic forces on both sides of the border coalesced to induce migration northward (Deverell 2005; Massey,

Durand, and Malone 2003). In the late nineteenth century, Mexican President Porfirio Díaz (who is widely regarded by historians as a dictator) opened up the doors of Mexico to foreign direct investment and triggered the expansion of commercial agriculture by reconfiguring Mexico's practice of land tenure. Land that was once held as public was divided up and sold, primarily to foreign capitalists and Mexican elites, and peasants were ejected from family farms (Gonzales 2002). By 1910, 95 percent of rural Mexicans who had survived on subsistence farming found themselves landless (Massey, Durand, and Malone 2003). Díaz's reforms led to economic development within Mexico, but the consequences of foreign ownership were that profits were not reinvested in Mexico in ways that would facilitate the creation of jobs or investment capital (Monroy 1999). While the purses of foreign capitalists and some of the Mexican elite were bursting at the seams under the Porfiriato, the majority of the Mexican population was suddenly landless and starving, and wages could not keep up with inflation. Compounding the declining fortunes of the poor was a significant drop in the mortality rate, which increased the Mexican population from 9.5 to 15.2 million between 1875 and 1910. The Mexican Revolution of 1910, supported by landless peasants and the provincial elite, was a direct response to the unbearable economic, social, and political conditions wrought by Díaz's neoliberal policies.[2] One tenth of the Mexican population migrated to the United States over the course of the revolutionary decade and the Mexican foreign-born population in California grew from 34,444 in 1910 to 86,610 in 1920 and reached nearly 200,000 by 1930 (Hayes-Bautista 2004). However, the Mexican Revolution was not the only factor that stimulated mass migration to the United States.

Coinciding with the Mexican Revolution, a number of changes within the United States created a demand for low-skilled workers that pulled displaced Mexicans north. By 1890, virtually all of Mexico's production centers were connected to markets and industries in all states of the United States by railroads such as the Southern Pacific and Santa Fe, a link that made mass migration from Mexico to the United States possible (Massey, Durand, and Malone 2003). Labor relationships built out of the agricultural expansion in the early twentieth century, especially in California, combined with U.S. restrictionist immigration laws born out of anti-Asian nativism, first limiting Chinese migration in the late 1800s with the Chinese Exclusion Act and with the Japanese in 1907 through the Gentlemen's Agreement, which curtailed the supply of low-wage Asian labor that agriculturalists and other employers had come to rely on (Ngai 2005; Zolberg 2006). Where were Southwestern employers supposed to obtain low-wage laborers now that low-skilled immigration from China and Japan had been brought to a standstill? Southwestern agriculturalists turned to Mexico and actively hired Mexicans through labor recruiters known as *engachadores*, or "hooks" (Massey, Durand, and Malone 2003).

Nativist federal immigration policies intending to prevent new immigrant entries did not stop with Asians immigrants. The 1920s were a time of intense nativism in the United States and long-settled Americans were particularly concerned that Southern and Eastern Jews, Italians, and Irish, all of whom were viewed as distinct racial/ethnic groups at the time, would dilute America's Anglo-Saxon roots with their supposed inborn deficiencies, inferior culture, and unassimilability (Foner 2005). Legislators responded to this period of anti-immigrant hysteria with the Immigration Act of 1924, which was the nation's first comprehensive immigration restriction law that established numerical limits, or national origin quotas, on immigrants (Ngai 2005). The legislation effectively brought immigration from Southern and Eastern Europe to a stand-still, but quotas were not placed on the Western Hemisphere at the urging of agriculturalists, who feared that their access to an exploitable low-wage labor supply—Mexicans—in the booming economy of the Roaring Twenties would also be obstructed (Gutierrez 1995). In short, the Immigration Act of 1924 was the final piece of legislation that left American agriculturalists, especially in the Southwest, dependent on foreign labor from Mexico. Thus began an insatia-ble taste for Mexican low-wage labor that continued for nearly a century, one that has resulted in patterns of selective low-wage Mexican immigrants to the United States (Feliciano 2005).[3]

It is often overlooked that it was not only the Mexican peasant who jour-neyed north to the United States in the early twentieth century. While the majority of recently arrived Mexican immigrants were low-skilled migrants, individuals belonging to the Mexican petit-bourgeoisie, including teachers, lawyers, doctors, and shopkeepers, also migrated to the United States. Historian Richard Garcia (1991) argues that the Mexican-origin population in both San Antonio and Los Angeles in the early 1900s boasted a small cadre of middle-class professionals, the majority of whom served their low-skilled counterparts, and a minute population of Mexican elites. However, their middle-class status did not automatically shield them from social and economic exclusion because "Middle-class Mexicans were still Mexicans, and thus associated with poor Mexicans in the eyes of the Anglo majority" (Monroy 1999: 33).

In response to their marginalized status, middle-class Mexican Americans in Texas created the assimilationist organization, the League of United Latin American Citizens (LULAC) that worked toward equality with whites by challenging school segregation and other forms of discrimination. Their rationale for claiming equality with whites hinged on the idea that Mexican Americans were white and thus not a racial group distinct from whites. To accomplish this, they attempted to separate themselves from poorer and less acculturated Mexican immigrants by restricting LULAC membership to U.S. citizens and by emphasizing their class status and English-language proficiency (Foley 1997; Orozco 2009). LULAC promoted an Americanization agenda that was built on separating middle-class Mexican Americans from immigrants, but it was the first Mexican American organization to challenge racism (Orozco 1992). While a middle-class Mexican American leadership was emerging in Texas during this time, the native-born middle-class Mexican American population in Los Angeles was small. Thus, prominent expatriate Mexicans in Los Angeles were primarily focused on promoting an agenda of Mexican nationalism, in concert with the Mexican consulate, rather than a larger agenda of social equality (Sanchez 1995).

The Great Depression and the Bracero Era

The large wave of migration in the early twentieth century would end with the stock market crash of 1929 and the Great Depression that followed it. As has occurred throughout American history, immigrants became visible scapegoats for the country's economic ills, and as unemployment rose to record levels in Southern California, nativism against Mexican immigrants and their descendants increased. Mexicans were portrayed in the media and by politicians as living off of welfare and stealing jobs from Americans, prompting calls for their deportation (Hoffman 1974). The Great Depression devastated the Southern California economy, and local governments, including those in Los Angeles and Orange County, sought to cut budgets by rounding up and repatriating Mexicans, many of whom were the American-born children of immigrants (Sanchez 1995). Mexican migration to the United States ceased for practically a decade, and low-wage agricultural jobs came to be filled by starving Americans, mostly the "Okies" who were suffering from the devastating dust storms that hit the Great Plains in the mid-1930s. This would be the last era in which native-born white Americans would be employed in low-wage agricultural labor (J. Gonzalez 2000; Massey, Durand, and Malone 2003).

The demand for Mexican labor grew once more when the United States entered World War II. As the economy rebounded and Americans joined the war effort en masse, growers were left with an extreme labor shortage and again turned to Congress to aid their efforts in obtaining foreign low-wage labor. In 1942 the United States and Mexico created a binational guest-worker program, the Bracero Program, allowing for the entry of temporary Mexican workers. Braceros were paid poorly and worked under the harshest conditions. As Roberto Suro argues, "It is easy to deny decent wages and working conditions to people who lack political standing and who have been marked as inferior creatures" (1998: 82). Employers viewed braceros as ideal workers because they were simply sent back to Mexico if they protested their poor living conditions or attempted to unionize (Monroy 1999). While the Bracero Program was supposed to be a temporary Band-Aid for labor shortages resulting from World War II, it was extended for two decades, resulting in the entry of four million Mexican immigrant men between 1942 and 1965 (Massey, Durand, and Malone 2003).

As the Bracero Program was being implemented nationally and a new wave of temporary labor migrants were journeying northward, nativism against long-settled Mexican Americans was widespread and officials and the media in Southern California inflamed the populace's fears about Mexicans by constructing them as violent hoodlums, particularly the most visible segment of the population, the Pachucos, or those who wore zoot suits. The social and economic tensions stemming from precarious Mexican and Anglo relations collided over two incidents. In what is known as the Sleepy Lagoon incident of 1942, twenty-two gang members were arrested for the alleged murder of a rival gang member at a party in East Los Angeles that had attracted zoot-suitors. The police had no concrete evidence upon which to charge those who were arrested, and the accused were found guilty by an all-white jury. In Southern California, the image of the zoot-suited criminal came to be associated with Mexican male youth and reinforced the idea that Mexican Americans, including the middle class, were far from white (Monroy 1999; Sanchez 1995). The positioning of Mexican American Pachuco youth as a threat set the stage for the Zoot Suit Riots, which occurred in East Los Angeles the summer following the Sleepy Lagoon incident. U.S. Navy sailors on shore leave viciously attacked Mexican Pachucos. Mexican American zoot-suitors were beaten, stripped of their clothes, shaved, and arrested by police for disturbing the peace. No sailors were arrested and the newspapers blamed the riot on Mexican Americans. The Zoot Suit Riots were emblematic of the historical tensions between the Los Angeles police and the Mexican American population and were the most visible outward manifestation of the discrimination they experienced (Sanchez 1995).

While native-born Mexican Americans were painted as foreign and a threat, many were participating in traditional American institutions, particularly the military. Up to 750,000 Mexican American men served in World War II (Rivas-Rodriguez 2005), and when those who hailed from Southern California returned home, wounds from the Sleepy Lagoon case and the Zoot Suit Riots were still fresh. Returning Mexican American GIs quickly became aware of the contradictions between the stated purpose of World War II, to rid Europe of fascist dictators, and the treatment of Mexican Americans in Los Angeles. The Sleepy Lagoon case and the Zoot Suit Riots helped develop a new political consciousness among Mexican Americans in Los Angeles, particularly among the returning veterans, some of whom enrolled in and graduated from college through the GI Bill. This small but newly educated and socially mobile middle-class segment of the Mexican American population began to question segregation and persistent discrimination and sought greater representation in the political process (Sanchez 1995). Los Angeles' socially mobile Mexican Americans translated their newfound financial and social resources into the Community Service Organization (CSO), a grassroots effort that registered voters, helped the foreign born attain citizenship, and advocated for equal educational opportunities (García Bedolla 2005; Monroy 1999). One of the CSO's early leaders was East Los Angeles–raised Edward Roybal, a war veteran and college graduate, who was elected to the Los Angeles City Council in 1949, largely as an effort by the CSO, and who was Los Angeles's first Mexican American council member of the twentieth century (Romo 1983).

The Civil Rights Era and the New Immigration

By the 1950s, the majority of the Mexican-origin population in the United States were the grandchildren and great-grandchildren of immigrants. And while most remained in poor, segregated communities, a minute middle-class population existed, largely as a function of the educational opportunities following World War II (Grebler, Moore, and Guzman 1970). Regardless of generational or class status, people of Mexican origin continued to be considered foreign, alien, and inferior. As was the case during the Great Depression, the recession following the Korean War in the 1950s resulted in "Operation Wetback" when the Immigration and Naturalization Service (INS) deported approximately 1.1 million Mexicans, the majority of whom were unauthorized braceros but some of whom were American-born citizens (Massey, Durand, and Malone 2003). Operation Wetback resulted in traumatic altercations with government officials who questioned native-born Mexican Americans about their citizenship status. Mexican Americans "watched federal agents engage in massive sweeps of their neighborhoods . . . and more and more of them began to realize how closely their civil liberties were tied to the legal and political status of Mexican immigrants" (Gutierrez 1995: 153). As had occurred after the Zoot Suit Riots and the Sleepy Lagoon incident, community activists, who were native-born Americans and many of whom were socially mobile middle-class Mexican Americans, began to understand that mass deportations and the dissolutions of families, the scapegoating of Mexican immigrants during hard economic times, and the positioning of Mexicans as inferior were symptoms of a larger system of exploitation (Gutierrez 1995).

As African Americans began to assert their identity and demand rights in the 1960s, so too did a new generation of Mexican Americans, the Chicano generation, who rejected the assimilatory strategies of the earlier generation. Mexican Americans campaigned for equal rights protections as minorities under the law as redress for their social and political exclusion, even though many legislators in Washington viewed civil rights as a black issue (Telles and Ortiz 2008). As Hayes-Bautista (2004: 42) argues, "Deportation-era Latinos had battled discrimination in their own way, suing to end segregated schools and military segregation, and organizing labor unions and community service organizations. The major generational difference was that the Chicano-era Latinos insisted on asserting a cultural presence that had been conspicuously lacking during the deportation-era efforts." Between 1965 and 1975, the prime era of the Chicano movement, culture and politics were intertwined for "La Causa" from Cesar Chavez and Dolores Huerta, who cofounded the United Farm Workers, which protested the working conditions of agricultural workers, to the 1968 Latino student walkouts in Los Angeles and San Antonio protesting inequality in education (Hayes-Bautista 2004). Emerging from this movement were national civil rights organizations that still exist today, such as the Mexican American Legal Defense and Education Fund (MALDEF), the National Association of Latino Elected Officials (NALEO), and the National Council of La Raza (NCLR), which fight for equality in education and politics and immigrant rights (Pachon and DeSipio 1994).

While Mexican Americans demanded equal rights for minorities and redress of institutional discrimination, federal immigration legislation and the allocation of visas, based on national-origin quotas, came to be viewed as antithetical to the ethos of the civil rights movement. A major change in federal immigration legislation occurred in 1965, which ushered in the contemporary era of Mexican migration to the United States. The 1965 Immigration Act, also known as the Hart-Celler Act, dismantled the racist system of national-origin quotas put in place in 1924 and replaced it with a three-pronged system that sought to fill jobs with workers, reunite families, and provide a haven for refugees (Chiswick 2008). The legislation established an annual quota of 20,000 visas for each country in the Eastern Hemisphere, while no quotas were established for countries in the Western Hemisphere. Total visas were capped at 170,000 for the Eastern Hemisphere and 120,000 for the Western Hemisphere (Alba and Nee 2003). The act's family reunification provision allowed the spouses and unmarried children (under the age of 21) of U.S. citizens to apply for visas outside of the hemispheric quotas. The intent behind family reunification was to privilege new immigration based on the existing population of European Americans, and therefore recalibrate and maintain the Anglo composition of the United States (Bean and Stevens 2003; Reimers 1985). Legislators did not foresee that family reunification would have the opposite effect, paving the way for large-scale migration from Asia, Latin America, and the Caribbean.

While the legislation opened up America's doors to new nonwhite immigrants, the act was extremely restrictive for Mexican Americans and failed to consider the long history and unique role that Mexican migration played in providing low-wage labor for the United States' economy. Mexican labor was still highly in demand by agriculturalists and low-wage manufacturers, but by counting immigrants from the Western Hemisphere under an annual quota for the first time, and by eliminating temporary work visas, the number of Mexican immigrants allowed to enter the country decreased dramatically. Approximately half of the visas allocated to the Western Hemisphere, 60,000, went to Mexican Americans in the decade after the act, but it was not enough to meet the demand for labor (Massey, Durand, and Malone 2003; Reimers 1985).

The new Western Hemispheric quotas triggered an era of large-scale unauthorized labor migration to the United States, the roots of which had taken hold during the Bracero Program (Massey, Durand, and Malone 2003; Ngai 2005). In the absence of a temporary labor program, agriculturalists actively recruited and hired unauthorized Mexican migrants. As Aristide Zolberg (2006: 335) notes, because "All applicants except for immediate relatives were subject to a rigorous labor certification. . . . The queues became even longer, and the regulatory process itself generated an incentive for illegal behavior. . . . The certification required all Western Hemisphere applicants to secure a job offer. But this of course was hard to obtain without prior contact with an employer, and given the admission queue, the applicant would not be available to fill the position for two to three years. Hence the most rational approach was to enter illegally, secure a job, and spend the waiting period working in the United States." Thus, employers, who lacked a federally sanctioned means to hire temporary low-wage labor migrants, were happy to recruit and hire unauthorized migrants, and the proportion of unauthorized entries increased exponentially in the two decades following the 1965 Immigration Act (Massey, Durand, and Malone 2003).

While Mexican immigrants could obtain a visa through family reunification or by securing labor certification from an employer, there was one additional avenue by which unauthorized migrants were able to regulate their status, a route that is virtually absent from the immigration literature. Unauthorized migrants who had native-born children in the United States were given priority over labor applicants and were granted legal permanent residency (Heer 1990). I stumbled upon this route to legalization only after a number of my respondents adamantly insisted that their parents successfully obtained legal residency when they or their siblings were born on U.S. soil. Terry Feiertag, a Chicago immigration lawyer, processed these "baby cases" in the 1960s and 1970s, and was co-counsel of the landmark 1978 *Silva v. Levi* court case initiated by their termination in 1976. As he explained,

> In the Western Hemisphere you could qualify under the Western Hemisphere quotas by labor or family if you were undocumented. One of the ways that you could qualify on the basis of family was if you had an infant born in the United States. What happened is you gave birth, you sent the birth certificate to the U.S. Consulate, and that gave you your ticket in line to get an immigrant visa. Tons of undocumented people were here living lives, giving birth, registering.[4]

As I detail in Chapter 3, a number of the parents of 1.5- and second-generation Mexican Americans in this study who migrated in the 1960s and early 1970s obtained legal permanent residency through their native-born children, helping to hasten social and economic mobility into the middle class because legal status allowed them to obtain stable jobs or open small businesses and purchase homes, often in middle-class neighborhoods. The "baby" provision under the quotas was not unprecedented, as federal statutes provided similar avenues for legalization under the Alien Registration Act of 1940 (Skrentny and Bell-Redman 2011). The ability to legalize through native-born infants was revoked in December 1976 when the Western Hemispheric quotas were decreased from 120,000 a year to 20,000 per country per year. Those who had been on the list to receive legal permanent residency under their native-born children now received deportation orders. Terry Feiertag was retained by several clients who had "a place in line" through their native-born children but suddenly received deportation orders once the quotas were enacted. Feiertag eventually discovered that the State Department had wrongfully issued about 150,000 visas under the original Western Hemisphere quota by giving them to Cuban refugees. Feiertag and his co-counsel filed a class-action lawsuit, *Silva v. Levi*, on behalf of those who had been in line for a visa before December 1976 but had been served deportation orders once the new quotas were enacted. He and his co-counsel successfully argued for an injunction against the deportations and eventual recapture of 150,000 visas. As Feiertag recalls,

> Part of the injunction was that anyone who had this ticket in line could go into a district office, present their letter of registration and get a notice, what came to be known as the Silva Letters, issued by the old INS, essentially saying you have the right to be here and the right to work. We don't know how many letters were issued; my guess is about 500,000 people all over the country who had been chased by deportation officers were now given the permission to remain. By getting these letters it allowed for mortgages and houses and jobs and many, many once undocumented immigrants, who now had this in-between status, were able to lead regular middle-class lives.

As Feiertag notes, the injunction and the Silva Letters provided undocumented migrants with authorization to remain in the United States and validated their residency, allowing them to integrate economically. Protections against deportations warranted by the Silva injunction, and justified by the Silva Letters, lasted until December of 1981. From Feiertag's perspective, the pressure to provide a pathway to legalization for unauthorized migrants, which was eventually granted under the 1986 Immigration Reform and Control Act (IRCA), was legitimized by the Silva Letters. Under IRCA, unauthorized migrants who could prove that they had been living in the United States since before January

1, 1982 or who had been working in agriculture for at least six months were able to legalize their status (Bean and Stevens 2003). As Feiertag contends,

> The protections under the Silva Letters lasted until late 1981. The pressure for legalization was legitimized by this. You had this built-in qualifying cohort. The trigger date for the 1986 amnesty was that you had to be here by January 1982. In my mind it is the most single impactful immigration case in terms of its effects. 150,000 people got visas but the injunction of four-and-a-half years covered a multiple of those people and allowed them to establish a presence in the U.S., and because it took so long, you had this judiciously imposed legitimacy to all of these people. What were you going to do with them when the injunction ran out? You said it was ok to set up your life and it went on for four and a half years and now you were going to say, ok go?

Between 1989 and 1994, approximately two million unauthorized Mexican migrants legalized under IRCA (Bean and Stevens 2003). In addition to the amnesty, the legislation also criminalized the hiring of unauthorized workers by applying sanctions to employers who knowingly recruited and hired them. IRCA also increased funding for border enforcement, leading to the expansion of the Border Patrol and the militarization of the border. Less than ten years after IRCA, the North American Free Trade Agreement (NAFTA) ushered in an era of economic integration between Canada, Mexico, and the United States, with the promise that foreign investment stemming from free trade would curb Mexicans' desires to migrate to the United States. However, NAFTA decimated Mexican manufacturers and corn farmers, who were driven out of business by the elimination of tariffs and the less expensive goods and corn that flowed into the country, leading many who depended on these industries to seek better fortunes north of the U.S.-Mexico border. Moreover, IRCA's provisions militarized the busiest unauthorized border crossings and increased internal enforcement and deportations, disrupting traditional patterns of seasonal circular migration, causing many male unauthorized Mexican migrants to remain in the United States and send for their wives and children. While legislators promised that IRCA and NAFTA would curtail unauthorized migration, their provisions actually had the opposite effect and ended up promoting not only unauthorized migration but also the permanent settlement of families in the United States (Cornelius 2001; Massey, Durand, and Malone 2003). Thus, the unauthorized population in the United States expanded yet again.

The 1990s to the Present

While unauthorized migration is not simply a Mexican issue (it is estimated that slightly more than half of unauthorized migrants are of Mexican origin), it is unquestionably associated with Mexican immigrants due to the rise of unauthorized migration to the United States in the 1990s after IRCA and NAFTA. Media and politicians portrayed the U.S.-Mexico border as a battleground that was under attack by a culturally distinct, unassimilable, and criminal ethnic group, which exacerbated ethnic tensions during a period of economic downturn (L. Chavez 2008; Massey 2009). When Senator Pete Wilson was elected governor of California in 1990, he inherited a state that was in financial ruins. California lost 830,000 jobs between 1990 and 1993, unemployment rates doubled, per capita income in California declined for the first time in almost one hundred years, and Wilson faced a budget deficit of more than $14 billion (García Bedolla 2005). Simultaneously, California was experiencing a significant racial and ethnic demographic shift. From 1960 to 1990, the foreign-born population in California increased from 9 to 22 percent while the Anglo population decreased to 57 percent (Hayes-Bautista 2004). As Paul Ong argues (1999: 21), "During this period, California was undergoing an immigration-driven demographic recomposition that created a backlash from an increasing number of whites who felt uneasy and displaced by cultural changes." This demographic change was particularly dramatic in Southern California, where over a third of the population was foreign born in the Los Angeles region, with the largest proportion of immigrants hailing from Mexico. The crumbling economy made these demographic changes obvious, and as in previous eras of economic crises, Mexican immigrants became scapegoats for the state's fiscal decline.

National anti-immigrant groups saw California as the battleground over immigration issues, and, capitalizing on anti-immigrant sentiment, organized three ballot initiatives, Propositions 187, 209, and 227, all of which were designed to impose restrictions on California's Mexican immigrant population and create an unfriendly context of reception aimed at discouraging migration to the state (Portes and Rumbaut 2001; Santa Ana 2002). Proposition 187 was a state ballot initiative sponsored by a grassroots movement, S.O.S., or Save Our State, that denied state services to unauthorized immigrants, including health care and education, and required police officers, teachers, and health care workers to report unauthorized migrants to the INS. While some justified

Proposition 187 by portraying unauthorized migrants as criminals and welfare dependent, others maintained that unauthorized Mexicans were unassimilable and fundamentally changing American culture by causing California to become a "third world country" (Jacobson 2008; Rodriguez 2008).

California Governor Pete Wilson made the issue of Latino unauthorized migration the cornerstone of his reelection campaign and officially endorsed Proposition 187. Wilson and the anti-immigrant organizations that positioned Latinos as a threat claimed that they were motivated by economic concerns, but his campaign, and the measures introduced, had strong racial overtones (Massey, Durand, and Malone 2003; Santa Ana 2002). Proposition 187 won with 59 percent of the statewide vote. While the measure was directed at immigrants, observers have demonstrated that Proposition 187 "thickened" the Mexican self-identification of native-born Mexican Americans, who developed a "reactive ethnicity" in the wake of perceived threat, particularly when they were mistaken for immigrants and subjected to discriminatory treatment (Portes and Rumbaut 2001: 148). Anti-immigrant initiatives did not stop with Proposition 187. In 1998, Proposition 227, which focused on eliminating bilingual education, was placed on the ballot. In the public discourse surrounding this initiative, the ability to speak Spanish was socially constructed as a marker of foreignness. Although Proposition 187 was subsequently struck down in federal court, the anti-immigrant sentiment it and Proposition 227 engendered has had a long-term effect on how Mexican Americans ethnically identify themselves and how they are viewed by others (García Bedolla 2005; Jiménez 2010).

By the year 2000, Latinos constituted 12.5 percent of the U.S. population and 32 percent of California's population. The hostile political and social environment experienced by Mexican Americans in the 1990s carried over to the first decade of the new millennium as the native-born Mexican American and unauthorized populations continued to increase. For example, in California, Jim Gilchrist, a retired accountant from Orange County, founded the infamous Minuteman Project, a citizen vigilante organization monitoring unauthorized migration at the U.S.-Mexico border. By 2007, more than sixty cities in California had passed ordinances prohibiting day laborers from congregating in specific areas, such as home improvement stores (A. Gonzalez 2007). Anti-immigrant sentiment toward Mexican immigrants and their descendants spread beyond California to states like Arizona that were experiencing a sudden influx of unauthorized migrants in rural border towns, a result of the militarization of the traditional points of entry along the U.S.-Mexico border (Massey, Durand, and Malone 2003), and to new destination states in the South and Midwest where the Latino population was growing most rapidly.

As the United States entered the Great Recession toward the end of 2007, media and politicians once again used immigrants as scapegoats for the country's economic ills and ramped up their portrayals of Latino immigrants as unassimilable burdens on society. The rapid growth and national diffusion of the Latino population, the Great Recession, and Congress's inability to reach a consensus on how to address high rates of unauthorized migration have led states to try to solve the "immigration problem" on their own by passing legislation aimed at promoting the attrition of immigrants through enforcement.[5] In April 2010, Governor Jan Brewer of Arizona signed into law Arizona Senate Bill 1070 (SB 1070), one of the strictest immigration measures in decades, giving police broad power to question and detain anyone they reasonably suspect is in the country without authorization. In 2011, Alabama, a state where the Latino population grew by 145 percent between 2000 and 2010 (although only 3 percent of the population overall is Latino), passed an even harsher law, HB 56, the Beason-Hammon Alabama Taxpayer and Citizen Protection Act (Passel and Cohn 2011). The Alabama law penalizes people who knowingly socially assist unauthorized migrants and requires public schools to confirm students' legal status through birth certificates or sworn affidavits. The law also makes it a felony to present false documents when applying for a job. Although sections of both of these laws have been blocked by federal judges, the criminalization of Mexican immigrants helps perpetuate what anthropologist Leo Chavez (2008) calls the "Latino threat narrative," a damaging narrative that conceals Latino socioeconomic advancement by portraying them as an unassimilable threat to American society. The pervasive idea that Latinos will never assimilate is perpetuated not only by media and politicians but also by scholars. The late Harvard political scientist Samuel P. Huntington (2004: 30) argued,

The persistent inflow of Hispanic immigrants threatens to divide the United States into two peoples, two cultures, and two languages. Unlike past immigrant groups, Mexicans and other Latinos have not assimilated into mainstream U.S. culture, forming instead their own political and linguistic enclaves—from Los Angeles to Miami—and rejecting the Anglo-Protestant values that built the American dream. The United States ignores this challenge at its peril.

The assertion that Mexican immigrants and their children will never assimilate into the fabric of American life and that they pose a threat to American values continues to have widespread consequences in everyday life for U.S. Latinos. Coinciding with the April 2010 signing of SB 1070, a 2010 report by the Pew Hispanic Center revealed that 61 percent of Latinos felt that discrimination against members of their ethnic group was a "major problem," as compared to 54 percent in 2007 (M. H. Lopez, Morin, and Taylor 2010). Polls that survey a broader swath of the population also report that Americans continue to view immigration as a major concern. A 2010 Pew Charitable Trust poll found that nearly half of people polled say immigrants are a burden on our country because they take our jobs, housing, and health care, an increase of 10 percent in this view since November 2009. And 44 percent of those polled agreed that immigrants threaten traditional American customs and values (Pew Forum on Religion and Public Life 2010).

In spite of the historical and presently nativist environment in the United States, some Mexican Americans in Southern California are achieving upward mobility and incorporating into the middle-class. Indications of this upward mobility, and the emergence of a Mexican American middle-class community, are evident not only in demographic data, as discussed in Chapter 1, but also in the increasing number of Mexican Americans entering the political arena in Southern California and California more broadly. For example, Antonio Villairagosa, a second-generation Mexican American, was elected mayor of Los Angeles on May 17, 2005, and reelected for a second term in 2009. He is the city's first Mexican American mayor since 1872. The California speaker of the assembly, John Pérez, is Mexican American, as are members of Congress, the Los Angeles school board, and the city council. As political scientist Lisa García Bedolla commented in a recent *Los Angeles Times* article about Latinos in positions of power, "It's coming full circle. That's what Los Angeles looked like before becoming part of the United States" (Decker 2010). Traditionally conservative Orange County has not achieved the same rates of Latino representation in public office, but strides are being made. In 1996, Loretta Sanchez, the daughter of Mexican immigrants who worked as an investment banker, ran and won against a six-term Anglo Republican incumbent to become the first Mexican American to represent Orange County in Congress. These shifts in political power correspond with the growing Latino population in Southern California and the rise of the contemporary Mexican American middle class, and may be a harbinger of what is to come throughout the nation as the Latino population continues to grow beyond California.

Conclusion

Mexican migration to the United States is both a new and an old phenomenon entrenched in a long relationship between the United States and Mexico. Contemporary middle-class Mexican Americans' mobility pathways and their experiences in the American middle class are embedded in the sociohistorical context of Mexican migration. As we shall see, the ancestral roots of some of today's middle-class Mexican Americans extend deep into American soil, from those who trace their ancestry to California's Spanish ranchos to those whose grandparents migrated during the Mexican Revolution in the early twentieth century. Others are the children of braceros, legal labor migrants, or unauthorized migrants who eventually garnered legal status under the "baby clause," or IRCA. Regardless of the length of its roots in the United States, the Mexican-origin population in the United States has a social, economic, and political history that is riddled with conflict and hostility but that also contains tenuous triumphs that have advanced its entry into the middle class, such as post–World War II prosperity, the civil rights movement, and immigration policy.

3 Barrios to Burbs: Divergent Class Backgrounds and Pathways into the Middle Class

Growing up it was poverty. My parents couldn't afford a house. We'd shop at the swap meets. . . . They had no idea about how to apply for college and couldn't afford it anyway.

—Lorenzo, second generation, writer

My parents did very well. My parents pretty much paid for undergrad and for graduate school they helped with a lot of it. . . . They've always given me stuff. When it came to graduate school I only had to take out one year of loans and that was like thirty grand that I saved.

—Karina, second generation, human resources

BRENDA GUERRERO GENTLY PLACED HER oversized vanilla latte on the wooden table, leaned toward me, and lowered her voice so that the patrons of the coffee shop would not be able to discern her words. "When I was growing up . . . we were really poor. We lived in a garage," she whispered. Brenda's parents, both from the same small rancho in Zacatecas, Mexico, have worked in low-level manufacturing jobs for the last thirty years. Her father is a machine operator and her mother assembles parts, day after day. Brenda's father never went to school and her mother only made it to the sixth grade in Mexico.

Traditional models of status attainment assert that the occupational and educational status of parents determines the educational attainment and socioeconomic status of their children (Blau and Duncan 1967). Others have argued that it is not only the individual attributes of parents that determine one's position in America but also the status of groups, such as whether particular groups face barriers to social mobility due to racial, ethnic, or gender discrimination (Horan 1978; Portes and Zhou 1993; Portes and Rumbaut 2001; Zhou et al. 2008). Some emphasize that the characteristics of social institutions, such as subpar schools in segregated neighborhoods or racialization in

schools, make entry into college difficult or nearly impossible, thereby per-
petuating racial inequalities in socioeconomic status (Bowles and Gintis 1977;
Telles and Ortiz 2008; Waters 1999). The segmented assimilation model combines the individual attributes of parents laid out in the status attainment
model with opportunity structures and the larger contexts of reception and
would predict that Brenda will likely follow a pathway of downward, or stagnated, assimilation due to her parents' low levels of human and social capital and the negative context of reception that Mexican Americans experience
in the United States. Taken together, we might expect that Brenda, a second-
generation Mexican American who was raised in a poor, inner-city community
with parents who have extremely low levels of education and human capital
and who toil in low-wage and low-status jobs, would not move beyond the
social status of her parents. Yet Brenda graduated from a subpar high school
at the top of her class, attended a prestigious women's liberal arts college and
law school, and now works as a high-powered attorney. While scholars are
concerned that Mexican Americans will attain only modest gains in socioeconomic attainment over the generations, the achievements of Brenda, and
of many others I studied, call into question the widespread fear that Mexican
Americans are overwhelmingly headed for downward mobility and not assimilating into the middle class.

Like nearly all in this study, Brenda's parents migrated to the United States
to "provide a better life, better opportunities" for their children. Brenda was
raised in a "bad" neighborhood of Santa Ana that was ruled by gangs, something she feels she could have easily fallen into if not for her identification as
"gifted" in second grade. In fourth grade Brenda was tracked into GATE, the
California Department of Education's Gifted and Talented Program, which
places elementary school and junior high school children in "differentiated"
classes with accelerated learning, challenging and advanced coursework, access
to the best teachers, individualized attention, and extensive opportunities to
participate in extracurricular academic activities, such as academic decath-
lons and educational field trips.[1]

Brenda's entry into GATE shielded her from attending the subpar schools
in her neighborhood during her elementary school years. Her parents could
not afford private school tuition, so she enrolled in a Santa Ana high school,
where 98 percent of the students are of Latino origin and where a high proportion, 80 percent, qualify for free or reduced-price lunches (FRL), a variable
that is used to measure economic disadvantage (Stein et al. 2008). Despite the

lower socioeconomic status of the high school, Brenda's pathway to educational achievement had been set in motion long before, when she was identified as a gifted child in elementary school. Because she was a GATE student, she was tracked into honors and Advanced Placement (AP) courses in high school, where she completed rigorous college preparatory coursework, engaged with teachers who expected she would apply to college, and received a constant stream of information on how to navigate the college application process. That Brenda even graduated high school was a major advancement in intergenerational mobility relative to her parents and a meaningful achievement within the extended family.

Brenda was awarded a scholarship at a women's liberal arts college in Southern California, where she excelled, but where she also felt out of place due to her poor background and ethnicity. While Brenda's classmates were traipsing off to ski glamorous Vail and Whistler over the winter holiday, she returned home to Santa Ana to work full-time to pay the balance on her tuition bill that was not covered by the generous scholarship she received. Her feelings of inferiority were exacerbated when she realized that although she had successfully completed college preparatory coursework in high school, her education and level of preparation were no match for those of her mostly white peers, many of whom attended private high schools or schools in upper-middle-class neighborhoods. As Brenda recalled,

The level of preparedness ... I remember sitting in freshman writing and the words these women would use, I would write them down, look them up later. They were so above and beyond what high school had provided me with, you know. I knew the level of education that I had received wasn't great, I mean it wasn't bad but I didn't realize how deficient it was until then.

Despite feeling out of place, Brenda worked diligently in college to prove her academic chops and eventually graduated from a top-ranked California law school. Looking back, Brenda feels that being identified as gifted and tracked into GATE was the crucial mechanism that shaped her education and occupational ascent. She contrasted her experience to that of her younger brother, Ben, who was labeled as a "troublemaker" and who was encouraged to enroll in trade school rather than college.

I was just lucky. . . . I think that the early channeling helped and I know that my brother was tracked as a troublemaker early on and it produced different outcomes. He didn't do anything for a while after graduation and now he's found an outlet for his creative energy [he's now in junior college] but he got tracked as a bad kid and there you go. I'm really not that smart.

Brenda also feels that "if the stars would have aligned differently" she could have been "one of those people" who does not achieve educational and occupational mobility. Not only were GATE and AP classes critical forces that fashioned a social structure for academic achievement; early educational tracking was also critical because it connected her with a cosseted peer group that was not involved in gangs or drugs:

> I grew up in Central Santa Ana and I was a straight edge[2] because I knew that should I fall into that [gangs and drugs], it was so easy and it was there and so easy to fall into that, there is no way that I could have gone to college if I would have chosen that lifestyle. . . . I just got lucky. I got so lucky that the people close around me didn't fall into that. That we kept each other safe you know. Just as easily you could make friends with X or Y and fall into that. I got lucky; I didn't fall into that and was identified as gifted.

Brenda has come a long way from living in a ramshackle garage in a "bad" area of Santa Ana, California. She now leases a large home in Santa Ana's most exclusive, and mostly white, neighborhood. She has traveled abroad and is carrying an oversized designer purse on her shoulder. A gold-foiled law degree from a prestigious university proudly hangs on her office wall, she works at an esteemed law firm, and in stark contrast to her parents' low wages, Brenda and her husband (who is half White and half Latino) together bring home more than $100,000 a year.

As Brenda's narrative illustrates, some middle-class Mexican Americans grow up impoverished in inner-city neighborhoods and achieve extreme rates of educational, occupational, residential, and financial mobility relative to their parents. Educational tracking buffers them from the deleterious conditions of the inner city, and as I will show, outside programs, along with mentors, set them on a path to educational achievement by providing them with the cultural and social capital that low-income families lack (Gandara 1995; Lareau 2003; Portes, Fernández-Kelly, and Haller 2009; R. C. Smith 2008; Zhou et al. 2008).

Whereas some middle-class Mexican Americans grow up poor, others have childhoods that are cloaked in middle-class privilege. Parental pathways to middle-class status differ by generation. The second generation raised in middle-class households generally has immigrant parents with low levels of education who forged a pathway into the middle class through high-paying jobs or business ownership. Third- and fourth-generation Mexican Americans raised in middle-class households are more likely to have parents with college degrees and professional occupations and have replicated the class status of their parents as the status-attainment model suggests. Regardless of generation, those raised in middle-class households reap the benefits that accompany having parents who make stable middle-class incomes. In addition to more financial resources, these benefits include living in middle-class neighborhoods and having access to high-quality schools, which provide youth with access to middle-class cultural capital.

One important mechanism that promotes social mobility into the middle class is parental legal status. The second generation who grew up middle class have parents who either migrated with legal status or were able to regularize their status soon after migrating to the United States. In contrast, many of the 1.5 and second generation who were raised in poor households have parents who were unauthorized for much of their childhood and adolescence, often until the 1986 Immigration Reform and Control Act, which offered legal status to nearly two million unauthorized immigrants who had lived and worked in the United States since 1982 (Bean and Stevens 2003). Recent research demonstrates that legal status has important implications for the social mobility of the children of immigrants, whose educational and occupational trajectories are tied to parental citizenship status (Bean et al. 2007, 2011; Zhou et al. 2008).

Like Brenda, Karina Martinez's parents also have very low levels of education. Both her mother and father only completed the third grade in Mexico. However, while Brenda's family lived in a garage in a low-income community, Karina's family lived in a white middle-class neighborhood of Los Angeles. Karina's parents migrated to the United States separately in the early 1970s to work in the fields of Central California. Karina's father migrated with a tourist visa that he overstayed. When he was caught working without the proper documentation, he was promptly deported to Tijuana. However, Mr. Martinez immediately returned to the United States on another tourist visa, upon which he met Karina's mother, who had crossed the U.S. border with the help of a coyote, a hired guide who helps smuggle unauthorized migrants cross the border by evading the Border Patrol (Cornelius 2001). Karina's father overstayed his tourist visa again, and both parents were unauthorized for several years and worked in low-wage jobs. When Karina's older sister was born on U.S. soil, her parents applied for and were given a visa and "a place in line" to apply for legal residency (which they eventually obtained) under the baby clause, discussed in Chapter 2, because they had a native-born child. Now armed with a Social Security card, Karina's father moved out of low-wage agricultural work and obtained a job at a manufacturing plant that paid a living wage and also gave employees profit-sharing opportunities, which is an arrangement where companies give employees a percentage of their yearly profits that grow tax deferred until their withdrawal upon retirement or when an employee leaves the company. Her father's salary, large yearly bonuses, overtime pay, and wages from her mother's thriving home-based Tupperware and Avon businesses provided the family with the financial means to purchase several rental properties, adding even more income to the family treasury. Their financial stability also allowed the Martinez family to settle in a largely white middle-class neighborhood by the time their eldest daughter entered elementary school and to afford private tuition at elementary and junior high schools. As Karina explained,

> For my parents, education was very important. They just thought that we would get a better education at private school. Their philosophy was to move to nice areas; we lived in nice areas where a lot of Americanos, the white kids, lived, because they are all going to go to college and go to school. So fortunately they were able to afford to live in nice areas. But that was their thinking. We will pay to live in these areas and there will be no other Latinos and we will be the little minority and that was our story throughout private school and high school. If they live in this area, they will go to college and have good friends, friends who have professional parents and all that.

After working at the manufacturing plant for more than a decade, Karina's father decided to cash out the $150,000 he had accumulated through the company's profit-sharing plan. He invested half of his shares in a retirement fund, and he used the other half as seed money to start a construction company, Martinez Construction. The construction company quickly became a financial success. By this time, the Martinez family was living in an upper-middle-class master-planned Orange County community, and Karina was attending an award-winning "California Distinguished" public high school. Karina always knew that she was going to college, not only because it was expected of her but also because that is what all of her middle-class friends were doing. And unlike those who were raised in poor households, Karina easily transformed her college aspirations into a reality, as she always knew that her parents could afford to pay her college tuition. Karina holds a bachelor's degree from a competitive California state university and a master's degree from Stanford University and now works in human resources. Unlike Brenda, who felt alienated from her white middle-class counterparts in college, Karina never felt out of place. Her class background provided her with middle-class cultural capital derived from a private school education and growing up in a white middle-class neighborhood that allows her to easily cross boundaries with middle-class whites (Bourdieu 1991), a finding that will be discussed in further detail in Chapter 5. Not surprisingly, Karina's sisters have also earned master's degrees from elite universities and work in white-collar jobs.

As Karina's case illustrates, legal status allows those who live and work on the margins of society to secure stable and relatively high-paying jobs, resulting in greater familial financial stability that translates into cumulative educational and social advantages for children. Living in a white middle-class neighborhood, having middle-class friends, and attending a private school provided the Martinez sisters with professional role models and access to middle-class social capital (contacts in networks that can lead to personal or professional gains) and cultural capital (specialized or insider knowledge stemming from elite classes) that their parents could not provide (Bourdieu 1977, 1991; Coleman 1990; DiMaggio 1982; Portes 1998). Movement into white middle-class neighborhoods accelerates acculturation and incorporation into white middle-class culture, whether or not this is the intended goal (Alba and Nee 2003).

Both Brenda's and Karina's parents wanted their children to obtain a college education, and both Brenda and Karina achieved remarkable levels of educational mobility relative to those of their parents. However, the two women's mobility experiences are embedded in different class contexts. Brenda's story of upward mobility is particularly remarkable, especially considering her parents' low-wage and dead-end jobs, the inner-city neighborhood in which she was raised, and the subpar high school she attended. Her identification as gifted and her tracking into GATE were an important mechanism that set her on a path to educational and occupational success. Educational tracking helped her build the social capital that could be parlayed into a college education, something her younger brother was unable to use to his advantage because he was labeled a troublemaker and was not placed on the gifted track. What is telling about Brenda's case is that many of those who were raised in poor households credit their high levels of educational attainment with the good fortune or "luck" of being tracked into GATE or AP classes, or, as we shall see, coming into contact with a mentor—sometimes a sibling, community member, or their parents' Anglo employers, who guide their education and their careers. Research has demonstrated that Mexican Americans from low-income backgrounds tend to have less access to financial, cultural, and social capital than other racial or ethnic groups have and that early educational tracking, outside programs that serve low-income minorities, and mentors are critical mechanisms that fill these capital gaps (Gandara 1995; Portes, Fernández-Kelly, and Haller 2009; R. C. Smith 2008; Zhou et al. 2008). Although Karina's parents also have low levels of education, her father's opportunity to regularize his legal status and find employment in a stable and relatively high-paying job led to cumulative advantages that greatly benefited Karina and her sisters. The family moved into a middle-class neighborhood and the sisters attended private schools, both of which provided Karina with constant access to middle-class cultural and social capital through her school and peer networks.

Brenda's and Karina's divergent class backgrounds are characteristic of the Mexican American middle class in Southern California. Some affluent Mexican Americans grow up poor while others grow up middle class, a within-group difference that is missed in large-scale survey research. Scholars assume that those who achieve middle-class status follow a path of straight-line assimilation into the white middle-class "mainstream," where their ethnicity becomes inconsequential to their further upward mobility, where boundaries between Mexican Americans and whites are blurred, and where ties to the immigrant ethnic community are severed. However, the story of the Mexican American middle class is more than just a tale of straight-line assimilation into the white middle class, especially because many middle-class Mexican Americans grow up poor, like Brenda, and retain extensive ties to impoverished parents and needy relatives, making them very different from their white middle-class counterparts. These differences in class backgrounds bear heavily on the lived experiences of Mexican Americans and shape their incorporation trajectories.

Divergent Class Backgrounds

Middle-class Mexican Americans who grew up disadvantaged explained in vivid detail the poor communities in which they were raised. Some lived in neighborhoods riddled with violence and walked through gang territory to get to school. Their descriptions of life in such neighborhoods contrast sharply with the gated communities and large tract homes with perfectly manicured lawns where I interviewed them. As we sat in overstuffed leather chairs in beautifully decorated living rooms or in kitchens with gleaming granite countertops and stainless steel appliances, several respondents broke down in tears when they recalled the abject poverty in which they were raised. One 1.5-generation respondent wept over the wave of shame she feels when she remembers standing in line for a free lunch at school, sometimes the largest meal of her day. A few respondents lived in garages or in homes with multiple families for a portion of their youth, several spoke of how their parents rented rooms to a constant stream of migrant workers to make ends meet, three respondents claimed they "ate beans for dinner every night," and the majority shopped at thrift stores for clothing and shoes or relied on "handouts" from local churches or social organizations. Andrea, a second-generation Mexican American who lacks a college degree but forged a pathway into the middle class through entrepreneurship, explained,

> I grew up in the second poorest city in the nation, in Cudahy, California. Born to immigrant parents. My father came to the United States seeking a better opportunity, you know, that American dream. He worked as a machinist, really hard labor. He would come home and his hands would really hurt. We couldn't afford Disneyland or anything. The first two of us grew up with secondhand clothes and shoes—thrift stores. And they used to take us to the park a lot [because it was free].

Similarly, Pablo Guzman, a second-generation Mexican American who works as a nurse, grew up in Lincoln Heights, a neighborhood in East Los Angeles where everyone was "Latino, Latino, Latino" and where "graffiti was everywhere and people [were] getting shot." Pablo's parents obtained legal status after the 1986 amnesty. His mother cleans hotel rooms and his father, now deceased, was a low-wage laborer. When I asked Pablo to characterize his socioeconomic background, he replied,

> Low income and below poverty line.
>
> JAV: Why do you say that?
>
> A: Because we didn't have the things that we needed sometimes for school or like clothes. I mean we had some types of food and we were fed, but basically it was rice and beans. It wasn't as bad as some people have it in the boonies if you know what I mean, but below poverty level. My dad never paid taxes. He never made enough money. A lot of it was cash. My mom too, I don't think she got paid much.

Growing up poor is a memory that never fades and is a critical factor that shapes their social identity as middle-class Mexican Americans, even among those who are further from the immigrant generation. When I asked Isabel, a third-generation Mexican American with a degree from Harvard University, to describe her class background, her eyes welled up with tears and she replied, "Poor!"

> JAV: You say that you were poor. What do you mean by that?
>
> A: Oh definitely. I mean now as an adult I know the technical version of poor. I would say my family definitely lived below the poverty line. As a child I knew I was poor because there were so many things that my parents had to say no to us and that was because of money. But all my friends were doing it so they had the money. I know that my parents would never say no to us because they didn't love us or because they didn't want us to. I understood that not having money was not acceptable. It was socially unacceptable and at that age it is not a good thing. You know children are cruel. They will point it out to you if you are poor and numerous people don't even have to use the word *poor* to make you aware of the fact that you are poor. On the up side my entire family was poor and all my cousins, so to us when we were together we were all comfortable because we were all the same. It was just interacting with people outside our family that would make my brothers and I feel . . . inferior.

Isabel lived in a low-income neighborhood for half her childhood, and she lived in a shack on a "ranch" owned by her grandfather for the other half.

> We probably spent half my childhood living in the towns and city and the other half living in the country. So when I did have a neighborhood when we lived in the towns and cities, it was pretty much like living in the poor house. I remember the streets that we lived on that weren't paved even though we lived in the city. We had no sidewalks. When we would go to shop for school clothes we would be on the other side of town and it didn't look anything like that and so we knew we were poor then. When we lived in the country . . . my grandfather owned a ranch, my mother's father. And when I tell people that they are like, "Oh wow" and they imagine it like a hacienda, but that ranch hasn't been operating since he passed away in the mid-'70s. It is just this big plot of land that is overgrown with brush and old buildings like an old house and an old barn. We did live there for a while, but that was because now that I am an adult I can understand this perfectly, but basically because our family was homeless, my

immediate family. What my father did was he went to my grandfather's ranch and he pretty much revamped this old log cabin that was there and we lived in it for about at least three years. We had no running water, no electricity.

The vivid descriptions of the impoverished backgrounds and neighborhoods of those from poor backgrounds contrast sharply with the descriptions of those who describe their upbringing as "solidly middle class." Those who grew up middle class became nostalgic when speaking about their *Leave It to Beaver* neighborhoods, which they primarily characterized as "safe" and "white," and where they were usually the only Mexican American family on the street. Vincent is a second-generation Mexican American whose father is an engineer. He explained that he was raised "solidly middle class, pretty much like whites." When I asked him to elaborate on being "solidly middle class," he replied, "We always had plenty of food and never had to worry about electricity or things like that. We were always very comfortable."

In sharp contrast to those who were raised in middle-class households where there was always plenty of food on the table and bills were always paid on time, the parents of those who were raised in poor households struggled to make ends meet. The more marginalized economic position of low-income households often results in premature entry into the labor force by 1.5- and second-generation youth who work to help families financially. A number of those who were raised in poor households worked while in high school or college and handed over their paychecks, or a portion of them, to help the family stay afloat, a finding that is in line with previous research that finds that low-income Mexican immigrant families must often rely on the labor of their children to make ends meet (Agius Vallejo, Lee, and Zhou 2011; Estrada and Hondagneu-Sotelo 2011; Newman 2000; Ong and Terriquez 2008; Zhou et al. 2008). Leo is a 1.5-generation Mexican American with a master's degree in architecture who started working in junior high school. As he explained,

> Growing up we all put money into the pot so when we all worked we all gave our paychecks to our father and he would give you an allowance based on what you earned and it was all distributed. . . . Growing up I didn't like that I had to work and give my whole check and only get forty bucks back. But I had to do it. It was a sacrifice that I had to do. I had to be part of the team and do it.

While those who grew up poor often had to work in high school and college to help support their families financially, none of those raised in middle-class households worked to support their families. When they did work prematurely it was often to earn extra money for personal wants, such as designer jeans or "going out." A few even received generous allowances. Vincent related:

> They would give me money all throughout high school and early high school. When I was going to college and playing baseball I wasn't able to work at all and I had to pay a lot of gas and my parents gave me a hundred dollars a month, money for me to manage.

I expected that many successful Mexican Americans, especially the 1.5 and second generation, would hail from disadvantaged backgrounds. This finding was not a surprise because of the selectivity of Mexican immigrants, who are generally low-wage labor migrants and who face a marginalized entry status, factors that shape the social status and opportunities of their children. Because Mexican migration is generally a low-wage labor migration, I was initially surprised to find a noteworthy number of second-generation Mexican Americans who have parents with relatively low levels of education yet were able to provide middle-class lifestyles for their children. Two patterns became evident as to how some immigrant parents are able to lead a middle-class lifestyle. First, research shows that legal documentation has deep implications for occupational opportunities and the long-term social mobility of the first generation (Hernández-León 2008). Parental legal status was critical in promoting Karina Martinez's family into the middle class, a pattern also exemplified by Vincent, whose father also obtained legal documentation. Manuel, Vincent's father, migrated to the United States in his teens with his mother and four siblings when his father died. The family was able to obtain legal residency through Manuel's father, who had worked in the mining industry in San Diego. Manuel joined the military, where he trained as an engineer and learned skills that he was able to parlay into a successful career in California's booming 1970s aerospace industry even though he lacked a college degree.

Second, the significant majority of the second generation who grew up middle class have parents who built successful small businesses after they migrated to the United States, oftentimes servicing the ethnic community. These businesses include car lots, car repair services, construction companies, or retail stores. While observers have argued that entrepreneurship is not necessarily a viable route to upward mobility for the Mexican-origin population (Farlie and Woodruff 2008; Raijman and Tienda 2003; Sanders and Nee 1996), small business ownership provides parents with greater financial resources to invest in their children, and it allows parents to buy their way out of low-income communities and establish residences in middle-class neighborhoods. This is one way in which the Mexican-origin middle class is different from the black middle class, who are more likely to remain in segregated neighborhoods that are in close proximity to inner-city communities because of a racially discriminatory housing market (Massey and Denton 1993; Pattillo-McCoy 2000). For some first-generation parents with limited educational credentials, business ownership becomes a pragmatic strategy to achieving intragenerational mobility (mobility that occurs within a single generation) and securing the trappings of middle-class life. The critical mechanism underlying the first generation's intragenerational mobility stems from the economic opportunities that follow legal status.

Those with immigrant parents who were raised in middle-class households are more likely to have parents who entered the United States with legal status, or if they entered the United States without authorization, they were able to regularize their status shortly after arrival. A few claimed that their parents regularized their status through labor certification, but what is particularly notable is that more than half of the second generation raised in middle-class households claimed that their parents were able to legalize through the "baby clause" or Silva Letters as described in Chapter 2. As one of my respondents who grew up middle class exclaimed, "I was my parents' anchor baby!"[3] Thus, legal status facilitates both intragenerational and intergenerational mobility. This research shows the importance of obtaining legal status early on in children's life-course trajectory because the financial returns allow for greater investment earlier in the life course and for a longer period of time leading to cumulative advantages that stem from better neighborhoods, middle-class schools, and middle-class peer networks.

While the 1.5 and second generation characterize their class backgrounds within a middle-class or poor dichotomy, the third- and fourth-generation respondents, regardless of whether they were raised in poor, low-income, or middle-class households, generally portray their families' mobility trajectories over the generations as the "typical immigrant story . . . just like the Irish and Italians," where each generation is doing better than the one before. Katie Ortega-Smith's tale is one of intergenerational mobility, where each generation surpasses the last in terms of income, education, and occupation. She is a fourth-generation Mexican American who grew up "lower middle class" in Riverside, a large, sprawling city just east of Los Angeles and Orange County.

Katie was raised in Colonia Casa Blanca, a segregated neighborhood that was once a citrus worker village but is now a low-income and blue-collar barrio composed of Mexican American families with long roots in the United States and more recent immigrant arrivals (G. González 1994). Katie's paternal great-grandfather fled Mexico with his family during the Mexican Revolution of 1910 and found work in Riverside's orange groves while her great-grandmother toiled in the packing house stuffing oranges into wooden crates emblazoned with bucolic renderings of perennially sunny Southern California. Katie's paternal grandfather and father were born and raised in Colonia Casa Blanca while her mother's family, also dating back several generations, settled in a different segregated neighborhood, Eastside, which also emerged from a concentration of citrus and produce workers. While Katie's great-grandparents labored in Southern California's booming citrus industry, her grandfather improved on his parents' elementary school education and occupation by graduating from high school and finding employment as a repairman for a large apartment complex, eventually working his way up to superintendent of all the properties owned by the firm. Katie's father, a third-generation Mexican American, improved on his father's education by attending two years of community college, although he dropped out when he was promoted to foreman of the construction company where he worked. Even though Katie's father did not graduate from college, his salary was enough to purchase a small California bungalow-style home in Casa Blanca. Her mother, who only graduated from high school, worked sporadically in fast food or retail but was generally able to stay home with their three children. Katie explains that they were neither poor nor middle class, but lower middle class: "We never went without."

Katie's parents emphasized that a college degree was the key to moving up and out of Casa Blanca. She did well in high school and was accepted to, and graduated from, the University of California. Katie's brothers have also improved on their parents' education, occupation, and income. "My older brother is a geek, totally nerdy. He's American; that's how he identifies himself. He's Republican and he works for a division of NASA." Katie's younger brother also holds a college degree and is a regional sales manager. Three generations of Katie's family were raised in a segregated neighborhood with long sociohistorical roots in the United States dating back to the Mexican Revolution, yet each generation has improved on the education and occupation of the last. Although it has taken four generations, Katie holds a college degree, is residentially assimilated, and, consistent with the linear assimilation model, which views intermarriage as the end point of assimilation, both she and her brother married Anglos. Many of the third- and fourth-generation respondents described a similar intergenerational mobility trajectory within their families of a slow but steady progression to socioeconomic assimilation over the generations.

As these case studies show, legal status is important in promoting intragenerational mobility and financial security among first-generation parents, the advantages of which stream down to children. Moreover, a legalization pathway that was once linked to the birth of a U.S. child has implications for public policy and debates about the utility of a pathway to legalization for unauthorized immigrants currently living in the country. This research also illuminates the extreme intergenerational mobility that can occur between an economically marginalized first generation and their 1.5- and second-generation adult children, the very population that is most feared to experience a downward mobility trajectory. Finally, my interviews with third- and fourth-generation middle-class Mexican Americans are in line with recent research demonstrating a pattern of intergenerational mobility that proceeds at a slow but steady pace over the generations (Alba and Nee 2003; Bean and Stevens 2003; Jiménez 2010).

Pathways to Educational Mobility

As I have demonstrated, the class backgrounds of successful Mexican Americans are not uniform. Some grow up middle class, while others grow up in poor or lower-middle-class households. How do those raised in poor households enter the middle class? Some socially mobile Mexican Americans forge a pathway into the middle class through business ownership, especially those who lack a college degree. Business ownership is a strategy to circumvent disadvantages in the labor market that emerge from not having gone to college. The reasons underlying the inability to obtain a college degree are structural. For example, Andrea earned a full scholarship to a small liberal arts college, but she had to drop out after one year to help support her family financially when her father fell ill and was unable to work. She eventually started a business because she grew tired of being passed over for promotions at her place of employment because she did not have a college degree. She now owns a successful employee staffing company.

While some enter the middle class through business ownership, the significant majority of those raised in poor households, regardless of generation, enter the middle class through higher education. A large body of research concentrates on the mechanisms that lead to educational failure among minorities. But what leads to success? Understanding the mechanisms that promote educational achievement among the Mexican American population is of critical importance because the Mexican-origin population has the lowest levels of education of any racial or ethnic group in the United States.

While laypersons might be quick to explain away Mexican Americans' relatively low levels of education by espousing the tired argument that Mexican "culture" simply does not value education, research has shown that the structural position of racial or ethnic groups shapes access to educational resources and cultural capital and is correlated with lower, or higher, levels of educational attainment among racial or ethnic minorities and immigrants (Bourdieu 1977; DiMaggio 1982; Lareau 2003; Lamont and Lareau 1988). Those born and raised in middle- or upper-class families have more favorable educational opportunities, which translate into better labor market outcomes, than those born into low-income or poor families (Conley 1999; Hout and Beller 2006). Moreover, schools mirror the class system of larger society and actively maintain class and racial or ethnic inequalities in education (Bowles and Gintis 1977; Coleman et al. 1966; Rist 1970). Microprocesses within schools, such as racial or ethnic discrimination, teachers' lowered expectations of minority youth, and the likelihood that minority youth, especially boys, are tracked into the non-college-bound vocational track, shape larger patterns of educational attainment among minorities (Carter 2005; Ford 1998; Roscigno and Ainsworth-Darnell 1999; R. C. Smith 2002; Telles and Ortiz 2008).

Mexican Americans who are raised in low-income households have limited financial capital, and the neighborhoods in which they are raised exhibit the injurious conditions of the inner city, including crime, lack of social and public services, and subpar schools, leading us to expect that they may not surpass the social status of their parents as the status attainment and segmented assimilation models predict. Mexican immigrant parents typically migrate with low levels of education and are unfamiliar with how higher education works in the United States. They are often unable to help their children with homework assignments or special projects, even in elementary school, because of their limited English ability and low levels of education. Middle-class parents in this study have more resources to overcome these obstacles if they are present, but low-income parents do not. As Zeke, a 1.5-generation Mexican American explained,

My mom was very, very interested in our school work but she only went through the sixth grade. My dad only went to the third grade. I realize now looking back that my mom's way of helping us was just encouragement. But we really didn't know anything about study habits. I have an encyclopedia that I saved. Our encyclopedia was one from 1955 and that was our reference. That's what we had. I saved it just because it means a lot to me. So if I had to look up stuff it was in that encyclopedia because I couldn't ask my parents.

Like Zeke, nearly all of the respondents, regardless of class background and generation, stressed that their parents expected them to go to college. In fact, a number of respondents related that a college education was their parents' dream: "It's why they moved us here, for education"; "My mom wanted me to have chances she didn't have"; "My dad is very smart, a big reader, but he didn't finish elementary school. It was a dream for me to go to college"; "My parents' dream was that we had to get a degree so we didn't have to labor like them." While parents have high aspirations for their children, they generally have no or limited knowledge of the "culture of college," which includes access to college preparatory classes and AP classes and the importance of extracurricular activities in building a precollege résumé. Parents also are unaware that preparing for, and taking, the Scholastic Aptitude Test (SAT) is a precondition for applying to a four-year university, and they lack information on the availability of financial aid and scholarships to defray college tuition costs.

Those who grow up middle class in the 1.5 and second generation also generally have parents with low levels of education who do not necessarily know how to navigate the education labyrinth, but they are able to bridge this parental knowledge gap by attending middle-class schools where a culture of college is built into the curriculum. Those who are raised in more affluent households also reap the benefits associated with living in middle-class neighborhoods, such as access to professional networks and institutions that help build the cultural capital that is valued in mainstream institutions (Bourdieu 1977; Bowles and Gintis 1977; Lareau 2003; Roscigno 1998). For example, Nicole, who was raised in a middle-class neighborhood in Los Angeles and who is now a partner of an accounting firm, explained that although her parents were successful restaurateurs, they knew little about how one actually goes about applying for college. "They encouraged me to ask my teachers and friends. They knew they could help me in ways they couldn't." Indeed, Nicole learned from her two best friends, who were white with college-educated parents, about the

SAT, and she accompanied one of the families on a tour of several University of California campuses, one of which she decided to attend. Similarly, Karina, introduced in the chapter's opening vignette, explained,

> Living in a middle-class neighborhood, you are around other people who are going to college and doing these things. You see their parents working in professional jobs. It is what you do. If you are applying [for college] you ask your friends for help and that is what you do. When you are around other people who are doing it and who have done it that's just what you do.

For those who grow up in middle-class neighborhoods, greater familial financial capital, combined with the social and cultural capital obtained through middle-class schools and peer networks, greatly facilitates educational mobility. Middle-class parents in this study also have more financial resources to invest in their children's educational mobility. Those resources include private school tuition and the ability to pay for tutors and other extracurricular activities such as music lessons, sports, and field trips.

Growing up in middle-class neighborhoods and having greater financial resources open the educational door for Mexican Americans. How, then, do some adult children of low-skilled, low-level workers who grow up in low-income neighborhoods, who lack financial capital and middle-class cultural capital, become psychologists, lawyers, vice presidents of corporations, engineers, and financial analysts, jobs that require high levels of education? First, as the opening vignette demonstrates in Brenda's case, educational tracking into GATE and AP classes is a mechanism that sets low-income Mexican Americans on a path to college attendance. In Patricia Gandara's (1995) study of low-income Mexican Americans who attend highly selective universities, nearly all of the subjects had been tracked into college preparatory classes in high school. Similarly, more than two thirds of those I interviewed who were raised in low-income households were tracked into GATE or AP classes or bused to middle-class schools outside their neighborhoods. These respondents were the most likely to attend more selective University of California campuses or Ivy League universities right out of high school. Pablo, introduced earlier, explained that the racial and ethnic composition of his neighborhood, and his elementary school, was

> Latinos Latinos Latinos! Mexican Mexican Mexican! Poor. And some Asians, but mainly Mexican, 90 percent Mexican. There [were] really no white people

and no Caucasians or whatever you want to call them and really no African Americans, just a couple [of] Asians. Mainly Chinese and Mexicans.

Pablo did not know that he attended a subpar school until he was hand-picked by one of his teachers to test for a new magnet program held at an upper-middle-class elementary and junior high school in largely prosperous Glendale, a city in the San Fernando Valley. Pablo passed the exam with flying colors. Starting in the fifth grade, he awoke at five each morning and took a forty-five-minute bus ride to and from Glendale. He immediately noticed the school was very different from the one he left behind in Lincoln Heights.

> When I got there I was like in a different world. It was a different school . . . just by the way people acted, dressed, [and] talked and the way they communicated. Just like the competition was incredible. People would fight for A's and B's. I mean they would just bicker over grades.

Pablo left the magnet program after eighth grade and returned to Los Angeles to attend a local urban high school. Because he did well at the magnet school, Pablo was tracked into a "one-of-a-kind university set-up program," which guaranteed college admission and a full scholarship to students who maintained a 3.5 GPA. Pablo applied to elite universities up and down the California coast but decided to attend UCLA so that he could remain close to home. By the time he entered college, his father had passed away and his younger brother had been initiated into the local gang. Like many middle-class Mexican Americans in this study, Pablo is the first in his family to graduate with a college degree, and a middle-class pioneer. His case points to the power of educational tracking and the divergent mobility trajectories that can occur within some families. As in Brenda Guerrero's case, Pablo's younger brother was not tracked into an accelerated program and attended the local elementary and junior high schools, where he too was labeled as a troublemaker. While Pablo was working toward a college degree, his younger brother dropped out of high school and was shot and killed in a skirmish with a rival gang.[4]

Brenda Guerrero's and Pablo's experiences demonstrate the paradoxical nature of educational tracking and AP classes. As the education psychologist Patricia Gandara (1995) found in her study of high-achieving Mexican Americans from low-income backgrounds, curriculum tracking provides opportunities by placing low-income Mexican American students in a college-bound peer group that is "cocooned" from lower-achieving peers. Tracking also exposes low-income Mexican Americans to the information they need to gain access to college and provides them with the academic background to apply for and attend selective universities, which regularly award more "points" in the admissions process to students who have taken AP classes (Burdman 2000). What is ironic is that tracking can also negatively affect students, as is evidenced by Brenda's and Pablo's younger brothers who were labeled and tracked as troublemakers from an early age and who have not achieved similar levels of success. Of course it is impossible to know whether Brenda's and Pablo's brothers would have gone on to college if they had been tracked into GATE, AP classes, or high school programs that guarantee a college education, or whether Brenda and Pablo would still have achieved the same rapid rise into the middle class if they had not been tracked into GATE and AP classes. Nevertheless, previous research has demonstrated that teachers act as institutional gatekeepers when they assess students and determine their eligibility for gifted programs, college prep, or AP class, or conversely when elementary school teachers slot Latino students into special education classes that place them on a course of remedial education throughout junior high and high school, a pattern that is more prevalent among Latino boys, resulting in gendered outcomes in educational attainment among Latinos (N. Lopez 2002; R. C. Smith 2002).

Tracking systems are cumulative, and begin at the elementary school level, when students are placed in accelerated or slower groups and classes (Rowan and Miracle 1983). The longer students stay in one track, the harder it is to move into another (Gandara 1995), and by junior high their educational trajectory has generally been determined (Kershaw 1992). The problem with tracking is that low-income black and Latino students are generally perceived by teachers as having less academic ability than white students and students from low-income backgrounds are disproportionately tracked into non-college-curriculum and vocational tracks (Oakes 1986). While tracking is a mechanism that leads to positive educational outcomes for some Mexican Americans who grow up poor, it is also a mechanism in which race, class, and gender intersect and which creates different opportunity structures that reproduce the racial hierarchy and exacerbate the education gap (R. C. Smith 2002; J. P. Smith 2006).

Mentors are the second critical mechanism in advancing the educational mobility of those who grow up in low-income neighborhoods. Low-income Mexican Americans cannot rely on parents for financial or cultural capital when it comes to applying for and attending college, and they generally lack access to middle-class mentors who can guide them and direct them into pro-fessional networks. For example, in her study of Mexican-origin and Japanese-origin high schoolers, sociologist Maria Eugenia Matute-Bianchi (1986) found that even the most achievement-oriented Mexican-origin youth have limited knowledge of how to pursue high-status, high-paying careers in the primary labor market. Individual family members, especially parents, are engaged in low-wage and low-status occupations and lack access to professionals in their familial and larger social networks. Mexican students' role models were more likely to be adults in the community, Matute-Bianchi discovered, whereas Japanese immigrants were more likely to have relatives who are vis-ible and intimate role models engaged in the professions within the family network. In this vein, researchers examining the exceptional educational out-comes of the children of immigrants or disadvantaged minorities who "beat the odds" in terms of educational attainment find that mentors or "significant others"—teachers, counselors, friends, or siblings—increase Mexican Ameri-cans' social capital and are an important mechanism that advances educa-tional attainment, as does knowing doctors, lawyers, or teachers (Levine and Nidiffer 1996; Portes, Fernández-Kelly, and Haller 2009; R. C. Smith 2008; Telles and Ortiz 2008). I also find that mentors are crucial in bridging the middle-class cultural and human capital gaps that are present in poor families. Men-tors provide access to knowledge, information, and connections, resources that those who grow up middle class have access to by virtue of their class status.

Poor Mexican American youth come into contact with "significant others," or educational mentors (Portes, Fernández-Kelly, and Haller 2009), in three primary ways. The first is through outside programs that provide educational support to students from low-income families. These outside programs may or may not be geared exclusively to Latinos. As Mateo, a lawyer and second-generation Mexican American, explained,

> My mentors taught me so much about things that I couldn't read about or learn from my own father because his experience was limited. The ins and outs of society and the workforce and different opportunities that exist. I wanted to go to UCLA, but I had no knowledge about how to apply to college and neither did my parents. I always assumed that I couldn't afford college. I couldn't perceive how my parents would have the money. My senior year, a counselor asked me, "what are you going to do?" I said, "I guess I'm going to go to com-munity college." And one weekend I attended a retreat given by the Chicano

students association. I heard an attorney speak who still practices law and he went there to encourage Hispanic students to be a lawyer. After I heard this guy talk—it had such an impact on me I was like, I want to be like him. I always remember that it was that one person who changed my life in terms of a career.

The Latino lawyer whom Mateo "serendipitously" met at the retreat not only acted as a role model by showing Mateo what was possible; he also took Mateo under his wing and helped him apply to college and, later, law schools. Thus, outside programs provide adolescents with a broader view of schools and colleges, and mentors and program staff act as cultural brokers by providing tools and long-term support that help minority youth negotiate institutions outside inner-city communities, such as selective colleges (Phelan, Davidson, and Yu 1991; Portes, Fernández-Kelly, and Haller 2009; R. C. Smith 2008).

The second way in which disadvantaged Mexican American youth come into contact with mentors is through their parents' employers. This occurs among those with parents who work low-wage immigrant jobs in the informal economy, chiefly through mothers who are domestic workers. Although these jobs can be fraught with interethnic conflict (Hondagneu-Sotelo 2001), mothers in these jobs build long-term relationships with their upper-middle-class white clientele, and they often bring their children to work with them, especially during summers or school vacations. This places Mexican American youth in "another world" and provides them with middle-class and professional contacts.

Geena exemplifies this pattern. Her father was a lawyer in Mexico and her mother worked at the firm as a secretary. Geena was raised by her single mother until her mother decided to join her extended family in Los Angeles when Geena was five years old. Geena then lived with her maternal grandmother because her mother worked as a live-in housekeeper, cleaning the mansions that dot the Hollywood hills and caring for other people's children there. Maggie would return home and visit her daughter on the weekends, and Geena would live with her in palatial mansions during the summers, where she would "enjoy the perks of those families, swimming in the pools, driving in the Mercedes and Rolls Royces." Geena attended a low-income urban school but was tracked into GATE classes. She always knew she wanted to be a lawyer, an aspiration that did not seem out of reach considering the cultural memory of her father's occupation. Although she never knew her father, and although she and her mother were now poor, her mother's occasional tales of her father's success and stature were a source of pride and a motivating force that shaped Geena's own aspirations (Fernández-Kelly 2008; Gandara 1995). While Geena's ambition and educational successes placed her on a track of educational achievement, she had no idea what applying to law school entailed. The most critical mechanism that helped her fulfill her goals was the intervention of her mother's white employer, a successful Hollywood lawyer, setting her on a rapid educational and occupational trajectory. As Geena recalled:

> Something kind of interesting or funny is that the family that my mom is working for since maybe 1988, he is a pretty successful attorney in, he's got his firm and all of that. In high school in maybe my sophomore or junior year, he asked my mom, "What is she thinking of doing?" and my mom said, "She wants to be a lawyer, like her dad." So he told her that he'd like to talk to me. So I went to meet with him and I was really nervous and he was very nice and basically I started talking to him, and I basically didn't know you had to go to college before you go to law school. He was wonderful, he was like a mentor and he told me what I had to do, he set me up, he knew a lot of people that knew a lot of people, whatever. I ended up being able to meet with a college counselor that was a good friend of his; he kind of helped me by going through my statement, my applications and things like that. So he is a USC alumni, so I got accepted into a few schools; he was very happy that I got into USC.

Geena earned straight A's at USC while working part-time on campus to help pay her tuition and living expenses. However, during her second year at USC, the department in which she worked part-time cut the student workers' hours and Geena was out of a job. She drove her mother to work one morning and subsequently ran into her mentor, who questioned why she was not at work.

> I told him that I lost my job and I was going to try to find another job. He left his office and a couple of hours later he called and said, "Can you work a computer?" I said, "Of course I can." So he asked, "Would you want to work at my firm?" and I said, "Yes!" So a week later . . . I was there. Yes, things happen; sometimes you don't know why things happen. So I think that the beginning of that school year, I started at his firm and later on I found out that he really didn't need anybody [laughter]. But I was there until I started law school, so for three or almost four years. It was great to work there; everybody was super nice because they didn't know my background, and they didn't know who I was really. They didn't know that I was his housekeeper's daughter; they just

knew she is a daughter of a friend, and that makes all the difference. I was their little baby for four years. It was great; I had all the hours I wanted or didn't. The summers were great. One summer I went to DC to intern—that was a nonpaid internship for a while and they all kind of put together money for me to be paid. Me wanting to be a lawyer to get that exposure, to get that level of comfort around rich attorneys. To me, I was comfortable in certain environments growing up. . . . At the same time it gave me more confidence because I was respected by these people; you know I was going to Christmas parties and hanging out with them, things like that. He would always tell me that he wanted this to help me. He is a great, great wonderful man. He has taken me as something of a project or something like that.

While Geena may have eventually figured out the necessary steps to apply for college and law school, her mother's Anglo employer became a conduit to an instantly rich source of social and cultural capital at a crucial time in her educational trajectory. As her mentor's "project," Geena has been able to continuously draw on him for advice, and she has gained entrée to an elite network of professionals who helped her secure a job at a high-profile firm.

Finally, some respondents who were raised in poor households also explained that their older siblings who had gone through college themselves acted as educational mentors. For example, Alejandra and Martha Calvo are sisters who were raised in a low-income area of Santa Ana. Alejandra was brought to the United States as a young child, and the family remained unauthorized until Martha was born, when their parents adjusted their status under the "baby clause." Their parents, both of whom have less than an elementary education, constantly emphasized the importance of obtaining an education. As Alejandra, the eldest, remembers, "My family for some odd reason would tell us that they would break their backs, but you just needed to get your degrees. . . . They said the biggest satisfaction they would get is for us to have our degree. So that constant reminder that they were working so hard for us so we could become something, that would be the biggest satisfaction for them." Alejandra was focused on attending college, but she had no idea how to make her parents' dream a reality. She was not tracked into the AP classes and she received no assistance from the counselors at her urban high school. After graduating from high school, Alejandra enrolled at the local community college and eventually transferred to the local California State University campus. Although she is thankful of the education she received, she wished she would have had the opportunity to attend an Ivy League school, something she pushed her younger sister, Martha, to do.

> My younger sister attended Brown, an Ivy League school, and she is the one who reaped the benefits of my knowledge. I like to take some credit in that I told her to apply, I helped her with her applications, I told her she needed to leave. So I have to take that credit. She went back east and she called one time and she was crying and told me she didn't belong there. She told me it was my entire fault, but I think it benefited her in the end.
>
> JAV: It was important for you to see her go to a better school?
>
> A: Well, I thought I couldn't do it right after [high school] . . . I will be very honest. I didn't have someone push me, I was very insecure about my skill set, I knew I couldn't get into an Ivy League school. I didn't think I was that smart in the class, I know I wasn't scored with the gifted children. I think in the back of my mind I was doubting my skill set because I saw smart kids in the class all the time. I had a high "B" average, or a 3.2 GPA in high school. I went to community college and I thought I can't just leave; it will be really hard on my mom. My sister was in elementary and my little brother was two years old. I felt like that somebody needed to stay back and help them out a little bit, so I couldn't leave.

Martha, interviewed at a different point in time, corroborated Alejandra's claim that she was an important mentor. "I would say that my older siblings, Alejandra and Jon, were key in laying the foundation so that I could follow a solid, strong college-bound path in high school." Others spoke of how their older siblings helped with their college applications, assisted in filling out financial aid forms, and advised them of which classes to take to compile a competitive application. More simply, older siblings also act as role models by demonstrating that a college education is attainable. Recent studies have also demonstrated the importance of older siblings in "showing the ropes" to low-income Mexican Americans (Bettie 2003; Gandara 1995; Portes, Fernández-Kelly, and Haller 2009). Particularly noteworthy is that socially mobile first-born Mexican Americans in this study are also an important source of financial capital for their younger siblings' education. As will be discussed in Chapter 4, socially mobile middle-class Mexican Americans often pay for costly private school tuition for their younger siblings, especially if their parents continue to live in inner-city neighborhoods. They purchase computers and books for their siblings, and they constantly help them with homework.

Conclusion

Middle-class Mexican Americans appear similar on paper in terms of their middle-class attributes, but their class backgrounds diverge, an important difference that is concealed in large-scale survey research. Some Mexican Americans' backgrounds are steeped in middle-class privilege where they reap the benefits associated with higher parental incomes stemming from their parents' high-paying jobs or successful entrepreneurial endeavors. The advantages associated with growing up middle class include living in middle-class neighborhoods and attending middle-class schools, which provide youth with the social and cultural capital that is critical for higher educational attainment. The underlying mechanism that allows some immigrant families to gain a foothold in the middle class is parental legal status.

While some grew up middle class, the majority of successful Mexican Americans I interviewed, especially those in the 1.5 and second generation, grew up in poverty and achieved extreme rates of intergenerational mobility relative to their parents and much of their kin. They were raised in long-established, low-income ethnic communities or *colonias* by parents who toiled in low-wage immigrant jobs. The majority attained social mobility through higher education; however, some moved up the corporate ladder even though they lacked a college degree, and others followed a pathway into the middle class through entrepreneurship. Overall, middle-class Mexicans' social mobility trajectories offset the widespread pessimism that the entirety of the Mexican American population is following a pathway of downward, or stagnated, assimilation.

The status attainment model, where parental income and education predicts the education of children, helps to partly explain the success of those raised in middle-class households, especially because higher parental incomes lead to middle-class neighborhoods and high-quality schools. However, this model does not explain the high levels of educational and occupational attainment achieved by those with poor and low-educated parents. The role of educational tracking, outside programs, and access to mentors cannot be overstated in helping to explain how some Mexican Americans from disadvantaged backgrounds achieve rapid intergenerational and social mobility and gain entry into the middle class. GATE, AP courses, and outside programs geared toward college are crucial in providing adolescents with a broader view of schools and other mainstream institutions, and they help fill the gaps in educational knowledge and professional networks that exist within low-income families. Outside programs are also important because they link low-income Mexican Americans to mentors and provide information about financial aid that makes college aspirations a reality. Professional mentors and older siblings also help fill gaps in resources and networks by providing social and cultural capital that low-income parents often lack. Together, these mechanisms advance educational and occupational attainment and ultimately entry into the middle class.

Scholars would expect the economically successful Mexican Americans detailed in this chapter to follow a traditional pathway of assimilation where they incorporate into the white middle class. Do middle-class Mexican Americans assimilate as middle-class whites, or might there be an additional pathway into the middle class? The remaining chapters of this book elucidate the ways in which class background—growing up poor or middle class—shapes the lived experiences of successful Mexican Americans and their incorporation pathways into the middle class.

4 Family Obligations: The Immigrant Narrative and Middle-Class Individualism
With Jennifer Lee

My mom will call and say, "Can I borrow money?" and I say, "I am not going to let you borrow." I tell her up front, "I will give you whatever you need." I have a loyalty to my family, especially because of the hardships we went through.

—Linda, 1.5 generation, nurse practitioner

My family didn't have that sense of communal interdependence. My parents just raised us to be competitive to get ahead.

—Joe, second generation, psychologist

MIDDLE-CLASS MEXICAN AMERICANS EXHIBIT the traditional indicators of middle-class status and at first glance appear to be a homogeneous ethnic group. Delve below the surface and a key difference comes to light: middle-class Mexican Americans hail from varied socioeconomic backgrounds. Some were raised in poor households and low-income ethnic communities and are the first in their families to enter the middle class, while others grow up in economically secure households and white middle-class neighborhoods. Contemporary theories of incorporation do not adequately consider whether, and to what extent, within-group differences in class background structure lived experiences and incorporation pathways. If we adhere to contemporary theories of incorporation, we might expect Mexican Americans to follow a path of linear assimilation into the white middle class where ties to coethnics and the ethnic community are severed following upward mobility (Gordon 1964; Portes and Zhou 1993). The minority culture of mobility model complicates the linear assimilation framework by drawing on the experiences of middle-class African Americans and predicting that socially mobile minorities face unique challenges that distinguish them from the white middle class, one of which is the maintenance of ties to poorer coethnics who make appeals for financial and social support

(Neckerman, Carter, and Lee 1999). This chapter tests these different frameworks by examining whether middle-class Mexican Americans sever ties with or remain connected to poorer kin, and moreover, whether they retain salient family obligations that manifest in financial and social support.

Patterns of Family Obligations and Giving Back

Research examining family obligations and patterns of giving back concentrates on middle-class blacks and whites and demonstrates that these two groups have different attitudes about family obligations and divergent patterns of giving back to coethnics. Patterns of giving back among whites are nearly purely unidirectional, flowing downstream from parents to children, and continue in this vein even after children reach adulthood (Bianchi et al. 2008; Hogan, Eggebeen, and Clogg 1993; P. Taylor, Funk, and Kennedy 2005). In contrast, giving back to kin is a well-documented multidirectional phenomenon among African Americans, who are also more likely than whites to give back to coethnics beyond the nuclear family unit, regardless of whether they are poor or middle class (Billingsley 1992; Dawson 1994; Hochschild 1995; Lamont 2000; Pattillo-McCoy 2000; Stack 1974). This variation partly stems from whites' and blacks' different orientations regarding individualism and collectivism. Whites are more likely to support the ethos behind meritocratic individualism, while African Americans are more likely to subscribe to a collectivist, group-based orientation.

Whites are less likely to give back to coethnics in need, or to ask kin for financial assistance even when they experience economic uncertainty, than other racial/ethnic groups. This resistance stems from their strong credence in the American dream, which supports the ideologies of equality of opportunity, individualism, and self-reliance (Hochschild 1995; Lee 2002; Lipset 1997). An inherent facet of the American dream is the notion that mobility opportunities are equal and that getting ahead primarily entails delaying gratification and hard work. Given that most middle-class whites strongly believe in the American dream, they view the act of giving back as a violation of the creed that success should be achieved through individual effort (Hochschild 1995; Lipset 1997; Newman 1988). For example, in sociologist Katherine Newman's (1988) study of the downwardly mobile white middle class, she finds that middle-class white families go to great lengths to camouflage their precarious economic situation as long as possible rather than asking friends or family for financial or social assistance. In fact, she argues that nothing disintegrates family relationships and friendships more rapidly than asking for financial help. Newman suggests that this is because middle-class whites have not traditionally fostered a network of asking for and receiving support, even in the direst of circumstances. Working-class white Americans also share the values embodied in the American dream, as well as the tenets rooted in the Protestant work ethic such as hard work, discipline, and responsibility (Higginbotham and Weber 1992; Lamont 2000).

While whites consider asking a relative or friend for financial assistance a violation of the norm of hard work and personal success, African Americans maintain a strong sense of a collective, group-based identity, regardless of class, both because they choose to and because they cannot escape their racialized ethnic origins (Dawson 1994; Hochschild 1995; Lamont 2000; Shelton and Wilson 2006). The sense of responsibility middle-class African Americans feel for poorer coethnics stems from a shared history of discrimination, legal exclusion, and economic subordination to other groups, producing what political scientist Michael Dawson (1994) refers to as a sense of "linked fate." Another reason that middle-class blacks may be more likely to give back to their less affluent counterparts is their geographic proximity to poorer kin, resulting in more class-heterogeneous ties. Patterns of residential segregation consistently reveal that blacks remain the most spatially isolated of all racial/ethnic minority groups, regardless of class (Charles 2003; Massey and Denton 1987, 1993). Consequently, middle-class blacks are more likely to live in class-heterogeneous communities or in neighborhoods that are adjacent to poor blacks, and they are more likely than whites to have impoverished parents or siblings (Heflin and Pattillo 2006; Pattillo-McCoy 2000). As sociologists Colleen Heflin and Mary Pattillo (2006: 819) argue, "This enduring familiarity with poverty" distinguishes the black middle class from the white middle class because their social proximity to poorer kin can lead to greater demands to give back to poorer coethnics, even if the flow of resources means impeding one's further economic mobility. If middle-class minorities regularly give back to poorer kin and coethnics, they may be less able to secure their middle-class status, accumulate assets and wealth, and transfer their assets across generations (Cole and Omari 2003; Conley 1999; Oliver and Shapiro 1995).

The models of middle-class white individualism and middle-class black collectivism also extend to the upwardly mobile. As historian Elizabeth Higginbotham and sociologist Lynn Weber (1992) find in their study of socially mobile black and white women, black women who move up the economic ladder feel that they cannot leave their families in the dust, and they are significantly more likely than socially mobile white women to embrace a collective orientation to mobility. For example, a professional black woman who was raised working class explains, "I feel that in many respects I'm stronger in terms of emotional and financial well-being than most of my family and I feel an obligation to give back" (1992: 18). In contrast, when Higginbotham and Weber asked upwardly mobile white women whether they feel a sense of debt to their families and an obligation to give back, many of the women were puzzled and asked what the question meant. Higginbotham and Weber argue that upwardly mobile white women feel less obliged to give back because they view their success as a result of their own merits, rather than as a collective struggle for upward mobility. For example, a white woman in their study relates, "I am appreciative of the values my parents have instilled in me. But for the most part I feel like I have done it on my own" (1992: 431).

Are middle-class Mexican Americans more like middle-class whites, who exhibit an ethos of individualism and unidirectional patterns of support, or more like middle-class African Americans, a racialized minority, who retain a sense of linked fate born out of a legacy of discrimination? Scholars have proposed that Mexican immigrants bring collectivist orientations with them when they migrate and that they and their children are often more family oriented, or familistic, than other racial or ethnic groups, especially non-Hispanic whites (Baca Zinn 1982; Fuligni, Tseng, and Lam 1999; Mindel 1980). Mexican Americans are also portrayed as more likely than whites to retain a sense of filial responsibility to older parents and to be tightly bound to the extended family (Griswold del Castillo 1983; Fuligni, Tseng, and Lam 1999; Keefe and Padilla 1987; Marin 1993; Vega 1995). For example, in their study of attitudes toward family obligations, biobehavioral scientist Andrew Fuligni and colleagues Vivian Tseng and May Lam (1999: 11) find that Latino adolescents "possessed stronger values and greater expectations regarding their duty to assist, respect, and support their families than their peers with European backgrounds." Fuligni, Tseng, and Lam further argue that "these findings suggest that even within a society that emphasizes adolescent autonomy and independence, youths from families with collectivist traditions retain their parents' familistic values." While these studies primarily attribute feelings of obligation to Mexican or Latino culture, others argue that patterns of giving back among low-income immigrant groups stem from the economic and structural disadvantage that accompanies their immigrant status and marginalized economic position

(Agius Vallejo and Lee 2009; Roschelle 1997; Rumbaut and Komaie 2009; Sarkisian, Gerena, and Gerstel 2007).

Do middle-class Mexican Americans provide financial and social support to poorer coethnics? If so, does giving back stem from a sense of linked fate with poorer coethnics that is born out of a racialized middle-class minority status as it does for African Americans? Or does giving back arise out of a strong cultural orientation to familism, rather than a sense of linked fate? Or do middle-class Mexican Americans cut ties to coethnics once they enter the middle class, as the linear assimilation model predicts, and come to resemble middle-class whites in that they are less likely to give back because it violates the tenets of meritocratic individualism? These questions provide insight into middle-class Mexican Americans' varied experiences and incorporation pathways into the middle class.

Remaining Tied in the First and Second Generations

The majority of the 1.5- and second-generation Mexican Americans described in this book live in middle-class neighborhoods where the median household income exceeds the national median. Middle-class Mexican Americans live in large, ranch-style, single-family homes in neighborhoods with immaculately manicured yards, gleaming hardwood floors, and crystal blue swimming pools. A few of the respondents live in the brand-new gated condominium developments that dot Orange County's famous Pacific coastline, and some live in hip loft-style apartments overlooking the Los Angeles basin. A smaller number continue to live with their parents in or near the lower-income communities in which they were raised. These homes and neighborhoods are older, but the homes are well kept, and many boast recently remodeled kitchens or bathrooms, typically paid for by middle-class children.

The middle-class and largely white (as described by the respondents) neighborhoods that most call home contrast sharply with the neighborhoods where the parents and kin of the socially mobile continue to live. Over half of the respondents characterize their parents' neighborhoods as "low income" and Latino. As Maria, a 25-year-old successful entrepreneur, described, "My parents live in a really bad area in La Puente [a city in Los Angeles County]. It's like right in the middle of the neighborhood, and there are always gang bangers walking by." While many socially mobile middle-class Mexican Americans no longer live in the ethnic communities in which their parents reside, the majority retain strong ties to poorer kin who live in neighborhoods that are predominantly Latino and very low income (Brown 2007). Those who classify their socioeconomic background as poor are more likely than those who grow up middle class to remain in very close contact with kin, speaking to their parents at least once a day, every other day or every week. Moreover, just over half of those who were raised in poor households responded that they return to their parents' neighborhoods every weekend or every other weekend on average to attend various family gatherings. As the minority culture of mobility predicts, socially mobile Mexican Americans retain strong ties to poor relatives and thus retain a more enduring familiarity with poverty, making their experience as middle-class Americans distinctly different from the experience of most middle-class whites. Because they did not grow up in middle-class households, their parents often continue to toil in low-wage, backbreaking jobs, and they may also be the first in their nuclear or extended family to attend college and to penetrate the middle class.

In sharp contrast, those who grow up in middle-class neighborhoods are further removed from poverty because their childhoods were steeped in middle-class privilege and because their parents are more economically secure. Nevertheless, while those who grew up in middle-class neighborhoods may not have parents or siblings who are poor, they retain ties to extended kin, including cousins, aunts, uncles, and grandparents, who reside in low-income ethnic communities. However, they come into contact with their poor kin far less regularly than those who grow up poor, and visit with them primarily during major holidays and celebrations, such as weddings, graduation parties, or funerals, rather than weekly or several times a month. That those with more privileged childhoods visit their poorer kin less often may be related to their middle-class upbringing, since middle-class children—regardless of race—typically have weaker ties to extended kin (Lareau 2003).

Family Obligations and Giving Back

The majority of the 1.5- and second-generation middle-class Mexican Americans remain strongly tied to kin and coethnics in less affluent communities, like many middle-class African Americans. However, those who were raised in poor neighborhoods and households are more likely to offer assistance to their kin, and are more likely to feel obliged to do so, than those who grew up middle class. Virtually all of the 1.5- and second-generation socially mobile respondents retain salient financial and social family obligations. The one socially mobile second-generation respondent who does not give back explained that, because he is the youngest of eleven siblings, the responsibility of financially helping his family has never fallen on him; instead, his older siblings have shouldered the burden.

While nearly all of those who grew up poor retain extensive family obligations and give back to poorer coethnics, they do so in three different ways. First, 20 percent fully support their parents and/or younger siblings. Second, 30 percent are the financial "safety net" of their parents, siblings, and extended kin in times of financial crises or economic uncertainty such as when kin experience a medical emergency or are laid off from jobs. Finally, half offer regular financial support to kin. The first two types of financial support are most common among middle-class pioneers, while regular financial support is most frequent among those who have siblings who have also entered the middle class and who can share the burden. While the socially mobile retain salient financial obligations, second-generation Mexican Americans who grow up middle class do not give back financially to kin even though they have ties to poorer kin in their networks. However, it should be noted that nearly all, regardless of class background, provide social support to their parents and/or extended kin. Social support includes such tasks as making phone calls on behalf of Spanish-speaking parents, translating documents, driving kin to doctor's appointments, and babysitting.

One fifth of the 1.5- and second-generation respondents who grew up poor fully support their parents. When asked whether he has ever had to help his family financially, Adrian, a second-generation Mexican American who holds a master's degree and now works as a teacher, explains, "I have to. Ever since I started working when I was fourteen I have given them everything I could. Now it's at about a thousand dollars a month I give them, just to help them out." In addition to giving his parents this lump sum of money every month, Adrian pays all of the household bills. Two patterns became clear about those who fully support their parents. First, compared to those who offer more fluid types of assistance, those who fully support their parents are more likely to be the only members of their nuclear families to have achieved middle-class status. Magdalena, a business owner who is a freshly minted member of the American middle class, summed up this trend perfectly when she explained,

I feel a little more pressure because I am the oldest and the only one [who is middle class], so I think it's affected me more than some of my friends because they have other siblings to rely on. For me, I feel like, in comparison to my friends, I hold a larger burden because it's just me. My friend has like six other siblings and they all help out.

The second pattern that became evident about middle-class Mexican Americans who fully support their parents is that their parents worked in low-wage, backbreaking jobs with no medical insurance or retirement benefits, putting them at risk for chronic medical conditions rendering them unable to work. The burden of support is thus shouldered by their socially mobile adult children. Jose, a 1.5-generation immigrant who legalized under the 1986 Immigration Reform and Control Act (IRCA) along with his parents, has a degree from a prestigious university, is a successful architect, and makes nearly $100,000 a year in income. However, Jose still lives at home with his parents, although this is not his first choice. Jose's father once worked in a meat processing plant, but a few years ago, at only 47 years old, he started complaining about pain in his eyes. Lacking medical insurance or other liquid assets on which he could draw to pay for medical care, Jose's father received only the most basic medical care and was eventually diagnosed with glaucoma. Now he is legally blind and cannot work at all, and Jose has had to use the money he had diligently saved up for a down payment on a house, as well as some of his own retirement funds, to pay for his father's expensive medical bills. Jose began to work extra hours to provide for his parents and to pay his younger brother's Catholic school tuition. "I took it upon me to be the main provider. I still am. I do all their errands; I shop for them. I shop for my mom's clothes, my dad's clothes, groceries, everything."

This type of extensive financial support is not relegated to the 1.5 generation. Maria, a second-generation Mexican American and entrepreneur who has two young children of her own, fully supports her mother, who lives in a small, rent-subsidized apartment in a "bad" neighborhood. Maria's mother is unable to work because of long-standing health problems that went untreated due to a lack of insurance. As Maria elaborates, "I fully support my mom. I pay her rent, I give her money, I take her to the doctors, I buy her prescriptions. I take care of my mom."

Not all 1.5- and second-generation middle-class Mexican Americans provide constant financial support to their family members like Jose and Maria. Thirty percent act as the familial "safety net" in times of economic crises. Lupe, a 34-year-old second-generation Mexican who works as the vice president of a national financial services institution, is the only person in her family who has attained middle-class status. Like many of the socially mobile, Lupe was identified as a "gifted" child and placed on the accelerated track at a magnet high school, where she graduated a year early at age 17. She was admitted to several selective colleges on the East Coast but decided to attend a private university in

Los Angeles so that she could remain close to her family. A few years after graduating from college, Lupe moved to a middle-class neighborhood in Orange County, where she purchased a brand-new condominium. Her parents and three siblings remain in Cudahy, a city in Southeast Los Angeles that has one of the highest population densities of any city in the nation. Cudahy's population is 96 percent Latino with a median household income of $41,783, well below the national median and 21 percent of the population live below the poverty line (U.S. Bureau of the Census 2010). Although Lupe's father owns a landscaping company, the family barely made ends meet, and her father was never successful enough to rise beyond the "low-income, working-class" labels Lupe also uses to describe the social status of her two brothers. One of Lupe's brothers was recently laid off from his job as a low-level supervisor in a manufacturing plant and the other is a long-haul truck driver. As a vice president of a bank who earns over $100,000 a year, Lupe is similar to many middle-class whites in terms of her education, occupation, income, and neighborhood, yet the ties she retains to poorer kin distinguish her from her white middle-class counterparts, leaving her with an enduring familiarity with poverty.

As a banker, Lupe lectured me on the importance of having something "in the bank for a rainy day," but she explained that her family has no savings to draw on in times of need and that they have a "different mentality" when it comes to finances, as she relates:

> JAV: So when you say a different mentality—
> A: With finances. Making sure that you have something set aside so that if you lose your job or anything happens, you know, what is going to be your safety net? They are living without one, and it scares me. But then again, they probably think that I am—that I am their safety net.
> JAV: So you think they might view you that way?
> A: It's not a view; it's just the way it is.

Lupe recently gave her parents—who have been supporting her younger brother and his two young children during his divorce—$5,000 so that they could make their mortgage payment and cover their household bills. Moreover, during her college years, Lupe financially rescued her father, whose landscaping business was in jeopardy at the time, by giving him $10,000 from her school loans, which she is still paying back.

> I had more than enough loans to pay for tuition, like some of the loans were to pay for day-to-day expenses, but back then my dad's business was really

hurting so I gave them probably close to $10,000 of my loans to help the business.

In addition to these sizeable financial contributions, Lupe also agreed to cosign for the loan used to purchase her father's new truck, which he could not obtain on his own based on his credit record. As she explained, her financial support is "Like a cyclical thing. If there is something going on where they require financial help then they—you know, it happens at that time."

Paco, a second-generation white-collar professional, spoke with emotion as he recalled helping his father, a janitor, clean offices on the weekends, and he spoke with pride when he vividly described how hard he worked to obtain a bachelor's degree from UCLA and an MBA from Harvard University. In fact, he explained that he deliberately employed "a more individual approach and detached myself from them [his family] so I could concentrate on getting ahead myself and finishing my education. You know, like what whites typically do." However, after Paco moved back to California from the East Coast, his proximity to his less advantaged relatives, and their economic need, proved hard to ignore. When I asked whether he has ever helped his family financially, his confident smile morphed into a hard line as he glumly explained that he is viewed as the family financial safety net by his mother and sisters.

> My grandmother died about a month ago with credit card debt, and I assumed the debt so as to avoid bankruptcy for my mother. That's slightly exaggerated but it was a pretty significant amount. . . . About $6,000.
> JAV: How come you had to assume the debt?
> A: I just did. I'm . . . my sisters aren't in a position to do that as quickly and that was my role. . . . My mother was in a bind, my sisters were not in a position to help, and I was the only one who could, so I did.

Having to fully support parents and siblings or being viewed as a financial safety net in times of economic crises is not unusual for the 1.5 and second generations, who have become upwardly mobile in one generation and now don the markers of middle-class status. Middle-class Mexican Americans share their earnings, drain their savings accounts by giving lump sums of money to their families, and they open lines of credit in their own names for parents and siblings when costly items are needed. Some respondents have had to support their family members when one has lost a job or they are called upon to cover the mounting medical bills of kin who lack medical insurance because they work in low-wage jobs with no benefits. As the housing market in Southern

California took a dive and the mortgage crises worsened between 2008 and 2010, a few of the respondents were asked to help make mortgage payments to stall foreclosures for relatives who entered into risky loans. As the sole members of their families who have graduated from college, attained professional jobs, and now reside in middle-class suburbs, they are viewed as the success stories who have ample financial resources with which to help others.

While some 1.5- and second-generation socially mobile Mexican American middle-class respondents fully support their families or act as their families' financial safety nets, the majority offer assistance that is more fluid. The third and most common type of financial assistance is the regular monetary support that socially mobile Mexican Americans provide their family members. In this case, their parents or extended kin may not rely on them for their livelihood, but family members depend on their regular contributions to supplement their incomes. Half of the respondents who grew up in poor neighborhoods regularly give their parents between $200 and $1,000 each month to help defray household expenses such as paying for groceries, bills, clothing, and expensive private school tuition for younger siblings. They also typically give their parents lump sums of money each time they travel home to Mexico to visit their extended kin so that "they can enjoy themselves." Regular financial support is most common among those with parents who have jobs with medical benefits and most importantly among those who have middle-class siblings who share the financial burden.

Alejandra and Martha Calvo, introduced in Chapter 3, present a sharp contrast to Adrian, Maria, Lupe, and Paco, who are the first in their families to achieve middle-class status and who have given large lump sums of money to coethnics. Alejandra, born in Mexico, and Martha, American born, are two of four children raised in a low-income area of Orange County. Their mother worked as a shipping clerk and their father as a machine operator. Their parents applied for legal residency under the "baby clause" when Martha was born, which allowed them to obtain stable, but low wage, jobs. Their mother was able to acquire medical insurance through her job and continues to work at age 64 because as Martha said, "health insurance is really important for my mother." Alejandra earned a bachelor's degree from California State University and now works as an executive for an automobile corporation headquartered in Orange County. Martha, who is two years younger, is a lawyer and her brother, who has earned an associate's degree, is a computer programmer. When I asked Alejandra if she has ever helped her family financially, she explained that she and her two siblings each contribute $200 a month spending money for their parents or they all pitch in when something in the house needs to be replaced or remodeled. Alejandra stated that the siblings also fund their parents' yearly trip to Mexico. "If they are going to fly to Mexico, here is some spending money and here is the ticket." Martha later corroborated this collective financial support when she recounted that she gives her parents $200 each month for "spending money" and $1,000 whenever they visit their hometown in Mexico, typically twice a year.

A significant number of socially mobile Mexican Americans also provide regular financial support in the form of private, generally Catholic, school tuition for younger siblings. While the older siblings might now live in middle-class communities themselves, the younger siblings often continue to reside in the inner-city communities in which they were raised and where their parents still live. Due to their own educational experiences, which may be shaped by attending subpar schools themselves or by being bused into middle-class schools outside the ethnic community, socially mobile middle-class Mexican Americans understand that the schools in inner-city communities do not measure up to those in wealthier neighborhoods. Frank, an engineer and second-generation Mexican American who was raised in a low-income Mexican neighborhood in Los Angeles, is a case in point. Frank has a sister who is three years younger and a brother who is fifteen years younger. Frank's younger brother, Josh, entered elementary school while Frank and his sister, Amelia, were working toward their bachelor's degrees. Although they were enrolled in college full-time, Frank and his sister worked full-time while in college, in part to help pay Josh's tuition. Frank and his sister each paid $2,300 a year for Josh's private school education through elementary school and junior high. Their tuition payments ended when their brother entered ninth grade and tested into a magnet high school located in a middle-class neighborhood. When asked how Josh ended up in Catholic school, Frank replied,

My sister and I pushed my parents to do it. And he would have a new teacher every month; they were all subs. At the time the schools were growing so much they were hiring all these people and he was like a second grader and we knew he would be affected and I said why don't we put him in Catholic school and that's how he went there. He started doing well and my mom was like, I'm not taking him out.

JAV: How did they afford to send him to Catholic school?

A: My sister and I paid for it. We [had] seen him excelling and he was doing well and enjoying it. My mom sat us down and said, why should we take him out? Being the fact that there is a fifteen-year gap it's totally different as opposed to three years; I'm fifteen and I have a baby brother. You can't not help. . . . So we just helped him out. We were having success and we wanted to share that with our families.

Frank's "success" allowed him to pay his younger brother's tuition, which subsequently buffered him from the affects of attending a subpar school system and ultimately facilitated his entry into a much-sought-after magnet school outside the ethnic community. While they no longer pay private school tuition for their brother, Frank and his sister continue to financially support his education. They purchase his school uniforms and supplies, and they recently bought him a brand-new, high-powered laptop so that he could "stay competitive with the other kids." They also pay for his extracurricular activities. Others exhibited similar patterns. Inez is 1.5 generation and the director of a nonprofit. She lives in a middle-class neighborhood, but travels home to Santa Ana several times a week to check in on her mother and sister. Inez is in charge of directing and financially underwriting her 15-year-old sister's education, something that her mother, a factory supervisor with a sixth-grade education, finds daunting. Inez explained,

If the computer is broke, I'll fix it. School clothes. Supplies. Extra stuff. I have made a plan for her for college. I hope that I can maintain my level of income so that when she goes to college she will be able to study abroad, she will be able to do things that I didn't get to do. I want my sister to have these experiences and not have to worry about not being able to do them because her parents can't afford it. I help my sister out with her homework a lot. She is at that level that there is no way that my mom can help her. Language barrier plus other . . . just the level of math and all that stuff that she's at.

In short, older siblings who have made it to the middle class often direct a significant proportion of their social and financial resources to their younger siblings, which advances their educational attainment.

Middle-class Mexican American pioneers become important sources of financial and social capital not only for parents and siblings but also for the extended family. Socially mobile Mexican Americans may also be asked to give back to extended kin. Again, because they have attained middle-class status, their less advantaged relatives regularly turn to them for economic assistance. As Martha Calvo explains,

> Because my Mom did such a good job with us, and we are doing very well, and we've always been close to our extended families, they always come to me or my sister. Always. For financial assistance, *always* [her emphasis].

Martha and her sister are regularly called upon by their *tíos* (uncles and aunts)—many of whom Martha admits are fictive kin (relationships based not on blood or marriage but on close relationships)—to make financial contributions when extended family members are in need.

Social Support Through Cultural Brokering

While there may be differences in the ways in which middle-class Mexican Americans give back financially, all of the 1.5 and second generation who grow up poor, and some of the second generation who grow up middle class, provide some type of social support to their families, primarily when they act as "cultural brokers" between their families and the English-speaking public (Lee 2002). Research has demonstrated that the English-speaking children of Mexican immigrants frequently act as language brokers for their parents (Orellana, Dorner, and Pulido 2003; Valenzuela 1999), and I find that this pattern continues beyond adolescence and into adulthood, even when adult children acknowledge that their parents become proficient in English. The immigrant parents of 1.5- and second-generation middle-class Mexican Americans constantly call upon their middle-class adult children to translate documents, draft letters, make phone calls, and accompany them to work-related and medical appointments. Both men and women engaged in these activities on behalf of their kin but women reported spending significantly more time helping coethnics, especially mothers, than their male counterparts (Silverstein and Bengston 1997). For instance, Natalie, a second-generation Mexican who works sixty- to eighty-hour work weeks running her own business, explains how much her mother relies on her English-translating skills to complete numerous day-to-day tasks, "Like I do a lot of phone calling for her and translating for her. Like if she needs to clarify a bill or something. She puts it off until I have time to do it."

As the adult children of immigrants, 1.5- and second-generation Mexicans are also called upon to help relatives deal with American bureaucratic institutions that many foreign-born parents and extended relatives find difficult to navigate. For example, Martha Calvo has taken days off from work to "bust" cousins out of jail who "get locked up," and has even missed work to help a friend of her father's negotiate the overwhelmingly complex Social Security system. When I asked Martha why she took a day off from work to escort her "uncle" to the Social Security office, she replied, "He's not really, um, he doesn't really speak English that well and his oldest daughter couldn't handle it, and he doesn't have anyone else to turn to."

As foreign-born persons with limited English-language abilities, many Mexican immigrant parents (and extended family members) rely on their middle-class adult children or kin to help them navigate what they perceive to be an intimidating middle-class world.

While those who grow up poor are more likely to help kin financially and socially, only a few of those raised in middle-class households act as cultural brokers for kin, and typically only for parents. For example, Karina, introduced in Chapter 3, grew up middle class, and her father now owns a successful contracting business. Although she and her sisters have never had to help their parents financially—her parents will not even allow her to pick up the check when they go out to dinner—Karina mentioned that she and her sisters regularly help their father by writing letters, translating documents, and preparing contracting bids. Although her father is now fluent in English, Karina continues to help him with these tasks "because we know how professional letters should look." Moreover, because his daughters lack a Spanish accent, their father often asks that they phone supply companies or government agencies on his behalf. He believes that his complaints or requests will be taken more seriously because his daughters do not have an accent.

While middle-class African Americans might also make loans to poorer coethnics or break extended kin out of jail, the experiences of the Mexican American middle class differ in an important regard. In addition to managing the demands of class-heterogeneous networks, middle-class Mexican Americans, especially those who grow up poor, must come to the aid of foreign-born parents, relatives, and coethnics who lack fluency in the English language and who have little understanding of American bureaucracy. This places an additional burden on the middle-class children of immigrants, who act as cultural and language brokers for their non-English-speaking kin.

Growing Up Middle Class

While those who grew up middle class might help parents or kin occasionally translate documents or accompany their parents to doctor's appointments, none of those who were raised in middle-class households offer financial assistance to parents, extended family, or friends, even though they have impoverished relatives in their kinship networks. For example, Vincent, who maintains that he grew up "solidly middle class" in a white middle-class neighborhood, talked at length and with some disdain about one of his uncles who is so poor that he must shower outside with a hose because he cannot afford to repair his indoor shower, which has been broken for years. Despite the class heterogeneity of his kin network, when asked if he has ever helped his family financially, Vincent immediately defines "family" as only his nuclear kin and replies:

> No, never had to. They [my parents] are not the type that would expect us to do anything for them. Now that I'm a parent and I have a family, they would never want to burden us like that. We help them out emotionally. If it doesn't conflict with anything on our end we will help them.

Most notable about Vincent's response is that while he had just finished explaining the dire conditions in which some of his relatives live, he does not feel compelled to offer financial assistance to extended kin who are clearly in financial need. Moreover, in stark contrast to middle-class Mexican Americans who grow up poor, Vincent feels that having to financially support his parents or extended kin is an onerous responsibility that he does not intend to shoulder. Like Vincent, none of those who grew up in middle-class households felt compelled to help poorer relatives financially. While those who grew up poor often view their financial assistance as a gift rather than a loan, Art, a second-generation Mexican American raised in a middle-class neighborhood of Los Angeles, explained that he does not help poorer coethnics, in part because once you loan someone money, "you never get that money back." Deena, another respondent who grew up middle class, invoked meritocratic individualistic ideals when she explained, "I see my cousins driving new cars and carrying Coach bags and then they can't afford their house payment? I went to college, got a degree, and I've worked hard and I don't feel that I should help them because they won't live within their means."

The Immigrant Narrative Versus Middle-Class Individualism

Socially mobile Mexican Americans are more likely to give back to kin and coethnics. Their patterns of giving back mirror the middle-class African American model of collectivism (Hochschild 1995; Pattillo-McCoy 2000). Do middle-class Mexican Americans give back because they retain a sense of linked fate with poorer coethnics, like African Americans, that emerges from a racialized minority identity? Or are patterns of giving back simply born out of a Mexican culture of familism? This pattern cannot be reduced to linked fate or to an overly simplistic cultural explanation. The 1.5- and second-generation middle-class Mexican Americans who grow up poor frame their family obligations within an "immigrant narrative" of parental struggle and sacrifice (Smith 2005). All of the respondents who grew up in low-income neighborhoods underscored how much their parents had sacrificed in order to migrate to the United States, and described the backbreaking, low-wage, low-status jobs their parents took upon their arrival in their new host country. From their perspective, their parents worked hard, delayed their own gratification, and placed their children's needs above their own because they wanted to provide them with better opportunities. Given the bleak economic prospects in Mexico, their parents were willing to do whatever was necessary to give their children a better education and a greater chance for educational and occupational advancement. Now that the children have become adults, they feel that it is their turn to give back, not only to their parents, but also to their less affluent relatives, especially to those who do not have middle-class children of their own.

For example, Martha's sentiments accurately reflect those of the other respondents who grew up with foreign-born parents in impoverished neighborhoods. When asked why she provides such extensive levels of financial and social support to her family, she paused for a long moment, became choked up, and then replied through her tears,

> You ask all these deep questions, Jody. I can't help to get a little emotional. I don't know, you have to understand that when you are second generation and you come from an immigrant family, you understand everything that they went through to get you where you are at today, and I am just really grateful.

Others invoke explicit immigrant images of their parents' sacrifice. Leo, an architect and 1.5-generation Mexican who started working in high school to help support his family financially, explains the sacrifices that his parents made when deciding to come to the United States, and describes the downward mobility they faced upon arrival:

> They wanted us to have a better education. My parents in Mexico had businesses and were well off but they thought that it was going to be better for us to come to the States, and that was the main purpose for us leaving. They

pretty much sold all their assets, and we left. They gave up everything . . . all the stores that they owned. . . . They ended up working in the fields picking strawberries, celery, and asparagus. I'll never forget that. They did all that type of work. I'll never forget that.

JAV: Do you feel obligated to take care of them?

A: I wouldn't say obligated but a responsibility. You have to think of your parents. You have to. There is no other option.

As Leo explains, his parents sacrificed everything to migrate to the United States and worked backbreaking jobs in the fields to support the family. While Leo has achieved mobility and is a successful architect, his parents were migrant workers with no retirement or health benefits, making it his responsibility to support them because "there is no other option." While the act of immigration creates the opportunity for the 1.5 and second generations to achieve middle-class status, the marginalized economic context of Mexican migration also means that close kin, especially parents, continue to have a substantial financial need. This enduring familiarity with poverty combines with the mobility struggle inherent in the immigrant experience and leads to a sense of financial and social obligation among those who grew up poor but have now achieved middle-class status.

While they draw upon the immigrant narrative to explain why they assist their parents and extended kin, some provided a cultural explanation for giving back. When I asked the respondents why they provided financial and social support, a few simply stated, "It's what is expected. It's our culture," and "It's an understanding. It's just the way it is in Mexican families." Maria explains that while Asians and Latinos adopt the same view about helping family members, giving back is something that clearly differentiates Mexicans from whites, who are individualistic and who do not "care about family."

Asians are very close to Hispanics on their theories of how they do things. They will all help each other. Their parents will take care of the children while their parents work.

JAV: What about whites?

A: I don't think so. They have nuclear families. They don't help out their cousins. They don't help out their extended family. It's like the extended family; that's different. When I talk to other people [whites] they don't understand why I would let my cousin and her kid live in my house, and live in my living room, and eat my food. They don't understand. I have a friend who's white and she's like, "Why don't you just kick your cousin out?" And I'm like, "You don't understand; I can't do that."

Although family obligations are made salient by class-heterogeneous social ties and economic need, some socially mobile Mexican Americans make sense of their behavior by viewing "giving back" as something that is tied up with Mexican "family values," even though they acknowledge that Asian Americans and African Americans also provide for their families. As Mexican Americans achieve upward mobility and interact with middle-class whites in college or in the professional workforce, they come to understand that giving back is something that distinguishes Mexican Americans from their white middle-class counterparts, who direct all of their financial resources to their children and who "forget" about their parents and the extended family. As Carmen, a 31-year-old second-generation socially mobile Mexican American, explained,

> I think black people respect their elders and want to take care of their elders. Especially the ones who have educated themselves. I think they feel the obligation to take care of their families. Whites, I don't think that they had that sense of obligation. In the white culture, I work with somebody, he's Jewish but they are white. His kids, they are the most ungrateful kids and they don't care about anything. All they care about is money and stuff. As long as he gave them money they are fine but when there's no more money they don't care. They are not worried about him; they don't call him or feel the need to visit him. I don't know a lot of white families, but [in] the few that I've run into at work, the kids at 18 are gone, out the door.
>
> JAV: How is that different from your family?
>
> A: We are closer. If you turn 18 you are not going to get pushed out the door. You can be 40 years old and still live at home. Hello! My Tío Armando and Tía Laura! They still live at home and take care of my grandma. And in our family, my brothers and me, we are not going to forget about our mom. She'll never be in a convalescent home where most Caucasian people end up. There's no way. Even if it's going to be a problem, too bad. But how much of a problem can it be to take care of your mother?

As socially mobile Mexican Americans enter college and the primary workforce, they come to understand that their family obligations set them apart from their white counterparts who do not have similar feelings of financial and social obligations toward their families. Some begin to view these different orientations to giving back as phenomena that are culturally specific to each group. Mexican American culture (along with that of blacks and Asian Americans) is familistic, while white culture is selfish and individualistic. But what these respondents define as "culture" or "family values" is better conceptualized as a subscription to the immigrant narrative that recognizes self-sacrifice on the part of the immigrant generation, which in turn leads to their willingness to offer assistance to their parents, siblings, and extended kin (even those who are not related by blood) who have economic need. By clinging to the immigrant narrative, they feel that they cannot turn their backs on less privileged "family" members—regardless of how distant the connection. Rather than a sense of linked fate born out of racial discrimination or a Mexican culture of familism, the collectivism exhibited by socially mobile middle-class Mexican Americans is born out of the immigrant struggle for upward mobility and the fact that close kin continue to struggle economically.

The question remains, why do those who grow up in middle-class households not give back financially, even though they, too, have class-heterogeneous kin networks? As detailed in Chapter 3, those who grew up middle class are more likely to have parents with higher levels of education or parents who obtained relatively high-paying jobs or who opened successful small businesses soon after their arrival, which solidified their middle-class status during childhood. Those who grew up in middle-class households did not watch their parents break their backs in the fields or arrive home with aching hands after working on the assembly line, and they have not personally experienced the blood, sweat, and tears that social mobility entails. Consequently, they lack an immigrant narrative that is born out of the struggle for upward mobility. In fact, those who were reared in middle-class households are quick to equate their upbringing to that of middle-class whites, who they feel are reared to be "individualistic and competitive to get ahead." The tug between the immigrant narrative, stemming from economic disadvantage, and middle-class individualism, stemming from growing up economically secure, is captured by a married couple that includes Linda, a 1.5-generation Mexican American who grew up in a poor, agricultural community, and Joe, a second-generation Mexican American who was raised in a solidly middle-class neighborhood in Orange County. Linda's mother cleaned houses in the San Diego Area, while Joe's parents owned Latino grocery stores. Linda has a master's degree in health and works as a nurse practitioner, while Joe has a PhD and a thriving psychology practice.

Joe and Linda own a three-story home in a historical neighborhood in Orange, a city in Orange County. When I arrived at the house, Linda was speaking on the phone to Joe, who was picking up dinner on his way home from work. Linda insisted on ordering me something, and even though I force-fully declined the offer, she made Joe bring me a chocolate shake because she said it was rude of them not to feed me. Linda was relieved to see that I was a "regular person," as she wanted to make sure that I was not "someone who was going to tie them up and steal their art collection." Linda and Joe frequently host fundraisers for the Latino community at their home, which is laid with rich hardwood throughout and contains antique furnishings and original paintings and sculptures by local Mexican American artists. Linda is particularly proud of their home and of her new convertible because she grew up in a three-room apartment with six siblings and drove a "beater" for many years in college where she "literally epitomized the definition of a starving student."

While they now enjoy a comfortable lifestyle, Linda and Joe continuously reflected on the stark differences between their class backgrounds and their families. Linda erupted in tears several times during our interview when she discussed how poor her family was and the constant teasing she endured from other children. Her husband, whose experiences were the polar opposite, comforted Linda as she recalled,

> L: I remember in elementary school, we were so poor. Oh my god! [Her eyes well up with tears.] I had to wear the same clothes for weeks. And I remember I had like [she's crying now] . . .
>
> J: Honey, it's all right. You should be proud of that.
>
> L: I got teased a lot—
>
> J: She got teased a lot and berated and was humiliated for being poor. Kids are mean.
>
> L: We always had the free lunches and it was humiliating. You had to get your ticket and get in line and get your lunch ticket. It really affected my brother.
>
> J: He is a very proud guy—and he was telling me that he would go hungry because he didn't want people to know that he was on the lunch program. That moved me when I heard that.
>
> L: My mom, she struggled so much.

Consistent with the immigrant narrative, Linda constantly referred to her mother's "struggle" and "sacrifice" and went on to detail how her mother always took them school shopping for secondhand clothes, which were all she could afford on her salary as a domestic worker. Even discount stores were too expensive. "Kmart was expensive for us. I remember. It was like, counting our pennies. Shoes! My god, we always needed shoes." Joe, on the other hand, detailed a life of middle-class privilege. He shopped at more exclusive department stores like Nordstrom or Macy's for his school clothes. In stark contrast to Linda, who says she received practical things like shoes for Christmas, Joe was showered with gifts under the tree like many middle-class children were. Linda said, "Atari—that was like the lap of luxury." Joe remembered, "We were enthralled with Atari, but that would have been unthinkable for your mom." Despite the economic struggles and emotional pain she endured from growing up poor, Linda insists she is not ashamed by her upbringing or by her poor but hardworking mother; in fact, she evokes an immigrant narrative and insists that she is extremely indebted to her mother, who toiled long hours as a domestic worker just to buy them secondhand clothes, feed them simple meals, and put a roof over their heads.

While Linda constantly reiterated the various ways in which she and her siblings help the family financially and socially, she also strongly asserted that Joe and his siblings are "selfish" and that Joe's mother raised her children to be "competitive" with one another. Linda emphasized that her siblings were raised to "take care of each other," even if it meant that one of them did not have enough to eat or the proper clothes to wear, because that was the only way they could survive. "We always looked after each other. The older one looked after the next youngest and so on." Joe admitted, "I envy her family because they are very cohesive; they take care of each other. My mother raised us to be competitive to get ahead." Linda replied emphatically, "They never had to struggle." Because Linda believes that Joe's family embraces individualistic values akin to those of middle-class whites, she places Joe's middle-class nuclear family in the same category as whites by derisively calling him and his siblings "coconuts—brown on the outside, white on the inside." Similarly, Vincent, mentioned earlier, exhibits these individualistic values when he relates that he and his wife will help their families only if "it doesn't conflict with anything on our end."

Another reason that those who were raised middle class are less likely to financially support their families is that, like the flows of support that move in a single direction from parents to children among middle-class whites (Bianchi et al. 2008; Mabry, Giarrusso, and Bengston 2004; Newman 1988;), the Mexican American middle class who were raised in more affluent households find themselves on the receiving end of financial support. An example of one who has benefited from the exclusively unidirectional flow of resources, Vincent elaborates that his upbringing was "similar to whites" in that it was "a one-way street where it goes from the parents down, and nothing comes back up from the kids as they get older." In the same vein, Karina explained that her parents "are fine. They do very well. Even if we just go out to dinner they won't take our money. They say, 'You guys are young. You save your money for your future. We are fine and we don't need you to pay for dinner.'" Similarly, Joe has never had to help his parents or siblings financially and freely admits that the resources have always flowed from the parents down to the children.

Socially mobile Mexican Americans recognize that those who grow up middle class lack an immigrant narrative, that they are more individualistic, and that financial support moves only in a unidirectional flow from parents to children, and not in the reverse, a pattern they view as more "American," which is a code word for "white." Lorenzo, a socially mobile second-generation Mexican American who is a successful writer, explained that some of his Mexican American friends were supported by their parents throughout college and into adulthood. Lorenzo asserts, "I call those Mexicans *minimo pocho* and Americanized like, you know—you guys aren't Mexicans because you guys need mommy and daddy to help you out." *Pocho* is a derogatory term used to describe a person of Mexican origin who has fully acculturated into American society.

In the case of those who grew up middle class, one might argue that the absence of financial support is a function of having more middle-class kin. This is true to a degree because their immediate family members, especially their parents, are not poor. In contrast to those who grew up impoverished, those who grew up middle class are more likely to have parents with medical insurance, retirement funds, and secure, well-paying jobs or successful businesses, which means that there has never been a need to give back financially to parents. However, while their parents and siblings might not be impoverished, even the second-generation Mexican Americans from middle-class backgrounds have poor kin in their networks. Yet despite their contact with poorer grandparents, uncles, aunts, or cousins, those who grew up middle class do not offer them financial assistance. Hence, while having more middle-class kin might explain in part why they do not feel compelled to support their parents, this does not explain fully why those with more privileged backgrounds do not have a more collectivist orientation or provide support to less affluent extended kin.

Moreover, the obligation to give back cannot be reduced to geographic distance from extended kin. All of the respondents reside in the greater Los Angeles metropolitan area, and all admit to having relatives throughout the region. Even those who grew up in "safe, middle-class, white neighborhoods" have poor kin who live in nearby communities. What explains these divergent patterns of giving back is that those who grew up in middle-class communities do not cling to the immigrant narrative because their childhoods were not fraught with struggle and disadvantage born out of the poor, immigrant experience. Consequently, those whose childhoods were cloaked in middle-class privilege are more likely to adopt an ethos of meritocratic individualism. By contrast, those who grew up poor and witnessed their foreign-born parents work hard to get ahead strongly adopt the immigrant narrative, which pushes them to give back to their parents and their extended kin who continue to struggle. Hence, culture, family values, or a sense of linked fate does not fully explain why those who grow up poor give back to coethnics. If giving back were a cultural orientation derived from Mexican familistic values, or a sense of linked fate, we would expect all affluent Mexican Americans to give back, regardless of whether one grew up poor or subscribes to the immigrant narrative. What scholars, and sometimes even the respondents themselves, often reduce to culture is a function of economic need (Agius Vallejo and Lee 2009; Roschelle 1997; Sarkisian, Gerena, and Gerstel 2007).

Is Giving Back a Choice or Constraint?

Some socially mobile Mexican Americans delight in their newfound middle-class status because they are able to provide a better standard of living for their families and give them a taste of the middle-class lifestyle. For example, one respondent explained that he and his sister

> got a little luxurious and bought everybody new cars. . . . My parents have never ever owned a new car. In fact, I don't think they ever owned a car in the decade that they are in. It was always a couple [of] decades old. My sister and I decided to buy my mom and dad new cars. My dad now enjoys himself in a Dodge Ram and my mother in a Tahoe. Now they are stylin' [current] when they go to work. It's awesome to see them driving in their new cars.
>
> JAV: So you enjoy that?
>
> A: Oh my god! I love it, I love it. It almost seems like I do it for a selfish reason because it gives me my own little pleasure of seeing my parents drive

around. . . . The car that my dad had before is like a '75 pickup truck that he fixed himself to run. I remember that he used to drive us to school and it was the most embarrassing thing in the world and when I got more mature I re- alized that he had nothing to do with it, but just to see that excitement he has with his brand new car, now that he has a new car he's more confident.

Others feel like it is important to share the financial and social capital that accompany their middle-class status beyond the nuclear family. As Frank explained,

I am drawing satisfaction from doing all the little things and that's important for me.

JAV: The little things?

A: Helping my brother with his education. Helping him with books at a young age. Helping my other family, my cousins, by saying, here's $75, go buy some books for college. Helping them to apply to college. Things like that that people will always remember. People helped me a lot. I was reminded really quickly when a professor told me the way to repay him was to help some- body else out. That was a life learning lesson. I tell people all the time, just help somebody else out.

While some derive an extreme sense of pleasure from giving back, others have mixed emotions. Martha Calvo explained that she gets personal satisfaction from paying for the remodeling of her parents' home, "the way I think it should be redone." Although she expressed the desire to "do more" for her family (the definition of which she does not limit to the nuclear family unit, unlike those who grow up middle class), she admitted that it is difficult to balance her family obligations and the demands of her white-collar job.

I wish I could do more. I wish I could tell my mom to stop working today and don't worry about anything, I will take care of you. And same with my dad. With my extended family, with my uncle who I mentioned earlier who has had a horrible, horrible past few years with his wife passing away and having to raise his children alone and two of them being locked up, I wish I could do a lot more. I wish I could be there and provide more mentorship to his kids but there aren't enough hours in the day to do all that. It takes a toll; with my pro- fession I just think it takes a toll on you when you come home really late and you have phone calls, a ton of calls, and it's your dad's sister who's calling you too but you got to do what you got to do.

Martha's ambivalence hints that not all who give back do so willingly and happily. Nearly half of those who give back to parents and extended kin expressed some ambivalence and even resentment at having to shoulder these burdens. For example, one woman replied that "it can be burdensome time-wise, having to juggle, to balance all these things." When I asked her what she meant by "things," she listed her career, wanting to live her own life with her husband, and dealing with the constant demands placed on her by her mother, her siblings, and her extended family for money and social support.

Others also admit that they resent the constraints that follow family obligations. Paco, the respondent who gave his mother $6,000 so she would not have to declare bankruptcy, explained, "I try really hard not to feel resentful because my mother has worked her entire life for me." Paco called me unexpectedly nearly two years after his initial interview to inform me that his financial obligations to his mother have increased steadily every year as he has climbed the corporate ladder. In an aggravated voice he said, "I've given my mom $40,000 since we last spoke." When I asked why he continues to provide for his mother financially, he explained, "Well, my sisters just are not in a position to help. And she really did sacrifice for me growing up." Paco resents having to provide such large sums of money to his mother, especially because he has been unable to fund his retirement account, leaving him without a long-term financial cushion. The ambivalence that the respondents convey is mixed with guilt, since they firmly believe that whatever they give back does not even begin to approximate all that their parents have given and sacrificed for them in moving to the United States for a better life.

I also asked the respondents who give back whether they feel that their family obligations impede their further mobility, and three quarters admitted not only that the familial demands are taxing but also that they prevent them from directing their resources elsewhere. Because they regularly support family members, the 1.5- and second-generation respondents who give back explained that they are unable to purchase their own homes, put money into their savings accounts, adequately fund their retirement accounts, pay off debts that family members have incurred under their names, or pay off sizeable student loans from expensive private universities. One woman even began to cry as she explained that she and her husband have delayed having children because of the extensive financial obligations that each has to their respective families, whereas a male respondent expressed his frustrations over his inability to save for his children's college education, and the fear that his children will have to enroll in community college rather than a four-year university.

In addition to the financial constraints, family obligations can also derail educational mobility. Carrying the burden of familial obligations means that some middle-class Mexicans have had to drop out of college or forgo college altogether, which in turn has prevented them from acquiring degrees that would propel them into more highly paid, prestigious occupations. For example, Carmen, the respondent mentioned earlier, has worked her way up to vice president of sales and has hopes that she will eventually be promoted to executive vice president or even CEO of the company when the white males in these positions retire. However, company policy requires that candidates have at least a bachelor of arts degree. She frequently considers returning to college to complete her education, but she feels constrained from doing so since this would mean that she would no longer be able to assist all of those who frequently look to her for financial support, including her mother, aunts, cousins, brothers, and younger sister, who has two young children. Carmen weighed the decision out loud by saying, "I think, God, I am going to stop working so much, and go back to school." She then immediately stops her train of thought and changes her mind when it occurs to her,

> No, what if someone needs money? They are used to me making good money, and what if something happens? I am always trying to make more money so that I don't have to have issues with money so if somebody needs something I can help them out.

In another case, Andrea, a second-generation Mexican American who is now a successful entrepreneur, revealed that her parents forced her to drop out of the prestigious private college she attended on scholarship in order to help run the family business selling clothes and other found items at swap meets, which failed shortly after she withdrew from school. Andrea was unable to continue her college education after the family business failed because there was no other choice but to find a job to help support the family. Unlike her colleagues at the corporation where she previously worked who held a bachelor's degree at the minimum, Andrea is at a disadvantage in a corporate career because she has not completed college. Recalling her former job, Andrea admits that she was passed over for a promotion on two separate occasions because the higher positions required a college degree, making her an ineligible candidate. She regretfully explained, "It's really hard. It's affected me big time. There were two job opportunities at very high levels that would have taken me to the next stage." Lacking a college degree, Andrea has turned to entrepreneurship. That some middle-class Mexican Americans have had to drop out of college to support their families is an important finding because Mexican Americans continue to have the lowest education levels of all racial/ethnic groups in the United States. If the adult children of Mexican immigrants retain salient financial obligations because their families are in dire economic need, they may not be able to finish, or even enroll in, college, potentially hindering their mobility trajectory (Agius Vallejo, Lee, and Zhou 2011; Zhou et al. 2008).

That the majority of socially mobile respondents in this study emphasize that their opportunities for personal wealth accumulation have been constrained is also important considering that the wealth gap between Latinos and whites has increased to record highs in the last decade, due to the bursting of the housing market bubble and the recession that followed. The median wealth (assets minus debts) of white households is eighteen times that of Latino households (Kochhar, Fry, and Taylor 2011). Wealth levels are significant because liquid assets are critical in providing protection against short-term economic crises, such as the loss of a job. Furthermore, liquid assets provide long-term security through retirement income. This means that considerable financial obligations to family and extended kin might not only affect the ability of some middle-class Mexicans to draw on wealth in times of their own financial emergencies but also limit the amount of intergenerational wealth that is passed on to one's children. Inasmuch as 1.5- and second- generation middle-class Mexican Americans may be the "safety net" for coethnics, the majority of middle-class Mexican Americans who grow up poor live without a safety net themselves because of the financial obligations they have to their parents, siblings, and extended kin.

Does the Immigrant Narrative Last over the Generations?

While the 1.5- and second-generation respondents who grew up poor exhibit a strong ethos of giving back, the question remains whether their children—who are American born and raised in middle-class households—will continue to feel the need to give back to their families and poorer kin, or whether their attitudes and behaviors will more closely mirror those of the solidly middle class who strongly adhere to individualistic ideals. It is likely that the immigrant narrative diminishes over time, especially for those who are further removed from the immigrant generation. For example, in their quantitative study of adolescents, Andrew J. Fuligni and Sarah Pederson (2002) find that first-generation Latinos are more likely to exhibit a sense of family obligation and support than their third-generation peers. Because third- and fourth-generation Mexican Americans are the grandchildren and great-grandchildren of immigrants, their parents do not have an immigrant narrative frame of reference, and they may be less compelled to give back to their less privileged kin.

In-depth interviews with third-plus-generation Mexican Americans reveal that the immigrant narrative disappears the further removed one is from the immigrant generation and poverty. And, not surprisingly, later generations of middle-class Mexicans who grew up middle class do not give back to parents or poorer relatives. For example, Jessica is third-generation Mexican American on her mother's side (her father is white) and was raised in a middle-class household in the Midwest. Neither her parents nor her extended family members, some of whom remain low income and working class, have ever turned to her for financial support, something she has noticed that starkly differentiates her from her Mexican-origin friends who grew up poor. When I asked Jessica whether she has ever had to help her family financially, she replied,

> No, they were economically solid enough to where I didn't have to have that burden of helping them out, which I see is a big difference between me and a lot of my other Mexican American friends that are from I guess I'd say a lower class background. My middle-class friends don't give financial help to their parents either. I give them gifts, I gave them a gift on their thirtieth anniversary, I gave them a trip, but I don't have to send funds back to them to help them out.
>
> JAV: And so you've noticed that it is different with your other Mexican-origin friends who grew up poor, for example?
>
> A: Yeah, they help their families out a lot or live at home so they can contribute to the household. Whereas the ones who are middle class and even my upper-class friends, and I have about thirty or forty that I know, and then the ones that don't have a poor background don't give back to their parents.

Similarly, Adriana is third-generation Mexican American who grew up lower middle class in Los Angeles. Her parents were able to afford their children a Catholic school education but they "lived simply." Even though Adriana has some poorer relatives who have not fared as well and remain "isolated" in East Los Angeles, she parallels the mobility experience of her family over the generations to that of white ethnic immigrants of years past. She explains that her immigrant grandparents migrated with nothing but the clothes on their backs and that the responsibility of providing financial support is something that fell on her parents, the second generation. In other words, Adriana views giving back as something born out of the immigrant generation that disappears with upward mobility as later generations become more individually focused, and as earlier generations need less financial assistance. As she related, "We are the ones that have educations and we don't give back because we have to be concerned about ourselves and making it. But my parents don't need it anyway."

Like their second-generation counterparts who grew up middle class, later generations of middle-class Mexican Americans, whose childhood experiences are not steeped in poverty and who have a more individualistic orientation to upward mobility, do not have an immigrant narrative. But what about later generations of middle-class Mexican Americans who grew up poor and have achieved their middle-class status in one generation? Do they give back to poorer relatives, and if so, do they draw on an immigrant narrative to justify their support? Not surprisingly, the immigrant narrative is also absent among third- and fourth-generation Mexican Americans who are one generation removed from poverty. This is not to say that third- and fourth-generation middle-class Mexican Americans who grew up poor do not provide financial and social support to their families—quite the contrary. Their reasoning for giving back also emerges from a narrative of sacrifice and the struggle for mobility born out of a disadvantaged background. However, the idea of struggle and sacrifice is framed in growing up poor, rather than the intersection of class background and the immigration experience. This is not surprising considering that their parents are not immigrants.

Isabel is a case in point. Thirty-three-year-old Isabel is third-generation Mexican American and came of age in Texas with two younger brothers. Isabel attended an Ivy League university on scholarship and earned two master of arts degrees from another top-ranked university. She now works as an administrator for a school district in South Orange County. Although her mother has an associate's degree and her electrician father attended community college on and off for a few years, Isabel grew up poor on a ranch without running water for a significant portion of her adolescence. Isabel has helped her family financially since she was in college, and she currently sends her mother at least $100 a month. She is also called upon frequently by extended family members, such as her aunts and cousins, for large sums of money when a family crisis occurs, like a medical emergency or death in the family. Because she is one of the first in her family to attain middle-class status, her kin view her as being financially stable and responsible, as she explained, "I know my brothers and my family look at me like well, you are the one that is successful and has done it and you have everything under control. . . . So we can look to you as the one to be financially responsible." When asked why she gives back not only to her nuclear family but also to her extended family, Isabel first framed her behavior within a Mexican cultural narrative. However, as she contemplated the question more deeply, she drew on a narrative of sacrifice and struggle rooted in her disadvantaged background. Absent from her explanation is the immigrant narrative. As she explained,

> I do feel it is my obligation to give back to them [her parents]. I guess because I watched them take care of their parents and watched their parents take care of their parents, so culturally it seems like it is the natural thing to do. That is one level or one reason I think I feel that way. [She pauses for a moment.] Another reason is that I also feel like they sacrificed so much for us to get beyond where they were and they saw the same by their parents. I don't know how else to repay them . . . because I don't think most parents would ask for repayment, but it is a way to express my gratitude.

Isabel later questioned if giving back to poorer coethnics is really something "ethnic" or if it is more related to class background. She related that her white friends who grew up middle class cannot understand why she often sacrifices financially to help her family, which includes delaying having children so that she has more money available to help her family. After giving the topic some thought, she explained that the unidirectional flow of support from parent to child among whites stems not from a lack of family responsibility among adult children but from growing up more affluent—something Isabel acknowledges is typical among whites because the majority grow up middle class. An absence of family obligations and giving back is something she has also noticed among Latinos who were raised in affluent households. She related one example from her college years:

> I guess I have also noticed that it [giving back] is sort of related to social class. I remember once there was this guy who was a friend of mine in college who is Puerto Rican who was shocked because he overheard my roommate on the phone. She was also Mexican American and we kind of had the same back-

ground. We were the first ones to kind of get out of where we were, going to a big-named school, and make our families proud and all that overachiever checklist stuff, but also both from very poor families. I remember her talking on the phone about sending some money for something. She was doing the exact same thing that I had done. A friend of mine was there and he was like, "I have never heard of anyone or seen anything like that. Why would she send her parents money when they should send her money?" But his family was very wealthy. It was just a totally different thing, a totally different understanding of relationships between parents and child as far as finances go where he had only seen that flow in one direction. So it was unnatural to him to see how a child would open up their wallet and hand stuff over to their parents. I just told him, "Well, if she can help then she can help them." He was like, "Hmmm." He was very perplexed, but he thought it was interesting. He was like "Whoa, I had never thought of that." So I know it is not something that occurs to everybody and that also just that little experience . . . kind of makes me wonder if it is really ethnic or not. . . . He is very Puerto Rican.

Like their second-generation counterparts who grew up middle class, third- and fourth-generation Mexican Americans who grew up middle class more closely resemble the ideal type of white middle-class individualism. They retain a more individualistic orientation to mobility because their own mobility experiences are not born out of struggle and sacrifice. In fact, some even view their upward mobility as typifying the "traditional immigrant story" of success over the generations like that experienced by white ethnic immigrants. On the other hand, third- and fourth-generation Mexicans who have achieved their mobility in one generation, and some of those who were raised "low income," retain an ethos of giving back born out of the experience of being poor alone, rather than the immigrant narrative. Later generations of middle-class Mexican Americans who are one generation removed from poverty are not embracing an immigrant narrative, but a class narrative of struggle and sacrifice. The findings that later generations who grow up middle class are more individualistic compared to those who grow up low income are important, as together they lend further credence to the importance of class, rather than an oversimplified explanation that Mexican culture is more family oriented than the culture of other groups, or that Mexican Americans retain a sense of linked fate with poorer coethnics, in explaining patterns of giving back.

Conclusion

This chapter focuses on an underexamined measure of incorporation by investigating whether 1.5, second, and later generations of middle-class Mexican Americans retain family obligations and "give back" to kin and poorer coethnics. Examining ties to coethnics and family obligations and patterns of giving back illustrates Mexican Americans' varied experiences and dilemmas as they enter the middle class. Family obligations are less salient among those raised in middle-class households outside ethnic communities. Those who grow up solidly middle class more closely resemble the model of white middle-class individualism and are significantly less likely to extend financial assistance to poor kin and coethnics, a sign that some middle-class Mexican Americans are approximating behaviors associated with middle-class whites. But, as the minority culture of mobility predicts, socially mobile minorities face unique challenges stemming from their rapid upward mobility. Middle-class Mexican Americans who are raised in poor households remain intimately connected to poorer coethnics, especially parents, which means that they must manage relationships with kin who look to them for extensive financial and social support. The freshly minted middle class feel an obligation to give back even if it threatens to derail educational mobility or inhibit their economic security. While research shows that middle-class African Americans also provide extensively for kin and coethnics, middle-class Mexican Americans' collectivism is born out of socioeconomic inequalities and the struggle for upward mobility, rather than a larger sense of linked fate with coethnics born out of a long history of racialization and discrimination. If Mexican Americans' patterns of giving back followed the middle-class African American model of collectivism and linked fate, we would expect the respondents to feel that their own self-interests are linked to those of their racial/ethnic group. And, if family obligations and giving back were simply a Mexican cultural attribute, we would expect patterns of giving back to be uniform across social class backgrounds. Likewise, individualistic behaviors are not culturally specific to white Americans, but something that is rooted in their generally higher class standing.

The retention of family obligations and giving back are not phenomena that are specific to Mexican immigrants and their descendants. Tensions between the socially mobile and poorer coethnics are present among other immigrant groups who face a marginalized immigrant entry status in the United States, or among those who experience downward mobility upon arrival because their professional credentials do not transfer (Agius Vallejo, Lee, and Zhou 2011; L. S. H. Park 2005; Zhou and Bankston 1998), which indicates that giving back is a class, rather than distinctly ethnic, phenomenon among today's new immigrants. In fact, family obligations among the socially mobile go beyond the United States. On a broader scale, research has shown that similar patterns of family obligations and giving back are exhibited by the socially mobile in immigrant-receiving nations across the globe, and as in this study, family obligations become less salient among those who are of a higher socioeconomic status and who are further removed from ethnic communities (Goldsheider, Berhnhardt, and Goldsheider 2004).

Mexican Americans or Coconuts?
Middle-Class Minority and
American Identities

At work they call me a coconut. Brown on the outside and white on the inside.

—Vincent, second generation, sales executive

We are middle class and definitely Mexican. Definitely Mexican.

—Brenda, second generation, lawyer

Being Mexican is part of my heritage but I'm American.

—Elisa, third generation, social services

VINCENT RECLINED ON the oversized floral couch in his shabby chic-themed living room and explained that he ethnically identifies "I guess as a Mexican American. I am Mexican American because I am Mexican born in America." I questioned Vincent about this ethnic identity choice because when I called to inquire whether he would be interested in participating in a study on middle-class Mexican Americans, he replied, "I'm white. I'm going to mess up your study." I reminded him about this comment during our interview and he explained:

Because I grew up in a white neighborhood and school district, friends and people at work have always assumed I was white. And also because I don't have an accent and I don't wear clothes that would classify me as Mexican and everyone just thought I was Italian because of that. And I don't speak Spanish that good so people always say I'm white. At work they call me a coconut. Brown on the outside and white on the inside.

At this moment Vincent's Chilean American wife, Mary, who had obviously been eavesdropping on our conversation from the other room, poked her head around the corner. She added that she always describes Vincent as "American-ized" because "if I tell people he's Mexican they think his mom is in the kitchen making tortillas." When I asked Vincent and Mary to define what *American-ized* means, they both agreed that the term means "white." Vincent's and Mary's comments reflect the white racial framing of U.S. society where the noun *Amer-ican* is understood to be white and where the process of becoming "American" for immigrants has historically been defined in law and in practice as achieving "whiteness" as a means to gain access to the material and social resources re-served for the majority group (Feagin and Cobas 2008; Huber et al. 2008). Vincent went on to explain that "We are very American pie and that goes back to my dad. He wanted us to grow up American because I think he experienced racism, which I think is why he brought us to Orange County. To mix in and have a life that was better for his family." Recall from Chapter 3 that Vincent's father had legal documentation and secured a well-paying job as an engineer after a stint in the military. Vincent's father intentionally moved the family from the barrio to the burbs, an act that helped Vincent to acquire middle-class cultural cues and "grow up American," or closer to white.

This chapter examines the ethnic identities of middle-class Mexican Amer-icans and explains how class background, generation since immigration, and social interactions in different class and ethnic contexts shape patterns of ethnic identification, ethnic boundaries, and the different ways in which Mexi-can Americans incorporate into the American middle class. Racial and ethnic identities are socially constructed and racial and ethnic self-identification is a dialectical process that is formed both by one's internal definition of self and by how one is viewed by others (Barth 1969; Nagel 1994; Simmel 1950). Ethnicity is embedded in perceptions of social and cultural convergence or differences, and ethnic identities are defined, preserved, or transformed through the inclu-sive and exclusionist boundaries that blur, harden, or shrink through social interactions with coethnics and outsiders (Alba 2005; Barth 1969). Examining ethnic identities and boundaries between Mexican Americans and whites illu-minates the different ways in which assimilation occurs. For example, bound-ary crossing occurs if an individual Mexican American person moves from the minority group to the nonminority group (whites) without any real change to the boundary itself. If individual boundary crossing occurs on a large scale, the social structure is being altered and larger ethnic boundaries can shift, ultimately resulting in the social inclusion of a once distinct ethnic group (Alba 2005; Alba and Nee 2003). Blurred boundaries occur if Mexican

American individuals are able to present themselves as belonging to, or comfortable, on both the minority and nonminority side of the boundary. Boundaries between Mexican Americans and whites can also remain firm where each group knows on which side of the ethnic boundary they belong (Zolberg and Long 1999; Alba 2005, 2009).

The dialectical nature of ethnic identity, and the ways in which some middle-class Mexican Americans are able to cross boundaries with whites, is clear in Vincent's case. Outsiders hold a narrow definition of what it means to be Mexican American and often expect people of Mexican descent to be unauthorized and short in stature with dark features and to speak with a Spanish accent or stereotypical East Los Angeles cadence like Cheech Marin in the cult classic *Born in East LA*. A long history of portraying Mexican Americans as foreign and unassimilable means that the stereotypical Mexican American is also expected to hail from disadvantaged ethnic communities and poor class backgrounds (Jiménez 2010; Lee and Bean 2010), and to be "making tortillas in the kitchen," as Vincent's wife notes, not American apple pie. Through interactions with friends and coworkers in the middle-class social settings in which his everyday life has been embedded since childhood, Vincent is keenly aware that he falls outside the range of these narrow characterizations because he does not wear attire that fulfills a Mexican stereotype, nor does he speak English with a Spanish accent, or really even Spanish at all, for that matter. Even when Vincent asserts his Mexican roots, his social interactions with white coworkers and friends constantly reinforce that Vincent is a "coconut" or "Americanized," and therefore much closer to whites than to the stereotypical Mexican. Vincent has "tanned" skin, but he easily crosses the white boundary because he was raised in a white middle-class neighborhood far from the ethnic community, he retains weak ties to poorer coethnics, and he displays the conventional status cues of the white middle class, such as childhood vacations, participation in sports and extracurricular activities during his youth, speech patterns, and consumption patterns (Lareau 2003; Messner 2009). Despite his "tanned" skin, Vincent's class background and the disappearance of perceived cultural differences places him closer to whites, a phenomenon that sociologist Herbert Gans refers to as social whitening (Gans 2005).

Vincent's identity choice as American and white conforms to what Milton Gordon (1964) defined as "identificational assimilation," a stage late in the linear assimilation process that follows acculturation and structural incorporation. Historically, this process is epitomized by nineteenth-century immigrants who hailed from Southern and Eastern Europe. White ethnics, such as the Italian and Irish, were initially viewed as nonwhite upon setting foot on American soil. Eventually, racial and ethnic boundaries between the dominant population and white ethnics shifted and the definition of whiteness stretched to include these once ethnically distinct Southern and Eastern European groups. Southern and Eastern Europeans were able to cross the white boundary for several reasons. First, European immigrants learned to negotiate America's black-white racial divide by drawing rigid boundaries between themselves and African Americans in an effort to locate themselves closer to white on the racial hierarchy (Foner 2000; Roediger 2005). Second, post–World War II prosperity opened up the possibility for non-zero-sum mobility, where "swarthy" Southern and Eastern Europeans and Jews were socially whitened when they achieved intergenerational mobility without threatening the group position of long-established white Protestants (Alba 2009). Finally, boundaries between European ethnic groups and longer-settled Americans disintegrated in part because of restrictive immigration policies, such as the 1924 Immigration Act, which halted immigrant replenishment from Southern and Eastern Europe (Jiménez 2010). The descendants of white ethnics now enjoy an ethnic identification that is symbolic, optional, and costless in their everyday lives (Alba 1990; Gans 1979; Waters 1990).

The burning question is, will Mexican immigrants and their descendants follow in the footsteps of their white ethnic predecessors and disappear into the established white population? Considering the historical conditions that led to a boundary shift between Southern and Eastern European immigrants and long-settled whites, Mexican Americans' efforts to establish their group as racially white, future changes to the age and ethnic structures of the population and opportunities for non-zero-sum mobility, and declining rates of Mexican migration to the United States make this prospect possible. Mexicans were counted as white in the Census until 1920, when widespread nativist pressure stemming from the economic downturn of the Great Depression led to their reclassification as a separate race in the 1930 Census. However, like Southern and Eastern European immigrants, Mexicans understood the stigma of being federally defined as a nonwhite racial group. The Mexican American community and Mexican government protested this separate racial classification, leading the federal government to drop the practice (Hirschman, Alba, and Farley 2000; Rodriguez 2008). While the federal government sometimes treats Mexican Americans as a separate racial group by making them eligible for affirmative action policies (Skrentny 2002), "Mexican" is now federally defined as an ethnicity, rather than a distinct race, which means that a person with Mexican ancestry can be of "any race," including white. About half of those who claim a Mexican ethnicity on the Census form identified racially as white in the 2000 Census (Rumbaut, 2009).[1]

While post–World War II prosperity led to non-zero-sum mobility for white ethnics, which facilitated their absorption into the long-settled white population, sociologist Richard Alba (2009) argues that the mass retirement of the baby boomers heralds similar opportunities for non-zero-sum mobility, as it could open up the professional labor market for the rapidly growing working-age Latino population if they can close the education gap. Rates of college completion among Latinos remain low, but their rates of college enrollment have increased 24 percent between 2009 and 2010, more than that of any other ethnic group.[2] As of 2010, 32 percent of young Latinos were enrolled in college (Fry 2011). Higher levels of education among Latinos and a period of non-zero-sum mobility in the future might lead racial and ethnic boundaries to soften and expand to include upwardly mobile Mexican Americans.

Finally, the heavy waves of low-wage unauthorized Mexican migration to the United States, which characterized the latter half of the twentieth century, have declined to historically low levels due to U.S. immigration policies, increased border enforcement, low-labor demand stemming from the Great Recession, and expanding economic and educational opportunities in Mexico (Massey 2011).[3] As discussed in Chapter 2, historically high rates of unauthorized migration have reinforced pejorative stereotypes of Latinos, which has "thickened" ethnic identity (Portes and Rumbaut 2001; Jiménez 2010). However, if the trend of low levels of unauthorized migration continue, tomorrow's second- and third-generation Mexican Americans will come of age in a society that is not being constantly replenished with unauthorized migrants, which may also help to soften the white boundary.

Because some Mexican Americans consider themselves to be racially white, because the possibility for non-zero-sum mobility is wrought by the changing age and ethnic structure of the population, and because unauthorized immigrant replenishment from Mexico has, at this historical juncture, declined significantly, some Mexican Americans might be able to cross boundaries with whites and disappear into the established white population, following the traditional linear assimilation model. Who is better poised to do so than those who have entered the middle class? Middle-class Mexican Americans might be a harbinger of this pattern. Observers argue that Mexican Americans undergo a slow social whitening of their ethnicity as they become further removed from the immigrant generation and live lives entrenched in the middle class (Alba and Islam 2009; Emeka and Agius Vallejo 2011; Gans 2005; Ono 2002; Perlmann 2005; Tienda and Mitchell 2006; Yancey 2003). Other measures of assimilation also indicate that boundaries may be fading between whites and Mexican Americans. Intermarriage rates, which are "a barometer of decreasing social distance between groups" and the linchpin of structural assimilation, increase steadily between whites and people of Mexican origin with each generation since immigration (Telles and Ortiz 2008). Intermarriage rates for people of Mexican descent are much higher than they are for African Americans, indicating that the Mexican–white boundary is not as impermeable as the black–white boundary and that whites increasingly view Mexican Americans, especially those with high levels of education, as more suitable marriage partners than their middle-class African American counterparts (Lee and Bean 2010; Perlmann and Waters 2007).[4]

While some scholars predict that perceived ethnic differences between Mexican Americans and native-born white Americans will become less distinct over the generations as they achieve class mobility, and that Mexican Americans could be the next immigrant group to become white, others maintain that Mexican immigrants and their children are a racialized ethnic group who will find it difficult to fade into the white population (Portes and Rumbaut 2001; Portes and Zhou 1993; Telles and Ortiz 2008). Race no longer has scientific validity. But when groups are racialized, the in-group accepts negative stereotypes as true, leading to a tightening of group boundaries that are reinforced through everyday interactions and political and economic relations (Omi and Winant 1994). Proponents of this perspective argue that even though Mexicans are not considered to be a distinct racial group, a legacy of labor exploitation and social and political exclusion, as discussed in Chapter 2, has positioned Mexican immigrants and their descendants as a disadvantaged racialized group, which blocks their upward mobility. The racialization framework contends that a negative context of reception and persistent discrimination leads to downward or stagnated mobility by hindering Mexicans' residential assimilation, educational trajectories, and occupational prospects and leads to the adoption of a racialized ethnic identification as Mexican or Mexican American (D. Lopez and Stanton-Salazar 2001; Portes and Rumbaut 2001; Telles and Ortiz 2008).

As exemplified by Vincent, some middle-class Mexican Americans follow the linear assimilation model and cross the white boundary where they identify, and are viewed by others, as "American" or "whitewashed." In contrast, boundaries between whites and the socially mobile remain rigid and ethnic identities remain salient. The majority of those raised in poor households underscore that they are far from white and find the idea that they are "whitewashed" absurd. As Brenda asserted, "We are middle class and definitely Mexican. Definitely Mexican." Brenda's identity choice runs contrary to the linear assimilation model, which correlates social mobility and economic incorporation with softened ethnic boundaries and identificational assimilation, *and* the racialization model, which equates identifying as a minority with downward or stagnated mobility. Thus, neither of these group-based models can explain why identities vary within national-origin groups and why middle-class Mexican Americans like Brenda retain a salient minority ethnic identification. However, the minority culture of mobility framework contends that one can be structurally assimilated yet identify as a middle-class minority, an identity that is formed by the challenges that accompany upward mobility and middle-class minority status (Neckerman, Carter, and Lee 1999). Ultimately, class background, and navigating between different class and ethnic contexts, leads to identificational assimilation or a minority, yet middle-class, identity.

The 1.5 and Second Generations

Navigating Interethnic Relationships: The Social Exclusion of Growing Up Poor

The socially mobile 1.5 generation generally identify as "Mexican," in line with research demonstrating that those born in Mexico are more likely to identify with a single national origin group (Portes and Rumbaut 2001; Telles and Ortiz 2008; Tovar and Feliciano 2009). Second-generation identities range from Mexican to Mexican American. However, unlike Vincent's sketch in the opening vignette of this chapter, the freshly minted middle class do not view themselves, nor are they viewed by others, as "coconuts" or "whitewashed." As the minority culture of mobility model predicts, those who grow up poor face challenges distinct to socially mobile minorities that ultimately lead to the adoption of a class-based minority identity. One of these challenges is the retention of ties to poorer coethnics and family obligations, as discussed in Chapter 4. Another distinct challenge is that rapid social mobility sorts middle-class Mexican Americans into class-diverse social spaces, resulting in social interactions that are, as one respondent described, "awkward" in the low-income ethnic community and "painful" and "out of my league" in what they perceive to be white middle-class social settings, such as elite private educational institutions or corporate milieus. The social and professional worlds that socially mobile Mexican Americans enter are likely multicultural and multiethnic; however, I asked the respondents to detail the racial and ethnic composition of their colleges and workplaces, and the resounding answer was "largely," "mostly," or "pretty much" white. Whether this is true or not, this is how socially mobile Mexican Americans perceive the middle-class institutions in which they are engaged, and it is partly through their interactions with whites, whom they regard as the majority group with social and political power, that the meanings attached to their identities are formed. Their social interactions with poor coethnics on the one hand, and middle-class whites on the other, lead to the development of a minority middle-class identity.

Brenda, the native-born child of immigrants, identifies ethnically as Mexican, an identity that is tied to her ability to speak Spanish and her childhood, which was spent in a low-income Mexican immigrant neighborhood in Santa Ana. Although she retains a salient ethnic identification as Mexican, she also asserted that she is definitely middle class. Brenda is the first in her family to earn a college degree and regularly mingle in middle-class social and professional spaces. She did not realize that she was a "minority" until she left Santa Ana and entered a prestigious private college where her "limited experiences" and poor-class background became evident and made her feel different from her white classmates, echoing recent research demonstrating that socially mobile Mexican Americans experience a "culture shock" when they leave ethnic communities and enter middle-class institutions (Tovar and Feliciano 2009). Reflecting on her college experience, Brenda exclaimed, "I knew we were poor, but I didn't know we were deprived until I went to college!" Brenda's classmates drove brand-new cars, wore designer jeans, and received hefty allowances. In contrast, Brenda did not own a car, she never dressed in designer attire, and she labored at a low-wage part-time job for spending money. As she explained, "I just realized in college that white people live very differently. Never having to work and that kind of thing." Brenda eventually graduated at the top of her class from a highly ranked law school and is one of only a handful of Mexican-origin people employed at the law firm where she works. Although she claims that she is now a member of the American middle class, Brenda's ethnicity and class background give rise to strained social interactions with her white coworkers that lead her to momentarily question whether she truly belongs in the middle class.

> It's so funny. Today I didn't feel middle class. We were sitting at lunch and they were talking about *Friday Night Lights* and reading *Fast Food Nation*, which I've read, and it's like, ok, I can relate. And then it was so funny because we were just talking and some of the ways that they were exchanging I was like, I am not used to that! It was at a level where I wasn't used to communicating like that. They were talking about nothing.
>
> JAV: What were they talking about?
>
> A: I don't even remember but I was like, hmmm, this is going to be fun for the next three years of my life. But I remember going, "Last weekend I went to see *The Motorcycle Diaries.*" It was so weird because they were like, "Oh? Who's in that?" And I was like, "Gael García Bernal." And they were like, "He's been in?" (She says this in a high pitched voice and affected British-like accent). And I said, "*Amor Es Perros*, and *Y Tu Mama Tambien.*" And it throws people off when I say Spanish with an accent and that's when I don't feel middle class. People get so weird about stuff like that.
>
> JAV: Who gets weird?
>
> A: The white people. They were all white. And I think that it was just like, "Oh yeah, the Latina would go see that kind of movie." I said them in Spanish the way they are, not "A-more, Es, Pay-rose" (speaking slowly in a monotone without a Spanish accent). It was one of those things that bring them back to who I am, you know? And then I didn't feel welcomed. I try not to think about it because I am just like, whatever, I went to law school.

Ethnic boundaries become rigid when socially mobile Mexican Americans display their ethnicity through ethnic cues such as speaking Spanish or when they express ethnic-specific tastes for foods and leisure activities. As Brenda describes, speaking Spanish words with the proper accent, and a preference for Spanish-language movies, "brings them back to who I am," which is a socially mobile Mexican American woman who does not belong on the white side of the ethnic boundary despite her prestigious academic credentials. The palpable distaste that emanates from her white coworkers when she exhibits ethnic cultural cues is a subtle message that despite her accomplishments, Brenda has not crossed the white boundary and is not "welcomed" as a member of the white middle class.

Other respondents agreed that ethnic cultural cues, particularly the use of the Spanish language at work, reinforce ethnic and class differences. Coworkers are often shocked or ill at ease when socially mobile Mexican Americans speak Spanish in professional settings, and middle-class Mexican Americans come to understand that Spanish generally has no place in a professional workplace, especially where whites are the majority. Respondents explain that their non-Spanish-speaking coworkers become paranoid when they speak Spanish to a coworker or while on a personal call, assuming that they are "talking *chisme*," or gossiping, about them. Some of their non-Spanish-speaking coworkers have even complained to their bosses, who subsequently request that they refrain from using Spanish in the workplace.

Language marks the boundaries of group identity, and Spanish has been socially constructed as a marker of foreignness in America through public policy, "English-only" referendums, and media (L. Chavez 2008; Jiménez 2010; Ochoa 2004; Portes and Rumbaut 2001). Spanish-language ability in professional settings becomes a symbol of Mexican authenticity that reinforces Mexican ethnic identities, stigmatizes Mexican Americans, and leads to feelings of social isolation (Flores 2011). But tensions over the Spanish language are not limited to interactions with middle-class whites. The socially mobile 1.5 and second generations also mingle with assimilated and monolingual later-generation Mexican Americans, and failed attempts to bond over the Spanish language reinforce class and ethnic differences. For example, Frank is an electrical engineer at a top firm who ethnically identifies as Mexican. Frank's rapid social mobility has left him feeling alienated in the engineering field, a domain he perceives to be largely composed of whites. When I asked whether he has any close friends at work, he replied that "It's tough. The biggest challenge socially." Frank's ethnicity and low-class background make it difficult to relate to his white coworkers, a feeling he "just knows" is mutual. Frank explained that out of a company that employs 150 people, only one other employee, Ben Garcia, is of Mexican origin. Frank hoped that he and Ben would be able to bond over their Mexican roots and find common ground by means of speaking Spanglish, a combination of English and Spanish. But to Frank's disappointment, he and Ben could only relate to each other "purely from a work standpoint."

> We could never relate because of our social background. I tend to do the Spanglish thing, which is a really bad habit and you identify with people when they do that and people from the community where I come from do that constantly.

> I am trying to break that habit, but as we would talk about certain things and lifestyles, we just couldn't relate.

Ben Garcia is far removed from the immigrant generation, he does not retain ties to poorer coethnics, he does not speak Spanish, he identifies racially and ethnically as white, and he was raised in a white middle-class community. Besides their Spanish last names, there are no ethnic or class similarities for Frank and Ben to bond over because their lives are embedded in vastly different ethnic and class contexts. In the ethnic community, speaking Spanglish builds connections and solidarity, but in professional settings, it becomes a marker of class, generational, and ethnic differences, even among those who share a common ancestry. As Frank attempts to incorporate into a white professional milieu, he has learned that Spanglish is not acceptable at work and he makes a concerted effort to curtail his "bad habit."

> There's a place for it. It's like slang. There's definitely not a place for it in the professional world. A lot of the times when I get comfortable with people I get into that habit but if I am at work most people don't agree with it. Sometimes I just feel like there's a place for it so I try not to do it.

As socially mobile Mexican Americans interact in middle-class social and professional settings, they come to understand that ethnic markers and their lack of middle-class cultural cues, such as exotic childhood vacations, white-collar parental occupations, and speech patterns, brand them as outsiders. For example, one respondent explained that he sometimes feels a sense of dread when colleagues or clients discuss their backgrounds because "It always gets silent when I tell people my dad worked in the fields." When socially mobile Mexican Americans enter middle-class institutions, they are thrust into milieus where the intersection of their ethnic origins *and* class background mark them as outsiders leading to feelings of social isolation and the realization that they cannot cross or blur the white boundary, which reinforces their ethnicity.

A few of the socially mobile respondents even feared that their class background and ethnicity might hinder their occupational opportunities. For example, Tom explained how his ethnicity combines with his low-class background to mark him as an outsider at the large investment firm where he works as a financial analyst. Tom broke down the racial and ethnic composition of his firm as "65 percent white, 30 percent Asian, and a few black and Mexican." Although the racial and ethnic composition of his workplace is multiethnic, Tom's identity is formed by his interactions with whites who hold the majority of the executive positions at the firm and from whom he feels estranged.

> Quite honestly between you and myself, I tell people that when I am at work I am at work. It's a business relationship. I don't view the people at work as being friends. They are acquaintances. I try not to make things too personal. But they never see the true me. The reason is [that] I have learned to always have my guard up. . . . At work we never get to a point where we can establish that bond. My boss is a really nice guy, I respect him, but as far as a family function or party were to come up I would not invite him.
>
> JAV: Would it be different if you worked in a workplace that was more Latino?
> A: Yes it would. Definitely. Because, you know, I just know that some things in your own life are understood. You can't explain. I am working in a culture that is not mine. I recognize that and work within it and at the same time I realize that there are certain barriers placed to me.
> JAV: What types of barriers?
> A: When certain critical clients come in, I am not the person they want; they wouldn't want me to be the face man for the company. A lot in the business world are based on first impressions and the company is very critical in who they send out as their representatives.
> JAV: Why would they not want you to be the face man for the company?
> A: My skin color, my background. Say you are a high-net-worth individual. They will think, "How much can Tom share with this individual coming from his background?"

Recall that Vincent, who also has dark skin, has experienced a social whitening of his ethnicity and has no problem navigating middle-class professional spaces. However, Tom's skin tone and ethnicity is magnified by his class background. Tom went on to explain that he keeps details about his ethnicity and social class background under wraps as a strategy to ward off inevitable questions about unauthorized migration and to avoid the looks of disdain on the faces of his white coworkers when he reveals that he continues to live in a low-income ethnic community close to his parents. Frank's ethnicity and class background are constantly salient, resulting in feelings of social exclusion. However, the boundaries that whites draw have additional consequences. Because it is perceived that his ethnicity and class background make him unable to relate to higher-net-worth clients, Tom is frequently passed over to attend important client meetings and social functions. When I asked whether he considers this to be discrimination, he replied,

> I don't like to blame discrimination or racism about why something didn't work out, but the reality is that certain individuals are in power that share a particular culture; that's the reality. If you are not in that culture you are going to have difficulty adjusting to that.

The social and professional exclusion that socially mobile Mexican Americans must deal with sends a clear message: they are not members of the white middle-class "culture" and are thus unable to reap the social and economic benefits that accrue to whites.[5] Political scientist Maria Chávez (2011) also finds that Latino professionals face an unwelcome environment where they are on the receiving end of the message that they are not white. Similarly, sociologists Joe Feagin and José Cobas (2008: 52) argue that whites in professional occupations "transmit subtle and overt messages of racial stereotyping, imaging and interpretation of Latinos/as. Such negative views seriously handicap them as they try to survive and thrive within white-controlled institutions." One such handicap is that minorities are regularly left out of the corporate socializing rituals of white professionals, such as an after-work brew or a day on the golf course (Deal and Kennedy 2000; Feagin and Sikes 1994). Not being assigned to meet with high-net-worth clients, or being excluded from happy hour, is not only an overt message that Tom belongs on the minority side of the ethnic boundary; it also limits Tom's opportunities to build the networks and social capital that could advance his career.

The 1.5- and second-generation respondents who grew up low income discussed how other types of ethnic markers, such as surname, intersect with class background to constrict racial and ethnic boundaries in middle-class professional settings. Mateo, a 42-year-old lawyer and second-generation Mexican, has dark hair peppered with gray, lightly tanned skin, and light hazel eyes. Mateo explained that because he does not fit the narrow definition of what a Mexican person looks like, people initially assume that he is Italian until they scrutinize his business card or hear his Spanish first and last names, which broadcast that he is "some kind of Hispanic." When people learn of his class background, Mateo becomes a Mexican from the barrio. Mateo's social interactions with whites in professional settings have been a constant reminder that he is Mexican, and has not become "American," and have led him to contest the "lie" that America is a "melting pot" where immigrants and their descendants melt into a unified American core after achieving social mobility. As he emphasized,

The reality of the melting pot is that no matter how American I wanted to be, I was always called the Mexican kid. Even as a professional, I was a young lawyer and they are always, "Oh, he's Mexican" or "Mexican American." I believe that it is white America who classifies you because as much as I want to be American, there is never a day that passes where you aren't Mexican. And I am proud of that, but I think the reality is that the melting pot can never be a utopian scenario where we are all one, because we are not.

Mateo's experiences in the American middle class are far different than Vincent's. While Vincent is constantly told that he is not Mexican but American and whitewashed, Mateo's social interactions reinforce the idea that although he is middle class, his ethnic and class background prevents him from "melting" into the white middle class. Socially mobile Mexican Americans' experiences in middle-class milieus underscore the dialectical nature of ethnicity and the ways in which both internal definitions of self and the reactions of others help shape self-identification. Mateo, for example, is now middle class, but his parents are immigrants who struggled for upward mobility, his childhood was steeped in an immigrant ethnic community, and he speaks Spanish, all of which combine to form an internal definition of self as Mexican, an identity that is reinforced as Mateo attempts to navigate white professional settings. Mateo explains that even though he is a prosperous lawyer, he will never experience a social whitening of his ethnicity or feel simply "American," because "white America" does not classify him as such. It is important to emphasize that it is not just surname or skin color that hardens ethnic boundaries, as those hailing from middle-class backgrounds with darker skin are regularly viewed as "coconuts," "whitewashed" and "American" despite their Spanish last names. It is the intersection of class background and ethnicity that leads to salient boundaries and reinforces an ethnic identification among the socially mobile.

Navigating Interclass Relationships: The Awkwardness of Becoming Middle Class

Mexican Americans who grow up poor experience rigid intergroup boundaries as they enter middle-class social and professional spaces. Through subtle and overt messages from their white middle-class colleagues, they understand that they have not "melted" into the white middle class despite their accomplishments, which reinforces their ethnic identity. The socially mobile receive a different set of messages about their identity from poor kin who cannot relate to their white-collar occupations and middle-class experiences and who sometimes resent their success. Negotiating between these two different ethnic and class contexts reinforces a salient ethnic identity on the one hand and a middle-class identity on the other, leading to the development of a minority middle-class identity.

Lupe, introduced in previous chapters, is second generation and vice president of a bank. Although she has moved away from the ethnic community, she remains strongly tied to poorer kin, as evidenced by her role as the family's financial "safety net" in times of economic crises. She is one of the first in her extended family to earn a college degree, and Lupe admits that her lower-class relatives are extremely proud of her success. They tout her educational credentials and the fact that she is a "career woman" to anyone within earshot at family events, but her everyday life, entrenched in a middle-class world and a white-collar profession, is unfamiliar to them. This often results in awkward situations with her low-income relatives who are not similarly educated or who have not experienced upward mobility. As Lupe explained,

> They don't understand what I do. They sort of, it's kind of, I mean, they are proud people. This Sunday I was at my grandfather's birthday party and my aunt I think wanted to open up a bank account because she doesn't have one. All they know is I work at a bank and my mom said, "No no no, that's not what she does." So it's always kind of a mystery and I think they are too proud to ask me questions and I don't think they would really understand anyway. They are not sure what I do on a daily basis. Kind of an interesting dynamic. I can't go to a family event and talk about what I do or tell them about my latest accomplishment or that I went to go speak in New York about this or that; they don't get it. I guess I could explain it, but because they are not in it every day they don't understand it. It's an awkward situation because . . . they just don't know what I do.

The "interesting dynamic" is the class homogeneity of Lupe's family, which makes for "awkward" situations because her lower-class family members do not understand Lupe's achievements and her experiences in the middle-class business world. Lupe does not even attempt to explain her occupation to her relatives because she feels that their lower-class position renders them unable to comprehend her middle-class experiences. Similarly, Frank related,

> To this day my dad doesn't understand what I do. I bought this house and it's a fixer-upper so there are all these major repairs and he will say, "The electrical wiring is messed up," and I will say, "I don't know about residential electri-

cal work," and he will say, "Well you are an engineer." I'm like "Dad, that's not what I *do*" [his emphasis].

Frank tries to avoid talking about his career when he visits his parents and extended kin because "their experiences are just so different. They just can't relate." And he has never revealed to anyone, except to his socially mobile Mexican American friends, the alienation and social exclusion he has experienced in middle-class settings. "They [his parents] think that I have nothing to worry about because I achieved their dream."

Not all interclass relations are merely as uncomfortable as those with coethnics who have no conception of what a bank vice president or engineer does. The socially mobile must also manage relationships with poor kin who resent their economic success and who even question their Mexican authenticity now that they are middle class. Andrea is second-generation Mexican American. She owns a thriving employee staffing business and lives in Newport Beach, a wealthy city in coastal Orange County. Both of her brothers barely graduated high school, they are employed in low-wage work along with her parents, and they live in a low-income community in Los Angeles. Andrea is the first in her family to enter the middle class, and although she has helped her brothers financially, they resent her social and economic mobility. When she attempts to assert a Mexican ethnic identity, her brothers draw a class boundary and question her authenticity as Mexican because she has moved up and out of the ethnic community and into a white middle-class neighborhood.

> They come over and think that I live in a rich area. They say, "You live in Orange County; what do you know?" Or, "There's no way that I could ever live in Orange County," or "You're stupid for paying so much to live in Orange County." And I am like, "This is where my clients are!" I live in a white middle-class neighborhood, something that we never lived in growing up. My parents never thought of themselves as middle class. And I realized that I had to establish my business outside of where I was living because if I stayed there, I would be limited.

Andrea moved her staffing business from the ethnic community to a white middle-class area for economic opportunity, yet her brothers view her social mobility as desertion from her roots.

> My brother calls me Miss Beverly Hills. He says, "You have it easy." He thinks that everything I have is because, I don't know, he thinks it's not fair.

JAV: He says things like that to you?

A: Oh yeah. That I'm Miss Beverly Hills, that I live in a white area so what the hell do I know about Mexicans or what they have to go through.

JAV: How do you feel when he says that?

A: It angers me because if there is anyone who advocates more for my community it's me. And I tell him, "Look, I advocate for those who want to do something." It angers me a lot.

While socially mobile Mexican Americans are painfully aware of their low-class background in professional environments, their newfound middle-class status becomes intensely salient when interacting with poor kin. Poor kin and coethnics are not aware of the pain and social exclusion that accompanies social mobility. They assume that their middle-class kin no longer understand "what it means to be Mexican" and that troubles vanish with economic success. One respondent explained, "When you become successful . . . it's weird, a weird feeling. Mexicans can turn on you for that. I was trying to explain it to my uncle the other day, to ask him why Mexicans turn on each other like that and he was like, 'Well now you are rich and so what do you have to worry about. Some of us can't even pay our bills.'"

The Making of a Middle-Class Mexican American Identity

Despite their structural incorporation, socially mobile 1.5- and second-generation Mexican Americans do not identify as white, nor do they easily cross or blur boundaries with whites in middle-class settings, contrary to the linear assimilation model. Yet, the retention of an ethnic identification, and salient ethnic boundaries, does not mean that socially mobile Mexican Americans have developed a racialized identity that is indicative of structural exclusion and downward mobility. As the minority culture of mobility model implies, the identities and incorporation experiences of the socially mobile 1.5 and second generations are shaped by their experiences straddling two different ethnic and class contexts leading to a minority middle-class identity. Their upward mobility produces tensions with poorer coethnics, while their class background and salient ethnicity distinguish them from middle-class whites and later-generation Mexican Americans who have crossed the white boundary. Lupe elucidated how her attempts to negotiate between different class and ethnic contexts have helped shape a minority middle-class identity.

When I go back [to visit her family] I remember growing up in rough neighborhoods. Now I have opportunities to buy a home and I finally get to be a professional and be middle class . . . but I look around at work and I am the only
Latina and they [her coworkers] know where I come from and I have to explain
to them why Latinos do this or that . . . like when they ask me how to solve the
illegal immigration problem. What, am I expert on illegal immigration? But
there are a lot more of us now [middle-class Mexican Americans]. We hang out
and we talk about things like politics and situations in business because they
went to college just like I did and they live in the same world that I do. But we
like to retain our culture and go to salsa dance and have carne asadas [bar-
beques]. I have to be different people; it's the reality, when I am with my family,
or with my friends, or at work.

As discussed earlier, Lupe's interactions with poorer coethnics who cannot
relate to her newfound class privilege reinforce a middle-class sense of self but
her exchanges with white coworkers, who expect her to be an authority on
unauthorized migration because of her immigrant parents, reinforce the
impression that although she is middle class, she has not incorporated into
the white middle class. In her study of high school students, Julie Bettie (2003)
finds that upwardly mobile Mexican American girls are acutely aware of class
distinctions and that they refuse to interpret upward mobility as assimilation to
whiteness. This pattern holds among socially mobile Mexican American adults
who remain intensely aware of class and ethnic distinctions within and outside
ethnic communities and who do not view themselves as middle-class whites
simply because they have achieved upward mobility. When I asked Lupe if she
ever considered herself to be white, or a member of the white middle class, she
shook her head "No" and replied that she is "part of a new breed of Mexican
Americans" who retain their ethnic and cultural roots yet "we are also middle
class." This "new breed" of Mexican Americans are those raised in poor households whose everyday lives are embedded in different class and ethnic contexts
that reinforce a minority, yet middle-class, identity. Lupe experiences tense relationships with family and at work, but, like Frank, she can be herself among her
socially mobile Mexican American friends who understand the dilemmas associated with living in two different worlds and who can empathize with the
ethnic and class tensions that accompany social mobility.

As Lupe also notes, a minority middle-class identification is facilitated by
the rise of the contemporary Mexican American (or Latino) middle class.

Some of Lupe's strong friendships with other middle-class Mexican Americans were forged in college, but Lupe has met the majority of her affluent Mexican American *"comadres"* through her civic participation in Latino professional associations. Such participation is not unusual. One strategy that the socially mobile employ to manage the challenges associated with their newfound class status, especially the social exclusion they feel in professional settings, is to join ethnic business and professional associations based in the Mexican ethnic community. Nearly three quarters of the 1.5 and second generations who grew up poor participate in one or more Latino business organizations that cater to the Latino middle class. Latino professional associations, such as the Hispanic Bar Association, the Society of Hispanic MBA's, the Society of Hispanic Engineers, and the Association of Latinas in Business (an ethnic organization examined in Chapter 6), are social and professional contexts in which a middle-class minority identity is reinforced and lived out. These civic and social organizations epitomize the minority culture of mobility because they draw on and reinforce a minority middle-class identity and, as I demonstrate in Chapter 6, they are ethnic environments that seek to provide strategies for upward mobility and social inclusion in the context of group disadvantage.

The institutionalization of a middle-class Mexican American identity is also reinforced by an era of multiculturalism and the increasing attention, and rewards, that are paid to the maintenance of ethnic difference. Unlike the generations before them, today's socially mobile Mexican Americans come of age in a society that, while overtly hostile to immigrants in policy and practice, also paradoxically celebrates diversity and ethnic pride. This institutionalized focus on diversity is a result of antidiscrimination policies born out of black and Chicano activism in the 1960s and 1970s (Jiménez 2010; Skrentny 2002). Multicultural ideals and initiatives now permeate middle-class institutions like colleges and corporations. Colleges reward attachments to an ethnic minority identity by providing diversity scholarships, and corporations tout their diversity initiatives, which encourage the hiring and advancement of middle-class minorities.[6] Large multinational corporations (including some where my respondents are employed) literally advertise themselves as "diversity champions" who are committed to hiring minorities and women and to purchasing products and services from diverse suppliers who become certified as minority-owned or women-owned businesses.[7] These corporations, and scores of others, have diversity officers who work exclusively to increase the diversity of the workforce within organizations and diversity councils that oversee efforts to hire minorities. Thus, diversity initiatives not only legitimize the retention of a minority middle-class identity, they also make a minority middle-class identity an asset in education and the labor market. Of course, as the experiences of socially mobile Mexican Americans demonstrate, a focus on multiculturalism and diversity in theory does not mean that discrimination and prejudice no longer exist in middle-class institutions. While an ethos of multiculturalism is now routine in many different types of American institutions, the primary motives behind diversity initiatives in corporations are not to remedy social and economic inequalities, topple the racial hierarchy, or minimize discrimination within organizations. A 2010 study conducted by the Society for Human Resource Management found that 77 percent of corporations measure the impact of their diversity initiatives by the number of minorities who are recruited. Only 24 percent measure the impact of these initiatives by evaluating employees' "sensitivity or knowledge of diversity." Moreover, the report found that the top-reported outcome for corporations is "Improved public image of the organization." Farther on down the list at number six was the "Retention of a diverse workforce" ("Workplace Diversity Practices" 2010).[8]

A middle-class Mexican American identity is also reinforced through the commercialization of ethnic affluence. Advertising agencies and marketing strategists have taken note of the growing Latino middle-class demographic and are encouraging advertisers to go beyond the "general market" of the white middle class to tap into the growing affluent Latino population with multicultural advertising campaigns (Grunert 2009). Middle-class Mexican Americans are keenly aware that media, retail outlets, and financial institutions actively target the affluent Latino demographic. As one respondent noted, "There's more of us every day [middle-class Mexican Americans]. I see that we have more than half a billion dollars' buying power, which has only happened in the last few years. And I can only say this because I've done some stuff with advertising and you know you don't get to be middle class until you have buying power. And so they are starting to cater to us."

Likewise, numerous print publications, some of which graced my respondents' coffee tables, target affluent Latinos, further supporting, and even lending a cosmopolitan edge to, a middle-class Mexican American identity. These publications range from *Hispanic Business* magazine; *Latina* magazine, a fashion and lifestyle monthly geared toward affluent Latinas; *Urban Latino*, "The first lifestyle and cultural publication geared to bicultural Latinos"; and *Hispanic* magazine, which targets "U.S. Hispanic professionals, entrepreneurs, innovators, and trendsetters." In sum, multiculturalism, ethnic professional organizations, and the commercialization of ethnic affluence through advertising and ethnic media have helped to institutionalize and legitimize a middle-class Mexican American or Latino identity. While the segmented assimilation and racialization perspectives view the retention of a minority identity as a liability to mobility, a minority identity can lead to benefits and opportunities in education and the workplace.

Becoming Whitewashed: Growing Up Middle Class and Mexican American

The messages that second-generation Mexican Americans from middle-class backgrounds receive about their identity and where on the racial hierarchy they belong relative to whites, are very different than those received by their socially mobile counterparts. Their ethnicity is less salient compared to the socially mobile because growing up middle class helps them to cross the white boundary. In contrast to the socially mobile, those who were raised in middle-class households rarely spoke of feeling "out of place" in college or the workplace or having to be two different people at home and at work. They are also significantly less likely to turn to the ethnic community for instrumental support and do not typically join ethnic professional associations. They feel, and are viewed as, "whitewashed" or "Americanized" and are much more likely to have a hyphenated ethnic identification, adding "American" onto their Mexican ethnicity.

Like Vincent, Karina grew up in middle-class neighborhoods in Los Angeles and Orange County. When asked how she ethnically identifies, she replied, "Mexican first, because my parents were born there. But I am American too; that is not a question. And even when I tell people I am Mexican they tell me, you are American, so it is really Mexican American." Karina does not deny her Mexican ethnic origins and identifies as "Mexican first," but she also explains that her white friends and coworkers correct her and insist that she is "American," which really means that she is closer to white. The second generation who grew up middle class exhibit what are perceived to be white middle-class cultural cues, and they assert that their middle-class consumption patterns and preferences for food, beer, clothing, movies, music, and weekend activities distance them from narrow stereotypes of Mexicans, placing them on the white side of the ethnic boundary, effectively making them "coconuts," "whitewashed," or *pochos*. The notion that those raised in middle-class households are "brown on the outside and white on the inside" is also reinforced by interclass interactions with poor or socially mobile kin. One respondent recalled taking a high-end micro brew to a weekend carne asada held at his aunt's house in a low-income Latino neighborhood. When his cousin peered into the cooler he emerged with a bottle of the beer and called out, "Art, did you bring the *gabacho* beer? You are so whitewashed!" (*gabacho* is a pejorative term for a white American). Similarly, when Karina mentioned to her lower-class cousin that she was attending a gala event at Los Angeles' Museum of Modern Art, her cousin promptly replied, "Oh Karina, you're so white!"

The freshly minted middle class in this study also draw intergroup boundaries with those raised in established middle-class households and view them as belonging on the white side of the ethnic boundary. Recall from Chapter 4 that Linda, whose formative years were steeped in abject poverty, referred to her husband Joe as a coconut because his background is cloaked in what she perceives to be white middle-class privilege and individualism. Some refer to their established middle-class counterparts as "Chuppies," which is a slang term for Chicano yuppies, assimilated Mexican Americans who express their ethnic background in a symbolic manner through commodified ethnic symbols. As Lorenzo, a second-generation Mexican American who grew up poor, explained,

> I think with middle-class Mexicans, sometimes they'll view their Mexican background as—almost as a novelty factor. So, you know, what do they call them, Chuppies, Chicano yuppies, where, you know, they decorate their house in like, Frida [Kahlo] paintings like Diego Rivera and, you know, they'll have, like, Gypsy Kings playing, like *how exotic* [his emphasis]. It's almost like they fully assimilate into American society but then they view their Mexican ethnicity as a novelty factor. And I mean that's what—I mean that's traditional American—the American assimilationist way where, you know, even the Irish are like oh, you know, St. Patrick's Day. We're gonna be Irish in this way. We're gonna be Irish in that way because we've fully assimilated to that. . . . I don't need to show off my Mexican culture because I'm so—like, I'm so in it already in my mind that it comes out naturally in whatever way it does. I think a lot of Mexicans—Mexicans who are already in the middle class—I think they have to prove or they have this idea that they have to prove that they're Mexican. And, therefore, they just go out there and, you know, go all Chuppie on everyone.

In line with the linear assimilation model, racial and ethnic boundaries with the majority group are less salient for those whose hail from established middle-class backgrounds and who have experienced a social whitening of their ethnicity (Gans 2005). The second-generation respondents who grew up middle class identify largely as Mexican American, but this does not preclude them from feeling and being viewed as "whitewashed" or "American," in different class and ethnic contexts. Unlike their socially mobile counterparts, none of those who were raised in middle-class households questioned whether they truly belonged in the middle class and none spoke of feeling socially excluded in middle-class spaces. Altogether, their interactions with whites, poor kin, and socially mobile Mexican Americans reinforce the idea that they belong on the white, rather than Mexican, side of the ethnic boundary.

This is not to say that those raised in middle-class households never experience rigid boundaries with whites or that their class status completely buffers them from discrimination. Nearly all recounted occasions where they have been subjected to ethnic, gender, or immigrant stereotypes. Ethnic boundaries are often rigid upon initial contact with whites, usually because of surname or skin color, but they relax once established. Mexican Americans demonstrate their class privilege, often by mentioning the neighborhoods where they were raised or the professions or businesses in which their parents were engaged, status cues that distance them from pejorative Mexican stereotypes and place them closer to whites. And unlike the socially mobile, those reared in middle-class households do not feel that their Mexican ethnicity affects their opportunities in corporate environments. Moreover, several emphasized, without any prompting from me, that being Mexican American is very different from being African American, a racialized group. For example, Nacio, a dentist, related, "My race never comes into play like it does with a black person," a sentiment echoed by Vincent. When I asked Jenny if her Mexican ethnicity has hindered her mobility, she replied,

> You know what? If it has it went over my head just because if I went on a job interview and I didn't get it, it's because I didn't get it and that was it. But I have gotten things like, "Oh wow you're 35 and you're not married? Well how many kids do you have?" Or it's like, "How many brothers and sisters do you have?" Just because they assume I already have several children and I must have ten siblings. So there's those things but that's the type of stuff that can be let go and once people get to know you it never comes up. Just because to me, hostility to me is if someone burned a cross on my front lawn, like they do with blacks. To me that's hostility, like if someone did something like that. That's hostile; that's scary because that is open hatred.

While Tom views his ethnic and class background as occupational "barriers," Jenny does not feel that her ethnic background affects her mobility. Even though she sometimes finds herself on the receiving end of pejorative gendered Mexican stereotypes, she does not view these exchanges as racially motivated, openly hostile, and on par with the experiences of African Americans. Class background does not completely shield middle-class Mexican Americans from discrimination. However, the white boundary softens "once people get to know you," demonstrating that the boundary with whites is an ethnic, rather than rigid, racial line that can be crossed by Mexican Americans who display markers of class privilege.

Later-Generation Mexican Americans: Situational and American Identities

Following the model of identificational assimilation, we would expect third- and fourth-generation structurally incorporated Mexican Americans to exhibit fading patterns of ethnicity and to identify as white. As the grandchildren or great-grandchildren of immigrants, they are far removed from the immigrant generation. They are well educated and residentially assimilated and they follow a traditional pattern of linguistic assimilation where the mother tongue is generally lost by the third generation (Portes and Rumbaut 2001; Rumbaut, Massey, and Bean 2006), although some claim to speak Spanish *"un poco"* (a little) and others have gone to great pains in adulthood to gain Spanish "conversational" skills. Contrary to the identificational model, recent studies examining ethnic identity among later-generation middle-class Mexican Americans show that socioeconomic advancement over the generations is not necessarily correlated with the loss of an ethnic identification and the adoption of an American or white identity. Recent research demonstrates that some later-generation Mexican Americans from middle-class families are subjected to societal and interpersonal discrimination and often espouse a salient ethnic identification regardless of their class status and distance from the immigrant generation (Jiménez 2010; Vasquez 2011). I also find that some later-generation Mexican Americans retain salient ethnic identities that are partly born out of discriminatory experiences. However, patterns of identification vary as some adopt "American" identities and nearly disappear into the white middle class. A comparison of later-generation Mexican Americans who hail from low-income households to those raised in families long grounded in the middle class adds a layer of complexity to patterns of identity and the mechanisms that affect ethnic identification and assimilation experiences.

Situational Identities Among the Socially Mobile

Third- and fourth-generation Mexican Americans raised in poor or lower-middle-class households generally identify as Mexican American or Latino. They are also more likely to assert that their identity is situational and constantly changing depending on the ethnic and class contexts in which they are engaged (Nagel 1994). Katie Ortega-Smith, a fourth-generation Mexican American raised lower middle class, is a case in point. When I asked Katie how she ethnically identifies, she raised her eyebrows and replied in a conspiratorial tone, "Maybe you can help me with this." Was she Mexican American? Chicana? Latina? Simply American? She explained that she identifies with all of these labels depending on the class and ethnic context. "In Casa Blanca I feel Mexican American or sometimes just American depending on who I am around. In college I was Chicana. But when I visited Mexico City everyone told me I'm American. Then sometimes it's Latina." Katie primarily identifies as Mexican American or Latina, and sometimes even American. However, for Katie, an American identity comes to the fore when she interacts with immigrants, who view her as American because she is far removed from the immigrant generation and because she cannot speak Spanish. Thus, an American identity emerges because of the intragroup boundaries immigrants draw with later-generation Mexican Americans (Jiménez 2010), and not because she is viewed as American by whites. Similarly, Isabel, who was raised in a low-income Mexican American community in Texas, related,

> Racially, I don't identify and that is because of grad school that forced me to rethink the whole racial thing and the construction of race and I just got really aggravated with the concept and decided for now I have never applied myself with a race. Ethnically, I would have to say these days I am using the term *Latina*, but you know that term has changed in our time, but only when I am in California. When I am in Texas I am a Tejana. When I was growing up in Texas I was a Mexican American and then when I got to college I was Hispanic. After being in college for about two years I was Chicana. After leaving college and making friends with a lot of people that were not Chicana, I became Latina and I have kind of been Latina wherever I am around, when I am in a community where there are a lot of different ethnicities, such as Hispanic or Latinas or whatever you want to call it, I say Latina because it is easier, but when I am in Texas I am a Tejana. I guess Latina hasn't really—at

least in a small community where my family is from Latino still hasn't—clicked. So in Texas, Tejana is like you are not white, but white people call you Mexican even though your family hasn't lived in Mexico for generations, so you are a Tejana.

As Katie and Isabel illustrate, third- and fourth-generation Mexican Americans who grow up in low-income households explain that the way in which they self-identify has changed over their life course, but never do they identify simply as Mexican or white. They strongly identify with their Mexican roots, yet they are American born, which leads to a Mexican American identity in their youth. In college they adopt a politicized Chicano identity after enrolling in ethnic studies courses where they learn about Mexican Americans' history of exploitation and the struggle for group rights during the Chicano movement. Although they might occasionally identify ethnically as Mexican American, they primarily settle on a "Latino" or "Hispanic" label in adulthood and come to see themselves as part of a larger Latino panethnic category. Observers note that the Latino label is a nonwhite/nonblack racialized classification that symbolizes minority group status for members of Latin American ethnic groups (Golash-Boza and Darity 2008; Rumbaut 2009; Valdez 2011). Although Isabel claims a Latina identity as her ethnicity, and not as her race, identifying as Latina allows her to connect with others in the minority middle-class community who hail from different Latin American national-origin groups.

Social interactions with whites in the workplace also make the ethnicity and class backgrounds of later-generation Mexican Americans salient. John is an English professor and third-generation Mexican American who grew up "lower middle class" in Boyle Heights, a multigenerational neighborhood near East Los Angeles. John is tall and thin with dark brown hair and is frequently identified by others as Persian or Middle Eastern. He retains strong ties and family obligations to poorer coethnics who remain in Boyle Heights and he acknowledged that his middle-class privilege is constantly salient when interacting with them, especially when they visit his spacious home, when he talks about work, or when other indicators of his class status come up, such as his ability to afford a Mexican-immigrant nanny. He primarily ethnically identifies as Mexican American and he also explained that his educational credentials and distance from the immigrant generation allow him to occasionally blur boundaries with whites. However, these feelings are tempered by discriminatory interactions with his white colleagues.

A white colleague approached me and said, "We need someone with a Mexican accent to be the narrator for this documentary on Olvera Street in Los Angeles. Referring to *me* [his emphasis]. I heard my voice on the answering machine and I don't think I have a Mexican accent. But I know that they were making an assumption because of my ethnic heritage.

What John fails to note is that his colleague was also making assumptions about his class background. The professors in John's department are well aware that he was raised in Boyle Heights, not far from Olvera Street in Los Angeles, a characteristic that, combined with his ethnicity, places him closer to the stereotypical Mexican immigrant who speaks with an accent, even though he is American born, highly educated, and far removed from the immigrant generation.

Overall, later-generation socially mobile Mexican Americans do not identify as white or feel as if they have assimilated into the white middle class. They also retain a salient, and situational, ethnic identity that is embedded in their social mobility experiences and formed through educational experiences, ties to poorer coethnics, their distance from the immigrant generation, and their social interactions with whites.

The Established Middle Class: Mexican American and American

Later-generation Mexican Americans who grow up middle class have a different pattern of ethnic identification than their socially mobile counterparts. They are raised in white middle-class neighborhoods far from the ethnic community, and while they admit to having poor kinfolk in their family trees, their kin networks are more class homogeneous than the kin networks of those who grow up poor. Their identity choices follow two patterns. Some have little attachment to their ethnic origins and identify exclusively as American (which is a code word for white), while others identify as Mexican American; however, identifying as Mexican American has a variety of meanings and emerges from different mechanisms. For some, Mexican American means that they are American with a trace of Mexican ethnicity that remains salient because of their skin color (Jiménez 2010). For others, identifying as Mexican American is an identity that is attached to ethnic cultural practices that are maintained over the generations (Vasquez 2011).

Tina exemplifies the first pattern of identifying exclusively as American. Tina has a medium skin tone and light brown hair. She is third-generation Mexican American on her father's side and fourth on her mother's and was raised in an affluent suburb of Los Angeles. She knows that her immigrant ancestors migrated during the Mexican Revolution, but the story of their migration has become diluted over the generations. She emphasized that her family's trajectory epitomizes the "typical immigrant story of the Italians and Irish," where newcomers progress from low-income immigrant to middle-class American over the generations. Tina identifies as American, or white, and she explained that her Mexican ancestry "has never been a problem" and that it seldom comes up in public or in the workplace because people "always assume I'm just American." Tina is shielded from inquiries about her background because she exhibits the typical status cues of white middle-class culture, because her appearance does not align with a Mexican stereotype, and now later in life because of her Anglo last name acquired through intermarriage with a "Heinz-57." But even before she married, outsiders whitened her Latin last name, never assuming that she is descended from Mexican immigrants. "If it would come up it was always 'Is this Italian?'" The only ethnic cultural practice in which she admits to engaging is stuffing a piñata for her daughter's birthday party, a now common practice in Middle America.

Akin to Vincent, Tina initially questioned whether she was an ideal candidate for a study on middle-class Mexican Americans because she does not identify ethnically as Mexican American. Thus, I almost missed out on interviewing Tina, as I was only referred to her by a coworker to whom she had revealed her Mexican ancestry. In line with the linear assimilation model and recent research examining Mexican American ethnic attrition—which is a process whereby assimilated descendants of immigrants stop identifying as Mexican and disappear into the white category—among later-generation Mexican Americans, some descendants of Mexican immigrants adopt an American, or white, identity and have joined the middle class through traditional mechanisms such as education, geographic mobility, and intermarriage (Waters and Jiménez 2005). Ethnic attrition poses important consequences for studies of Mexican mobility because if the most successful Mexican Americans cease to identify themselves and their children as Mexican American, research may underestimate the extent of intergenerational progress achieved by Mexican Americans (Alba and Islam 2009; Duncan and Trejo 2011; Emeka and Agius Vallejo 2011; Perlmann 2005). A pattern of ethnic attrition, and some Mexican Americans' identification simply as American or white, is institutionally supported by the fact that Mexicans are federally defined as an ethnic group and can therefore make a claim to whiteness.

That some identify strictly as American does not mean that distance from the immigrant generation and middle-class privilege shield Mexican Americans from immigrant stereotypes or discriminatory attacks by whites. Elisa is a third-generation Mexican American who was raised in a middle-class household in Los Angeles. Both of her parents graduated from college, and Elisa holds a master's degree. Elisa does not hide her Mexican roots, but she emphasized that while she has Mexican ancestry, she is American. "Mexican is my history. It is my heritage. It is not who I am. I am an American. I am not more Mexican American, but American." However, when we arranged our meeting at a local coffee shop, she instructed me to be on the lookout for a "short, dark, Hispanic-looking woman." During our interview, Elisa related that she is frequently approached by immigrants asking for directions in Spanish, which she cannot give because she is monolingual. Conversely, non-Mexicans often speak to her in broken Spanish or react with visible surprise by her perfect, unaccented English. She understands that people initially view her as an immigrant because of the large population of Mexican immigrants in Southern California.

> I live in California so I understand it because the area has changed so much that I am not even sure who speaks Spanish and who speaks English. But they assume that I am going to speak Spanish. The assumption is like that because of the way I look, and how does that make me feel? Annoyed, but I mean, what can I do? So when I open my mouth when people talk to me, depending on who it is, they are just surprised because I am not Mexican because they assume that I am going to speak Spanish and I must be bilingual and not educated. . . . I am an American. I am a professional. I am a mother. I am in public service. But people will look at me, not all people, but some and say, "Oh, she is Mexican or Hispanic." It is kind of degrading.

Elisa also explained that her dark skin leads her white coworkers to expect that she will display stereotypical ethnic cultural cues.

> Or people assume things and they want to grace me as being the mother goddess and I am like, "Wait a minute!" I am not that into my culture and I am not a representation of whatever her name is, the mother goddess of Mexico? I don't even know who that is! I work with a [white] woman who is a wonderful person and she gets so upset that I'm not into my culture and she has tried to get me involved in the mother goddesses' horizontal life and she loves the

whole culture. She always asks why I don't embrace my culture and I am like, "What do you mean of my culture? I serve my culture. My culture is America. I drive a car. I know baseball and football; what do you want from me? That is my culture." I grew up with Friday night football and that was my growing up. I grew up as an American kid and people find that hard to deal with because of the expectations.

Because of her dark skin, Elisa is expected to epitomize the Mexican ideal of a Spanish speaker who remains close to her cultural roots, and she must frequently prove that she is not one of *those* Mexicans but a later-generation assimilated American with little connection to the culture of her immigrant ancestors. Elisa finds these social interactions in public and in the workplace annoying, and even degrading. She attempts to distance herself from the stereotypes associated with her appearance by asserting her distance from the immigrant generation and class background. When she meets someone new, inquiries about her ethnic ancestry inevitably arise and Elisa always emphasizes that she had a middle-class upbringing, professional parents, and that she holds a master's degree. Her appearance correlates to a Mexican stereotype at first glance, but Elisa stresses that her inability to speak Spanish and her class background distances her from more recent immigrants, making her "not Mexican." These attempts at social distancing are not surprising in a society that has not only portrayed Mexican Americans as unassimilable but also is stratified by race and ethnicity and where social and economic rewards are allocated to those who are defined as white (Bonilla-Silva 2003; Feagin and Sikes 1994; Haney-López 1996; Valdez 2011).

While skin color makes Mexican ethnicity more salient among some, studies support mixed results about whether skin color actually leads to a more salient self-identification as Mexican (Jiménez 2004, 2010; Lee and Bean 2010; Murguia and Telles 1996; Ono 2002; Telles and Ortiz 2008). Along these lines, I find that some established later-generation Mexican Americans with dark skin identify exclusively as American. For example, Melissa is dark skinned with long black hair. She identifies as American, and when I asked whether people ever see her as Mexican or Mexican American, she replied, "Oh, I get that at first but I'm just used to it because I'm dark. I mean, but everything I do is American. I don't speak Spanish; my parents don't. My friends say I'm white. I can't even eat salsa." Thus, some middle-class Mexican Americans with dark skin identify as American because they do not exhibit ethnic markers and because they perceive that their everyday activities place them closer to whites.

Only a few of the later-generation respondents who grow up middle class retain a strong attachment to their ethnic background, which is typically pursued through ethnic cultural practices. Amy is a case in point. Her father, a child of a bracero who also worked in the fields as a young child, is a lawyer, and she descends from an upper-middle-class Mexican American family on her mother's side ,that worked tirelessly for Mexican American rights during the Chicano movement. Her family members have always danced the Ballet Folklórico (traditional Latin American dances), and her mother was a professional Ballet Folklórico dancer who toured with a well-known dance troupe throughout North America. Amy was weaned in the dance studio, and dancing Folklórico also became her passion. She now runs a Ballet Folklórico dance studio. Amy was raised in a white middle-class neighborhood with "Anglo" friends and views her involvement in dance as the one thing that keeps her Mexican ethnicity alive. She feels very fortunate to be involved in dance because "the Folklórico gave me that cultural awareness by teaching me about Mexico, about my heritage." Amy has dark brown hair and light skin, and she is frequently identified as Persian. When asked about her identity, she replied,

> Actually, I'm Mexican American. It's funny, 'cause that's always a big thing, you know, is the term *Chicano*, is the term *Hispanic*, is the term—you know, what's the proper term? And the terminology changes all the time. I've always said I'm Mexican American. . . . So it's been a huge struggle for me. So I don't identify—I identify Mexican American. And I don't say Chicana because that was a thing in the '70s. And I don't say Hispanic because what is Hispanic? Sometimes I say I'm Latina I guess. But that's Latin; that could be anything.
>
> JAV: And what does Mexican American mean to you?
>
> A: American and Mexican descent; that's how I see it.

Amy went on to explain that she was "born into an American family that just happens to be strongly involved in the cultural aspect of it, of our heritage." Of course, an era of multiculturalism and historically high rates of Mexican immigration has bolstered the demand for ethnically linked activities and practices, thereby making them available for consumption by later-generation Mexican Americans (Jiménez 2010). For Amy, the Ballet Folklórico is the one ethnic tradition that is her medium for ethnic and cultural maintenance (Vasquez 2011). As this research demonstrates, identifying as Mexican American does not always mean that one retains a racialized ethnic identity or is privy to discrimination. Amy could easily disappear into the white population based on her phenotype, and she feels like she has never experienced discrimination, yet her involvement in ethnic cultural practices keeps her ethnicity alive.

In all, later-generation, established middle-class Mexican Americans espouse a range of ethnic identities. Some follow the identificational assimilation model, identify as American, and disappear into the white middle class. However, the effect of skin color is unclear. For some, skin color does not preclude them from feeling whitened. For others, skin color is a constant reminder that one has not assimilated into whiteness, no matter how strongly one feels that they are ethnically and culturally "American." Others retain a strong ethnic identity as Mexican American, a choice that is not linked to skin color or class background but to ethnic cultural practices.

Multiethnic Mexican Americans: Becoming Symbolically Mexican American

It was not my initial intention to interview later-generation multiethnic Mexican Americans. But as I sampled respondents for this study, I was referred to, and contacted by, people of Mexican origin with one white parent who view themselves as middle-class Mexican Americans. I did not exclude them from the research because ethnic self-identification is subjective. Thus, the Mexican American middle-class category includes some later-generation individuals who identify as Mexican American even though they have one parent of white ancestry. Their self-identification as Mexican American does not mean that they experience discrimination in their everyday life and rigid ethnic boundaries with whites or that they are subjected to derogatory Mexican stereotypes. In fact, outsiders are often shocked when they claim a Mexican American ethnicity because it is assumed that they are white based on their appearance. Their experiences and their identity choices point to the emergence of a voluntary ethnic identification among later-generation multiethnic Mexican Americans that is actively pursued through ethnic cultural symbols such as food, dancing the Ballet Folklórico, and valiant attempts to learn Spanish while in college in an effort to connect with their ethnic origins (Jiménez 2004; Lee and Bean 2010).

Jessica is a 33-year-old writer whose maternal grandparents were born in Mexico but moved to Illinois in the early twentieth century. Jessica has dark hair, dark brown eyes, and a medium skin tone. Jessica's second-generation Mexican American mother experienced constant bouts of discrimination growing up in a town primarily populated by people of German origin, where "girls were throwing her down in high school and trying to bleach her. They threw bleach on her to make her less brown." Jessica also learned later in life that her father's German family did not approve of the wedding and that "my German grandmother threatened my mother with a shotgun. Nonwhite ethnicity was looked at as very, very bad." Although Jessica knew she had Mexican ancestry, she did not identify as Mexican American growing up because her mother made every effort to separate the family from their Mexican roots, a pattern echoed by other multiethnic Mexican Americans in this study and illustrative of historical timing as the cohorts before lived in a period where the Mexican-origin population experienced little access to the social and economic opportunities eventually imparted by the civil rights movement (Rodriguez 2008; Sanchez 1996). It was not until Jessica went away to college that she rediscovered her Mexican ethnicity by joining a Ballet Folklórico dance troupe at the university.

> For four years that was a big part of who I was. I wasn't the best dancer in the world but I loved the people I met and just being able to dance. I remember performing in the Mexican folkloric dance skirt, and my dance partner in a Mexican hat and mariachi suit, and it was just so surreal in so many ways but it was very neat, and I just sort of found my way through that. I remember having a fight with my parents. My father in particular was really uncomfortable with me embracing that Mexican side of my culture, and told me to "cut out this Latin shit!" at one point.

The availability of a Mexican dance troupe at the university allowed Jessica to explore her ethnic ancestry, something that was forbidden in her youth. Family members, especially parents and grandparents, often cannot understand why their descendants want to cultivate what they worked so hard to leave behind, a phenomenon that Marcus Hansen (1938) termed "the problem of the third generation immigrant." Jessica also worked diligently to learn Spanish in college, something her parents did not support. And although only her mother is of Mexican origin, Jessica subsequently qualified for an extremely prestigious academic fellowship in Mexico that is awarded to Mexican Americans, and she has since forged a lucrative career writing

Spanish-language telenovelas. Jessica has worked hard to cultivate an ethnic identification, and she continues to dance Ballet Folklórico. In line with a symbolic ethnic identification that third- and fourth-generation white ethnics express, Jessica's ethnic origins have not hindered her mobility, and in fact, in an era where attachments to a minority identity are institutionally rewarded, becoming Mexican American as she transitioned into adulthood has actually furthered Jessica's career (Lee and Bean 2010).[9] Unlike the socially mobile and those with dark skin who have an ethnic identification imposed on them, Jessica can choose to be Mexican when she slips into her embroidered Jalisco de Ranchera dress:

> It [dancing] was an important way of connecting with my Mexican heritage. You can never look at somebody wearing a Mexican folkloric dance dress and say "Oh, that person must be Japanese." You just assume they're Mexican and I've always just sort of liked that. . . . I kind of like that; there's no ifs, ands, or buts; if you're wearing a Mexican folkloric dance dress, you're Mexican, at least for the time you're dancing.

When I asked Jessica what identifying as Mexican American means to her, she replied:

> It means that my family has roots in Mexico at some point. For a while I identified, growing up, as not having ethnicity. I didn't want to be anything. And then you know, I got a little more comfortable as an adult embracing all of them and it's just too confusing and difficult to say that I am a Polish, Mexican, Scottish, Irish, Cherokee, Russian, German, American. You know, I got to choose one or the other at some point because I don't want to go through the rest of my life explaining to every person I meet what am I. If I strongly identify with Mexican American, then I get to be Mexican American; end of discussion. We can move on to more important things like talking about the weather and politics, and art, and books and nature and life.

Jessica details a long list of possible identity choices, but she chooses to identify as Mexican American because it is enjoyable and because it provides tangible benefits in terms of her education and career. Janie is another case exhibiting how Mexican ethnicity is lucrative and also optional and symbolic among multiethnic Mexican Americans. Janie's father is white and her mother is third-generation Mexican. Janie grew up in a wealthy North Orange County town and lived a privileged childhood. It is no secret that her family has Mexican ancestry, as they can trace her mother's maternal side back to the Mexican revolution and her mother's paternal side, who migrated northward in the 1920s, to a rancho near Guadalajara. Her family is proud of their roots, but they "encouraged us to assimilate," especially because her grandparents experienced constant bouts of discrimination, something that Janie does not understand "because today that's not the reality [discrimination]. And so let's wake up and join the modern world."

Janie always felt like something was missing in her life and now feels "whole" because she has fully embraced her Mexican ancestry, a choice that can seemingly be made in the modern world, a world where, in her view, minorities no longer experience discrimination. Capitalizing on the growing Latino middle-class population, Janie recently decided to write novels appealing to affluent Mexican American women. Janie also added García, her mother's family name, as her middle name in order to display "my Mexican heritage." She currently identifies as Mexican American or Latina and, like the later-generation white ethnics studied by sociologist Mary Waters (1990), she invokes Mexican stereotypes as an explanation for her mannerisms and "fiery Latin attitude." She has also joined a number of middle-class ethnic organizations in an attempt to forge relationships with other Latinas and to further her career. The ways in which Janie promotes a Mexican ethnicity to her two children (who are one quarter Mexican American) and how she classifies her own identity further demonstrate the voluntary and symbolic nature of Mexican ancestry for later-generation Mexican multiethnics (Lee and Bean 2010). Janie explained,

> And my son asked me the other day, "If I eat more salsa will I become more Mexican?" [Laughter.] I said, "Yes!" [Laughter.] Because to me it's identification and it's not necessarily a bloodline. I gave him the answer that he wanted to hear and I really wasn't lying as far as I was concerned. My last two books have been about Latina culture in one way or another, you know, so I consider myself, I don't even go through the other ethnicities from my father. If someone were to press me I'd go, "Oh yeah I'm also a quarter German and a quarter Yugoslavian." But for me it doesn't even register. Because, pretty much anybody who knows me knows that I'm Mexican. It's one of the first things I let them know about myself! [Laughter.] I mean, I remember I had one friend just recently who didn't realize I was Mexican and I thought, "Oh, shit, I'm slipping!" [Laughter.]

Janie's ethnic identity is clearly symbolic. She did not grow up steeped in an immigrant struggle for upward mobility. She does not retain ties to poorer

coethnics and she does not experience discrimination based on her phenotype and surname. Most telling is that she is able to choose when and how she
wishes to identify as Mexican American—it is not an identity that is imposed
on her (Gans 1979; Waters 1990). Janie makes a concerted effort to display her
Mexican ancestry, not only because it makes her feel unique but also because it
furthers her career. For Janie, her Mexican ancestry is expressive, rather than
instrumental, and costless in her everyday life. These findings correspond with
sociologists Jennifer Lee and Frank Bean's (2010) study of multiracial adults.
They find that many Latino multiracials describe their Latino identity as optional, suggesting that some Latino identities are taking on the character of
white identities.

Conclusion

The nuances of ethnic identity emerge when we compare middle-class Mexican Americans from different class backgrounds and generations. Traditional
assimilation theorists expect that structurally incorporated immigrants and
their descendants will exhibit fading patterns of ethnicity and identify with
the dominant group—whites. While some middle-class Mexican Americans
follow this model, the Mexican American middle-class category includes individuals who adopt many different ethnic identities, from Mexican to Mexican
American to Latino to American, a label that is a code word for white. These
socially constructed identities have different meanings in everyday life and
range from instrumental to optional and symbolic. They are shaped by a long
history of portraying Mexican Americans as foreign and unassimalable, and
are fashioned by class background, an underexamined component of ethnic
identity. Interactions with coethnics within and outside the ethnic community and with whites, especially in the workplace, are mechanisms through
which class and generational differences in ethnic identification materialize
and through which middle-class Mexican Americans learn on what side of
the ethnic boundary they belong. Ultimately, Mexican Americans who grow
up in middle-class households are following the linear model and crossing
boundaries with middle-class whites. In contrast, those raised in poor
households and communities experience challenges stemming from their
low-class background, which leads to a minority pathway into the middle
class.

Second- and later-generation Mexican Americans who are raised in
middle-class households and neighborhoods do not deny their Mexican

ancestry, but they are more likely to view themselves as closer to whites and they easily cross the white boundary. Their middle-class cultural cues distance them from narrow Mexican stereotypes in the eyes of whites. Likewise, their middle-class status cues and individualistic behaviors whiten them in the eyes of both poorer and socially mobile coethnics. However, the ethnicities of those who claim to be "whitewashed" or "coconuts" are not entirely symbolic, as class status does not shield middle-class Mexican Americans from discrimination. Even the established middle class are on the receiving end of racial and ethnic stereotypes based on skin color, gender, assumptions about class background, and generation. Even so, they do not view these brushes with prejudice as discriminatory acts by whites that relegate them to an inferior position of racialized difference. When established Mexican Americans distance themselves from negative stereotypes of Mexican immigrants by asserting middle-class status cues, they are able to present themselves as belonging on the white side of the ethnic boundary, a pattern made possible by Mexican Americans' ability to make an institutionally legitimized claim to whiteness. Although Mexican immigrants are portrayed as a threat to American society, Mexican immigrant stereotypes are not viewed as innate, and Mexican Americans are socially whitened when they have the "right" middle-class status cues, demonstrating that Mexican Americans are not racialized in the same sense as African Americans. Further evidence that boundaries between whites and Mexican Americans are flexible is that some later-generation Mexican Americans identify ethnically as American and have disappeared into the white racial category altogether, as the linear assimilation model anticipates. Finally, those with one white parent have an ethnicity that is the most optional and symbolic in nature, demonstrating that some Latino identities are taking on the character of white identities (Lee and Bean 2007, 2010).

Socially mobile second-generation Mexican Americans retain a salient ethnic identification. Their strong ties to poorer coethnics keep them embedded in ethnic communities, and their freshly minted middle-class status is glaringly salient when interacting with poorer coethnics who cannot relate to their white-collar occupations or who resent their success and question their Mexican authenticity now that they are middle class. As the socially mobile leave ethnic communities and enter middle-class social and professional spaces, they experience rigid class and ethnic boundaries with whites, especially in white-collar workplaces, leading to feelings of pain and social exclusion and the realization that they cannot "melt" into the white middle class. As the minority culture of mobility portends, interactions with poorer coethnics reinforce their newfound class privilege, while interactions with whites make their class background and ethnicity salient, leading to the development of a minority middle-class identity.

While the identificational model expects ethnicity to fade among later-generation Mexican Americans, growing up poor is a memory that never grows faint and is a critical factor that shapes the ethnic identities of those who are further from the immigrant generation. For the socially mobile third and fourth generations, identities are the most fluid and situational and shift over time and space. They remain embedded in ethnic communities and experience rigid boundaries with whites stemming from their ethnicity and class background, which reinforces an ethnic identity. While they sometimes identify as Mexican American, they are also unable to resist the external classification and homogenization of Latin American groups under the Latino category. Regardless of generation, middle-class pioneers do not feel that they are incorporating into the white middle class, but rather as middle-class minorities.

It is critical to underscore that just because the boundaries of whiteness are expanding to include some Mexican Americans does not mean that American society has transcended race and racism. On the contrary, some Mexican Americans claim to be "whitewashed," and "coconuts" reflects the cultural premium of whiteness in America. Claiming a whitewashed identity is a way to distance oneself from derogatory and narrow stereotypes, but it also legitimizes the racial hierarchy and perpetuates the subordination of Mexican Americans who are perceived to be nonwhite (Haney-Lopez 1996; Feagin and Cobas 2008). While some Mexican Americans are able to cross the white boundary, a wholesale boundary shift, where Mexican Americans as a group are disappearing into the white category, is not occurring at this historical juncture. If this were the case, the socially mobile would not develop a minority middle-class identity that is partly born out of a context of discrimination or rely on a minority culture of mobility to provide strategies that help them navigate white social milieus. As we see in Chapter 6, one tactic used to manage the challenges that accompany minority middle-class status, especially among the 1.5 and second generations, is to create and join professional ethnic associations that provide strategies for economic mobility in the context of discrimination and group advantage and that ultimately support a minority pathway into the middle class. Thus, everyday racism and discrimination against Mexican Americans is systemic and continues to structure the daily lives of some, especially the socially mobile. However, as economic differences and perceived cultural differences diminish, the descendants of middle-class Mexican Americans are largely perceived by others, and perceive themselves, as closer to whites.

6

Ethnic Professional Associations and the Minority Culture of Mobility

We wanted to address the needs of Latinas who want to start a business or who want to move ahead in their careers. We haven't typically had that in the community because our parents, they worked hard, but they were focused on survival. So it is a way for all of us who are successful to give back.

—Elena, second generation, small business owner

MEXICAN AMERICANS ARE FOLLOWING different pathways into the middle class. Those from middle-class backgrounds generally follow the traditional linear route into the middle class, where they eventually cross boundaries with whites and where they come to view themselves, and be seen by others, as whitewashed. However, as I have shown in the preceding chapters, assimilation into the middle class does not require that immigrants and their descendants become members of the majority group, as asserted by both canonical assimilation theory and segmented assimilation theory. Socially mobile Mexican Americans experience unique challenges as they attempt to manage interclass relationships with coethnics within and outside the ethnic community and interethnic relationships with the white majority in professional environments. These challenges reinforce a class-based minority identity and lead to a minority culture of mobility, which is a group-specific mobility strategy that emerges out of a larger context of discrimination and group-based disadvantage that accompanies minority middle-class status (Neckerman, Carter, and Lee 1999). The most visible manifestation of the minority culture of mobility is the formation of, and participation in, ethnic professional associations that revolve around a minority middle-class identity and that seek to advance the mobility of coethnics.

This chapter focuses on the Mexican American middle-class community by using a Latina professional organization, the Association of Latinas in Business (ALB), as a strategic research site to study the ways in which social mobility and a larger social context of discrimination intersects with civic and ethnic re-sources in the ethnic community to produce a minority culture of mobility. Two questions guide this chapter. First, what types of ethnic institutions do middle-class Mexican Americans create and why? Second, what functions do ethnic professional associations perform and how do they advance a minority pathway into the middle class?

Civic Participation and the Class Context of Mexican American Communities

Research emphasizes that Asian and black immigrant communities in the United States provide benefits that buffer against downward assimilation into a minority underclass culture and improve chances for adolescents' upward mobility by fostering educational attainment (Gibson 1988; Portes and Rum-baut 2001; Portes and Zhou 1993; Waters 1999; Zhou and Bankston 1998; Zhou and Kim 2006). However, Mexican immigrant communities are not character-ized as having robust ethnic institutions or a strong entrepreneurial presence that fosters social and community capital, which are the ways in which social ties and shared norms help individuals become better educated, find jobs, accumulate economic capital, and advance in their careers (Coleman 1990; Portes 1998). This gap in ethnic resources within Mexican communities, com-bined with the reality that the majority of Mexican immigration is a low-skilled labor migration, has led a number of scholars to reach pessimistic conclusions regarding the social, organizational, and financial resources that the Mexican ethnic community can muster and offer to recent arrivals and the second gen-eration (Baca Zinn and Wells 2001; D. Lopez and Stanton-Salazar 2001; Portes and Rumbaut 2001; Portes, Fernández-Kelly, and Haller 2005). For example, Maxine Baca Zinn and Barbara Wells (2001: 256) argue:

> The social class context of the Mexican community is overwhelmingly poor and working class. Mexicans remain over-represented in low-wage occupations, especially service, manual labor and low-end manufacturing. These homoge-neous lower-class communities lack the high-quality resources that could facili-tate upward mobility for either new immigrants or second- and later-generation Mexicans.

These conclusions are drawn from scholarly research that overwhelmingly focuses on the economically marginalized immigrant- and second-generation youth who are just starting out in the labor market, leading to the erroneous conclusion that Mexican ethnic neighborhoods are "homogeneous lower-class communities" and therefore unable to provide ethnic resources to support upward mobility and incorporation into the middle class.

The significant majority of the socially mobile Mexican Americans I spoke with not only retain an immigrant narrative born out of disadvantage that drives their willingness to give back to poorer kin and coethnics; they also have an ethos of giving back to the ethnic communities where they came of age. Mexican American communities are not homogeneous lower-class communities devoid of ethnic resources that can foster upward mobility. Socially mobile Mexican Americans do not abandon ethnic communities, even when they reside outside of them, and are civically engaged—which is defined as any individual or collective action that aims to positively impact the collectivity—in activities that infuse the community with ethnic resources (M. Chávez 2011; Macedo 2005; Skocpol and Fiorina 1999). One respondent, who was raised in Santa Ana, California, explained the rationale behind her extensive community involvement:

> You know, I really like Santa Ana. I grew up there and people always dump on Santa Ana so much and you know part of it is because it's a Latino community, highly immigrant and they dump on it so much and I am just like, you know what? I know so many people in Santa Ana who are doing good things that went on to college that come back and are doing great things in the community that would love to change it, change it but in a good way. I just wanted to come back and be like, you know what? I grew up in this environment and look at me now and I am going to try and make it a better community kind of thing. It sounds arrogant but now that I've made it, I can give that back.

Socially mobile middle-class Mexican Americans give back to the community in different ways. Some make an impact individually by starting mock trial, mentoring, or college scholarship programs at the inner-city high schools they attended. Others are involved in larger collectivities and are active members and leaders in organizations that promote the educational attainment of inner-city youth. Some are actively involved in organizations that revolve around specific professions, like the Hispanic Bar Association, or their education, like the National Society of Hispanic MBAs. Still others are active in more general professional and business associations headquartered in ethnic communities, like local chapters of the Hispanic Chamber of Commerce or the Association of Latinas in Business (ALB). Civic participation in ethnic professional organizations is a way to gain valuable business skills, networking opportunities, and social support from other socially mobile Latinos who face rigid ethnic boundaries in professional milieus. Thus, a focus on civically active Mexican American middle-class adults, who have social and financial resources and who are dedicated to influencing the lives of the collective community demonstrates that Mexican ethnic communities are not class homogeneous and contradicts the assertion that ethnic communities lack "high-quality resources" that can promote the mobility of immigrants and the second generation.

It is primarily the socially mobile who retain an ethos of giving back to the ethnic community and who are civically engaged in ethnic professional associations. When I asked those raised in middle-class households whether they participate in ethnic professional organizations or other groups that revolve around a Mexican American or Latino ethnicity, they replied, "No, never have," "I don't see the point in separating myself out," and "I went to one meeting and I just didn't find it helpful so I never went back." The majority of those who were raised in middle-class households and communities do not become card-carrying members of ethnic professional associations because they have access to greater social and cultural capital resources than their counterparts who grow up poor. And, because they more easily cross the white boundary in business and professional settings, as detailed in Chapter 5, they do not need to rely on the ethnic community for social support. There are two exceptions to this pattern. First, some Mexican Americans from middle-class backgrounds who own businesses join ethnic professional organizations. Joining an ethnic organization, such as the ALB or the Hispanic Chamber of Commerce, is viewed as a strategy to obtain more clients and increase revenues and not as a means to obtain business skills. Second, those in the third and fourth generations who grew up middle class and who have one white parent are also more likely to join ethnic organizations. As Jessica and Janie mentioned in Chapter 5, their participation in ethnic organizations makes them feel more ethnic. Because they easily cross boundaries with whites and already have middle-class capital by virtue of their class background, those who grew up middle class become civically active in ethnic organizations for economic gain or pleasure, rather than for instrumental support.

I now turn to a discussion of the Association of Latinas in Business, an ethnic professional organization spearheaded by middle-class Latinas, which illustrates how middle-class Mexican Americans become civically engaged in ethnic communities by using class and ethnic capital to create ethnic professional organizations that infuse communities with social and human capital resources. Low-income and working-class Mexican American women have a long history of community activism and volunteerism (García Bedolla 2005; Grasmuck and Pressar 1991; Hondagneu-Sotelo 1994; Jones-Correa 1998; Naples 1991), and this ethos of giving back to the community remains as class status changes. Middle-class Latinas are creating ethnic institutions in the ethnic community that act as a minority culture of mobility and a springboard for upward mobility into the middle class.

The Association of Latinas in Business

The Association of Latinas in Business, or the ALB, is a 501(c)(3) nonprofit organization with chapters in several major metropolitan regions of California, and chapters are also popping up in new immigrant destination states in the American South. The chapter studied here is based in Santa Ana, a city in Orange County. The ALB's Orange County chapter has nearly 300 members, 22 percent of whom are men.[1] The organization's members are Latino entrepreneurs or professionals. The majority are first- or second-generation immigrants with about a quarter being third generation and later. Membership in the organization costs $100 and must be renewed yearly. Members must also pay to attend all business and social events, but at a discounted rate.

The ALB differs significantly from venerable civic organizations created by middle-class Mexican Americans in the early 1900s like the League of United Latin American Citizens (LULAC), or those created by Mexican American women during the Chicano movement, not only because it is so new but also because the activities in which the members are engaged focus exclusively on promoting social and economic mobility, rather than political advocacy (Marquez 2003). For example, political scientist Benjamin Marquez (2003) details the social and political rise of the Mexican American Women's National Association (MANA), a Mexican American women's association that was founded in the 1970s by feminist Chicana activists to combat racial and gender discrimination. MANA works to promote the mobility of its members through networking and leadership training, but the primary goals are to lobby at the national, state, and local levels to protest issues affecting the Latino community, such as the deportation of Mexican nationals and English-only legislation, while bringing attention to issues that male-oriented Mexican American organizations, such as the Hispanic Chamber of Commerce, have routinely overlooked, like reproductive rights and domestic violence. The ALB is different from MANA because the ALB is a 501(c)(3) nonprofit community-level organization, which means that it is a nonpartisan charitable group focused first and foremost on providing resources at the local level, rather than advocacy at the national level. The ALB's founders specifically filed for 501(c)(3) status because they wanted to set themselves apart from 501(c)(6) groups, like the Hispanic Chamber of Commerce, that primarily focus on advocacy rather than "business education." For example, like MANA, the Hispanic Chamber of Commerce can endorse political candidates or lobby for issues affecting business owners, while the ALB cannot. The intention was that the ALB would be a charitable organization that provides tangible resources and opportunities to the local Latino community in cities across the nation. As one of the founding board members explained, "We are not a chamber of commerce organization. A (c)(3) is more of what you are doing for the community and helping those in need."

The nonpolitical focus is constantly reiterated during board meetings, particularly because a number of the board members are highly engaged in Latino political causes and are on the speed dial of California's Latino politicians. For example, as the national immigration debate heated up in early 2006 when Congress was contemplating the Sensenbrenner Immigration Bill, the president of the ALB distributed a typed statement at April's board meeting, just a few weeks before the May Day immigration march (protesting the Sensenbrenner Immigration Bill) that was scheduled to march down the very street where the ALB's offices are located.[2] The president reminded the board members that the ALB is a nonpartisan organization and they were not to discuss immigration policy issues, especially unauthorized migration, at official ALB events or while they were acting as representatives of the organization; otherwise, they would be in violation of their 501(c)(3) status. The statement listed a few approved banal phrases, written by the organization's lawyer, that the board members were to articulate if they were asked about their stance on unauthorized migration or "the immigrant debate." Similarly, heated debate ensued a few months later when some of the members wanted to invite Loretta Sanchez, the Mexican American democratic congresswoman whose district includes Santa Ana, and whom some of the board members tirelessly fundraise for, to speak at an ALB-sponsored event. A few of the board members, chiefly the handful of Republicans, were vehemently opposed to this idea, which they felt would be the organization's official endorsement of the candidate a few months before the 2006 midterm elections and thus a violation of their 501(c)(3) status, and their own political leanings. As one board member insisted, "We do things differently. We keep politics out of it." Thus, the ALB does not lobby the government or support local or national political candidates who are sympathetic to what they term "Mexican" or "Latino" causes, like comprehensive immigration reform. The sole focus of the organization is to provide education and resources to promote the mobility of Latinos at the local level.

While I observed, interviewed, and constantly conversed with the membership at large, the majority of my day-to-day contact was with the ALB's nineteen female board members, eight of whom are entrepreneurs. Some of these small business owners are the proprietors of service-oriented companies such as accounting and marketing firms, staffing agencies, and retail stores. One of the board members works for a large nonprofit organization, and the remaining board members are employed as bankers, accountants, lawyers, and high-ranking executives in medium to large corporations. Those with college degrees or who work in corporations are more likely to work in white middle-class business settings. While the majority hold college degrees, several of the small-business owners, and a few of the bankers, have only graduated from high school or technical schools. As I discuss in Chapter 3, business ownership is often an avenue to social mobility and middle-class status for those without college degrees. They are more likely to own businesses because they understand that not having a college degree restricts opportunities for upward mobility in corporate settings or because they have been overlooked for promotions in corporate settings because they lack a college degree. Three of these small businesses cater to the ethnic community, both to upwardly mobile Latinos and the more recently arrived.

The board members exhibit the traditional indicators of middle-class status. They are employed in professional occupations or own businesses, some have college degrees, most are homeowners, and all make well over the national median income. A few of the board members live in middle-class neighborhoods scattered with historic homes in north Santa Ana. Everyone else lives in affluent, primarily white, towns in the surrounding area and a few live in exclusive gated communities. However, a number of those who live in upper-middle-class areas beyond Santa Ana came of age in the city's poorer neighborhoods. Like middle-class African Americans, the majority of these middle-class Latinas are strongly embedded in the lower-class Mexican ethnic community in Santa Ana through their social ties to poorer coethnics who remain there (Pattillo-McCoy 2000). Finally, their ages range from 24 to 65 and mirror that of the organization as a whole.

While the majority of the board members are of Mexican origin, a handful of the board members are from Central and South American countries, such as Ecuador, El Salvador, and Argentina. Two primary differences exist between those of Mexican origin and those of other Latin American ethnicities. First, the Mexican-origin board members are more likely to report that they grew up poor, and second, those who are not of Mexican origin are more likely to be first-generation immigrants who achieved some modicum of mobility in their country of origin prior to migrating to the United States. For example, two women from South American nations were school teachers before they migrated to the United States in their early twenties. All official business is conducted in English, but the board members speak Spanish and Spanglish (a mix of Spanish and English) frequently to convey a particular point or when informally speaking among themselves. The board members, and the general membership, also run the gamut in phenotype, from dark skin and dark hair to blond hair and blue eyes.

The Community Context of Santa Ana

In order to fully understand why and how a minority culture of mobility evolves as socially mobile Mexican Americans incorporate into the middle class, it is important to detail the ethnic community in which these organizations are embedded and the larger social context within which Mexican Americans in Southern California, and Latinos more generally, negotiate their upward mobility. The ALB chapter under study here is headquartered in the city of Santa Ana, which is located in Orange County, directly sandwiched between San Diego and Los Angeles Counties. Orange County is an area made famous by television shows like *The O.C.*, *The Real Housewives of Orange County*, and *Laguna Beach: The Real Orange County* that glamorize the lifestyles of Orange County's wealthy white population. Santa Ana is only nine miles from Newport Beach, the backdrop for *The O.C.*, and only fifteen miles from affluent Laguna Beach, but the city is an entirely different world. As Table 7 demonstrates, Santa Ana exhibits glaring inequalities in housing, income, and education compared to Orange County as a whole. For example, Santa Ana's residents have attained much lower levels of education than the average Orange County resident. Fewer than half of Santa Ana's residents over the age of 25 have graduated from high school, as compared to 80 percent of Orange County, and only 9 percent

Table 7. Demographic characteristics of Santa Ana, Orange County, California, and the United States, 2000

	Santa Ana	Orange County	California	United States
Median household income ($)	43,412	58,605	49,894	44,334
Home ownership (%)	49	61	57	66
Below poverty line (%)	20	10	13	13
Race/ethnicity (%)				
Non-Latino white	12	47	43	66
Latino	76	33	36	15
Black	2	2	7	13
Asian	9	16	12	4
Foreign born (%)	53	30	26	11
High school graduate or higher (%)	43	80	77	80
Bachelor of arts or higher (%)	9	31	27	24

SOURCE: U.S. Bureau of the Census (2000). This table also appears in Vallejo (2009).

hold a college degree (U.S. Bureau of the Census 2000). Orange County's poorest zip code is located in Santa Ana (where the median household income is only one third of that of the county) and many neighborhoods are marred by high levels of poverty and ruled by gangs, notorious for the sale of narcotics and weapons (Bridenball and Jeselow 2005; Gittelshon 2008). Housing density is greater than in any Orange County city and Santa Ana has been hit particularly hard by the housing crisis (Gittelshon 2008).

Santa Ana's relatively low median income, high housing density, and low rates of education reflect the racial and ethnic composition and generational status of the city's residents. Santa Ana's population is 76 percent Latino (65 percent ethnically identify as Mexican), as compared to 33 percent of the county, and more than half of the city's residents are foreign born (U.S. Bureau of the Census 2000). Like other urban areas that have seen an increase in their minority populations, Santa Ana has experienced a substantial amount of white flight over the last forty years. The non-Hispanic white population decreased from 70 percent in 1970 to 12 percent in 2000 and the majority of the white population live in Floral Park, a ritzy upper-middle-class neighborhood at the northernmost tip of the city, a bucolic neighborhood dotted with historic homes on wide, tree-lined streets, separated from the lower-income neighborhoods by a long, one-way boulevard (U.S. Bureau of the Census 1972, 2000). Despite Santa Ana's largely immigrant population, the median household income among Latino residents in 2000 was $42,000, just under the median income for the U.S.

population, but nearly 25 percent lower than the median income of Orange County (U.S. Bureau of the Census 2000).

The stereotype that Santa Ana is a poor immigrant city pervades Southern California, but the community is an interesting study in contrasts of socio-economic difference. Unlike some inner-city business districts, downtown Santa Ana, where the ALB's office is located, is a bustling consumer center with a steady and reliable business climate derived from a socioeconomically and ethnically diverse cast of patrons (Venkatesh 2006). For example, down-town Santa Ana features a fusion of businesses that cater to the professionals who work in the city, to those that attract a young and hip crowd drawn to the Artists' Village, to enterprises aimed at more recently arrived immigrants. As Santa Ana is the county seat of the Orange County courthouse and district at-torney's office, it is not uncommon to see men and women in business suits walking the streets and dining at expensive restaurants scattered about the area. Downtown Santa Ana has also experienced a significant amount of gentrifica-tion with the opening of the Artists' Village that caters to an urban crowd with its work/live lofts, trendy lounges, environmentally green boutiques and restau-rants, and monthly art exhibits. While this newly "revitalized" area seeks to draw more affluent patrons, recently arrived immigrants can also fulfill their needs in a Spanish-speaking environment on Fourth Street, an area adjacent to the Artists' Village.

The multilayered social spaces of Santa Ana provide a unique opportunity to examine how the growing middle-class Mexican American presence in ethnic communities reinforces a class-based minority identity and facilitates the creation of a minority culture of mobility. For example, the city council is made up entirely of Latinos, and the president of Santa Ana City College is Latina. Moreover, many affluent Mexican Americans who grew up in Santa Ana but now live elsewhere return to the community to shop the ethnic grocery stores and businesses and to participate in community events, such as yearly Mariachi, Cinco de Mayo, and Día de los Muertos festivals. Downtown Santa Ana is a class-diverse social space where one can dine at a hip restaurant; wire money to Mexico; buy a book from Libreria Martinez, the only Spanish bilin-gual bookstore in the county; get fitted for a *quinceañera* dress; peruse one-of-a-kind works of art at expensive art galleries (many owned by Latinos); and purchase refreshing fruitas and refrescos from street vendors.

While Santa Ana's neighborhoods and businesses provide a supportive point of entry for the large immigrant population and a cultural social space for middle-class Latinos, Orange County has a long history of institutionalized discrimination and exclusion of the Mexican-origin and Latino population. For example, the Mexican-origin population historically experienced de facto segregation with "Mexican seats" in movie theaters and "Mexican Day" at the public swimming pool, and de jure segregation, as each school district had its own "Mexican" school until the historic *Mendez v. Westminster* decision in 1946, which desegregated Orange County schools, setting a precedent for *Brown v. Board of Education* (Arriola 1997). During the 1990s, the majority of California's population voted for Propositions 187 (initially drafted by an Orange County resident), 209, and 227. As detailed in Chapter 2, these anti-immigrant initiatives largely targeted the Mexican-origin population and were intended to restrict state services and outlaw bilingual education (García-Bedolla 2005; Portes and Rumbaut 2001). The founder of the civilian vigilante group that targets unauthorized migrants, "The Minutemen," is from Orange County, and in March 2010, the City Council of Costa Mesa, the municipality wedged between Santa Ana and Newport Beach, declared itself a "Rule of Law" city in an effort to demonstrate that unauthorized migrants are not welcome in the city. The social and historical context of Orange County has led journalist and pundit Gustavo Arellano to consistently refer to Orange County as the Mexican-hating capital of the United States (Arellano 2006, 2008). The cultural landscape of the community, combined with a historical legacy of exclusion and a negative context of reception in Orange County more generally, provides the social context that leads professional Latinos to create a minority culture of mobility.

Building an Ethnic Professional Association

The founders of the ALB were originally members of a different organization, the Society of Mexican Business Women (SMB),[3] also headquartered in Santa Ana. Although the SMB is similarly geared toward Latina professionals and business owners, the ALB's founders feel that the SMB's model is ineffective in promoting individual mobility and the advancement of Latinos as a group because the organization does not focus on business training and resources that can be put into practice in everyday life. The ALB's founders explained that the SMB is predominantly social and does little to help professional business owners take their businesses to "the next level." Laura (my initial key informant into the organization), a founding board member, explained,

When I was asked to launch the Orange County chapter I was hesitant but I felt like there was a big need to bring information and resources for women in the community who are starting their businesses could really walk away with and not just make it a social *comadre* thing [like the SMB]. There is another organization in the community for women and I support them; I just think their focus is different.

JAV: They are more social?

A: If you ask me for my opinion, yes. That's what it is. I saw it more as really strictly a networking group, more socializing, not as a business group that benefits the community. You can join both of them but I think that we both bring different things to the plate.

Lydia, another founding board member, recalled,

There was some confusion at SMB about the definition of a business woman. They just thought that if you are employed in any job you are a business woman. A lot of these women had day jobs but wanted to start hobby jobs, like selling Tupperware for example. Just informal, not even registered. We wanted to take our businesses to the next level and were not getting the information to do it.

Laura had contacts within the original chapter of the ALB, located in Los Angeles. Several women left the SMB and attended a few meetings of the ALB-Los Angeles before deciding to start the Orange County chapter. The ALB is based in Santa Ana but aims to serve members throughout Orange County. A few of the founding members looked perplexed that I would even question why they decided to head-quarter the Orange County chapter in Santa Ana rather than a more affluent city like Newport Beach. One woman said that "Anything Latino happens in Santa Ana." Another explained that Santa Ana is the only city in largely white Orange County where Mexican Americans are the majority and where there is the political and social support to create and sustain professional ethnic institutions. The historical presence of Latinos in the city, the current concentration of Latino residents, and the cultural memory of those who grew up or still live there (even if they live in the most exclusive neighborhoods) make Santa Ana a natural choice for the ALB, even if many of the members must traverse the county to participate in the ALB's monthly events.

The ALB makes it clear through their marketing materials that they are an organization that seeks to provide the Latino middle-class community with resources, educational programs, networking opportunities, and strategies that will help socially mobile Latinos move ahead in white-collar professions or business. One of the ways they try to achieve these goals is through monthly breakfast meetings, "as a way to start your day off right, before you go to work." The breakfast meetings cost $20 and are held in the ballroom of a local hotel. They begin at 7:30 in the morning with anywhere from sixty to one hundred people in attendance. Members are encouraged to arrive on time, pick up a name tag, and network until breakfast is served at eight. There is always a table set up where members can lay out their business cards and marketing materials for others to gather. Attendees sit at round tables in groups of ten people and by eight o'clock a typical breakfast of coffee, scrambled eggs, hash browns, and bacon is served by Latino waiters clad in white shirts and bow ties. Laura, the founding president, leads the members in the Pledge of Allegiance, thanks the sponsors, and then introduces the guest speakers. The first topic the organization presented at a breakfast meeting was "How to Build Your Business Team," which was followed by subjects like "The ABC's of Marketing," "The Art of Negotiation," and "Etiquette Is Power: How to Outclass Your Competition." In addition to the breakfast meetings, the organization puts on one event per quarter, such as an evening networking mixer, where members are encouraged to meet and exchange information with at least three new people in order to extend their professional contacts.

While members of the ALB strive to present a professional appearance, their common rhetoric reinforces a sense of community and ethnic identity that revolves around their minority middle-class status. The ALB draws on a class-based minority identity to recruit members who consider themselves to be Mexican American, or Latino, and middle class. The message that the ALB targets for this specific demographic comes across in its marketing materials, which include stock photos of women with dark hair and medium skin tones dressed in suits and diligently working in office settings. At the same time, the group's slogan is *Sí, se puede*, or "Yes, we can," the iconic motto of the United Farmworkers, originated by Cesar Chavez and Dolores Huerta during the Chicano movement. Besides in their written marketing materials, the board members also refer to themselves frequently as Latinas or Mexicanas when speaking informally with each other, and they use phrases like "our community" and "the Latino professional community" at formal events. These visual cues, "code words," and slogans help separate the ALB from the largely white professional organizations in the community, which ALB members feel are generally not welcoming to minority professionals and business owners. Moreover, while ALB members may be middle-class professionals, these words generate and strengthen a sense of empowerment that revolves around a class-based minority identity (Snow 2001). To illustrate, when the board posed for a formal portrait, the photographer, a Latino male in his late twenties, instructed the women to pose like the white supermodel Cindy Crawford. Laura, the president of the organization, looked at the photographer with contempt and replied loudly, "Cindy Crawford? Ladies, pose like Eva Longoria. Latina power!" The board members echoed her cry to arms by replying, "Latina power!" as the photographer snapped the photo. This incident illustrates that the structurally assimilated board members of the ALB strongly identify as an ethnic minority rather than white (a pattern also detailed in Chapter 5), invoking the image of a successful Mexican American actress and businesswoman to distinguish themselves from a white supermodel. While previous research theorizes that upwardly mobile immigrants and their descendants will shed their ethnic identities, cut ties to the ethnic community, and incorporate into the white middle class, the members of the ALB take pride in and actively reinforce a distinct class-based ethnic identity to create institutions in ethnic communities where the socially mobile middle-class Mexican American can thrive.

Creating a Minority Culture of Mobility

What are the underlying social mechanisms that lead middle-class Mexican Americans to create and foster a minority culture of mobility? The minority culture of mobility perspective asserts that a minority pathway into the middle class is activated in the context of group disadvantage and discrimination. As demonstrated in Chapter 5, middle-class Mexican Americans, particularly those who grew up poor, interact regularly with whites who hold narrow views of what it means to be Mexican in America. These views are bound up in perceptions of race and ethnicity, class, and gender and reflect the larger social context in which Mexican Americans negotiate their mobility. Professional ethnic organizations are an important element of a minority culture of mobility because they are created, in part, to mitigate pejorative group-based stereotypes about Mexican Americans and Latinos. The board members of the ALB feel that the organization promotes a more positive image of the Latino community in Orange County, "showing another side of our community." They hope that a Latina business organization can help combat the "immigrant

shadow" or the idea that Latino immigrants and their children are unassimilable, poor, uneducated, and unauthorized (Zhou and Lee 2007), stereotypes
that continue to follow them despite their prestigious degrees, corporate jobs,
and social mobility. This objective is not explicitly stated in the organization's
membership materials, but it is frequently discussed informally at board
meetings and events. As Beatriz, a second-generation Mexican who was raised
in a low-income community in North Orange County, explained during our
interview,

> If we as a community are going to prove to everyone that we are here not be-
> cause we are lazy and that we just want to speak Spanish and take over the
> country and make it our own little country, that's all I ever heard. And I say
> that the ALB has a responsibility to show the real side of our community
> where business owners are educated and we are lucky enough to share two
> cultures, the heritage of our parents and the country we are born into.

Beatriz feels that the ALB helps correct the commonly held belief that
Latinos are not incorporating culturally and economically into the fabric of
American society. She does not disparage immigrants as individuals, and she
feels "lucky" to share the "heritage" of being Mexican with her parents. However, Beatriz hopes that the ALB's successful members counteract the idea of a
monolithic Mexican population by demonstrating "the real side" of the Mexican community, where "business owners are educated" and savvy enough to
navigate the white business world without relinquishing their ethnic identity.

The board members of the ALB draw on a minority middle-class identity
and actively work to reinforce the notion that although they are middle class,
they are not white. However, recall from the previous chapter that socially
mobile Latinos experience class and ethnic boundaries when interacting with
middle-class whites in professional milieus. These experiences lead them to
believe that Latinos must be socialized to normative middle-class standards
of business in order to succeed in Orange County's largely white business
community. An example of how the ALB attempts to promote normative
business standards was particularly evident during one breakfast meeting.
The title of the meeting was "Etiquette Is Power: How to Outclass Your Competition and the Art of Knowing How to Relate to Others in the Business
World." Belinda, a Mexican American woman who was the guest speaker, owns
a professional development organization that trains Latinos how to interact in
high-powered corporate environments. She emphasized to a rapt audience

that proper business etiquette and table manners are vital in forming lasting business relationships and can make or break a business deal. She spoke about the importance of a firm handshake, making eye contact, and how to exchange business cards, and she related tricks for remembering names. Brenda's discussion of table manners received the most attention. She demonstrated which forks to use for different dinner courses, instructed the audience to never dig in before everyone at the table is served and the host has taken the first bite of the meal, and made clear that mopping up sauce with your dinner roll raises an immediate low-class red flag. Some of the women and men at my table reacted in surprise to Brenda's tips. One board member responded to the nervous laughter by saying, "That's why we are here. To provide you with this information so you can make these contacts and shatter the stereotypes of us in this community."

Women and minorities are regularly left out of the corporate socializing rituals of white males, such as being invited to partake in an after-work brew with upper management, which provide important informal networking opportunities and that can lead to career advancement (Deal and Kennedy 2000; Feagin and Sikes 1994). The board members of the ALB understand from experience that it is critical to gain access to these corporate rituals, and they specifically devise meetings that arm middle-class Mexican Americans with the strategies to blur boundaries that will provide opportunities to build social capital. For example, one theme of another breakfast meeting, this time held at an affluent country club in a neighboring beach city, was how to conduct business on the golf course, which was followed by a hands-on golf clinic that taught fundamentals in swinging and putting. Business golf was frequently a subject of hot debate, as many of the board members lamented that Mexicans are not brought up playing golf because of their marginalized economic positions as children. In a region where executive golf is a year-round event and an institutionalized corporate social practice, the board members understand that not being able to play golf puts socially mobile Mexican Americans at a distinct disadvantage as professionals when trying to negotiate large business deals that are informally consummated on the golf course. The first speaker, a male member of the organization who is president of another Latino civic group, explained to the ALB's members that the "Latino community is missing the boat with their lack of interest in golf" and that playing golf had doubled his organization's revenues in the last year. As Laura concluded the meeting, she reiterated that the golf clinic was a "great opportunity" not only for the members but also for the larger Latino community and that the ALB "does things differently in the way that they create opportunities for Latina entrepreneurs to get ahead in business. Today, I am going to learn how to play golf. That's because women, Latina women in the community, have a direction and a goal and we go after what we want."

As these examples illustrate and as the minority culture of mobility emphasizes, the board members of the ALB retain a salient ethnic identification even though they are economically successful, and they make a concerted effort to publicly espouse their ethnic origins. Moreover, they rely on a salient middle-class ethnic identity to recruit members. But at the same time, the board clearly communicates to the members through its monthly breakfast meetings that in order to be a successful entrepreneur or corporate professional in Orange County's white business world, they must shed behaviors that signal a lower-class status. Moving up and out of the barrio is often accompanied by pain and social exclusion as Mexican Americans who grow up poor incorporate into the middle class and attempt to bridge ethnic and class boundaries with whites in professional settings. Therefore, the underlying message of the ALB is that successful Latinos should approximate a normative image that revolves around a carefully constructed middle-class persona—business education and networking skills alone are not enough to secure mobility or "shatter stereotypes" in Orange County. The board members know from experience, and from their own faux pas, that middle-class leisure activities such as golf, styles of dress, and etiquette are just as essential for mobility. As sociologists Ivan Light and Steven Gold note (2000: 107), "Studies of minority men and women have consistently found that competence in the folkways of the male white Protestant upper middle class are vital to success, even if such skills are unrelated to actual job performance." Through a combination of business education, presentation of business etiquette, and learning how to play golf, the organization creates and transmits "middle-class ethnic capital"—by socializing Latinos to partake in middle-class business culture and advocating a middle-class presentation of self while retaining their ethnic identity—so that they can generate social and economic capital (Coleman 1990; Portes 1998; Zhou and Kim 2006). Instead of formally challenging the racial and ethnic hierarchy that privileges white middle-class business practices, the ALB encourages individuals to achieve mobility by adhering to conventional business standards in order to blur ethnic boundaries in the white upper-class business world (Alba 1999, 2005; Loewen 1974).

Combating Immigrant Stereotypes

Merely being a member of an ethnic professional association does not automatically shield one from an "immigrant shadow." The name of the organization, the Association of Latinas in Business, clearly connotes that its members are business professionals, yet a stigma remains because the word *Latina* figures prominently in the title and immediately signals a lower-class status and ethnic stereotypes to white professionals. For example, at one board meeting, Lydia, the president elect, explained that she originally desired to hold the golf clinic at Green View, a public golf course in Orange County. She told the other board members that she would "never set foot in Green View again," and that if the group decided to go forward with the breakfast there she would "absolutely not be a part of it." She continued, "I felt very discriminated against when I spoke to the managers about the breakfast. They felt that our group was not the caliber of people to bring to the golf course." Lydia, a successful entrepreneur in her early forties with light brown hair and fair skin, is college educated but speaks with a slight Spanish accent. She mentioned to me later that her accent must have served as a marker for the characteristics of the entire group, especially because she wore her best business suit and introduced herself as the president of a Latina business organization. As Lydia suspects, the managers at Green View engaged in statistical discrimination, "the practice of using group membership as a proxy in the absence of clear information about individuals" (Phelps 1972). Green View's managers seemed to associate Lydia's ethnic background, her accent, and her affiliation with a Latina organization with low-class Latinos. The other board members were not shocked by Lydia's encounter. One person suggested that they hold the golf clinic at a country club that had hosted events for the Hispanic Chamber of Commerce, because the white managers at this club would know that "not all Latinos in the community are illegals who only speak Spanish."

I personally encountered the negative group-based stereotypes that socially mobile Mexican Americans are subjected to once they mingle socially and professionally outside ethnic communities that lead professional minorities to seek refuge in the middle-class minority community. I worked at the ALB's booth during Orange County's Largest Mixer, a yearly business networking event held in Costa Mesa. Orange County's Largest Mixer is touted as the "ultimate business networking event" and brings together hundreds of corporations, small businesses, and business associations under one roof. I managed the ALB's table along with four professionally dressed female members with the goal of signing up new members or sponsors who could underwrite the breakfast meetings and networking events in return for valuable face time in front of hundreds of middle-class Latinos. The president of the organization requested that I stand in front of the table, with membership brochures in hand, in order to greet and speak with people as they walked by the booth. I wore a well-tailored pinstriped business suit, black high heels, light makeup, and my dark hair was styled in a shoulder-length bob. The table was draped with a large white banner featuring glossy images of medium skin-toned women with dark hair in business suits and the name of the organization, "The Association of Latinas in Business," spelled out in large letters. One of the organization's members, who owns a company that makes Mexican desserts, donated several cases of Jell-O that we handed out as an enticement to stop by the booth.

When an older white male with a ruddy complexion and red hair approached the table, I handed him a membership brochure and inquired about his line of work. He replied that he was a cosmetic surgeon in Laguna Beach, an affluent city located in South Orange County, and that he specialized in "lunchtime procedures" for women professionals who just want to perk up their appearance and who may not have a lot of time to go under the knife. I suggested he join the ALB, as it might be a good opportunity to obtain new clients because the majority of the ALB's members are female entrepreneurs and professionals. Without delay, the plastic surgeon handed back the membership brochure and exclaimed, "This is a Latina organization? I don't think your members are my caliber of people. I usually deal with the Newport Beach type of ladies." As the comments from this cosmetic surgeon indicate, and as Lydia's experience at the golf course also signifies, for most whites, *Latina* connotes something of a "caliber" other than middle class and professional, even when followed by the word *business*. Like middle-class blacks, who cannot escape the poor and uneducated stereotypes associated with their racial background, Latinas cannot escape the immigrant shadow when interacting with whites in their everyday lives, even when they display clear markers of class mobility (Feagin 1991; Feagin and Sikes 1994; Lee 2000; Zhou and Lee 2007).

Besides providing business education and socializing middle-class Latinos to white middle-class business culture, one focus of the ALB is to combat the immigrant shadow that remains significant in the everyday lives of socially mobile Latinas. As Beatriz emphasized, a professional Latina business organization is a way to publicly show the "other side" of an ethnic community that is often touted as being poor, unassimilable, and uneducated, while at the same time providing an avenue for middle-class Latinas to signal their more affluent class positions to the white majority. However, it is clear through my interviews and participant observations that affluent whites do not view all middle-class Latinos as members of the professional business class, especially those who have achieved their mobility in one generation. As this research confirms, ethnic stereotypes and a negative context of reception do not vanish just because immigrants and their adult children achieve social mobility and enter the middle class. The reasons for this are twofold. First, high rates of migration from Mexico, or immigrant replenishment, have reinforced immigrant stereotypes (Jiménez 2010). Second, the mobility experiences of middle-class Mexican Americans are embedded in a region that has a long history of discrimination and social exclusion toward the Mexican-origin population. Even though they are middle class, their ethnic identity is not an optional and symbolic choice, as the linear assimilation model predicts. Interpersonal interactions with whites often conjure feelings of exclusion by reinforcing that they are not legitimate members of the white middle class. But just because they self-identify and are identified by others as nonwhite does not mean that they have not incorporated into the middle class. Quite the contrary. Orange County's 1.5- and second-generation Latinas are accomplished middle-class professionals whose identity intersects with their racial and ethnic background and class status as they attempt to create a social space in the ethnic community where the minority middle-class population can thrive.

Combating Gender Stereotypes

Recent research has demonstrated that Mexican Americans in particular, and Latinos in general, must deal with disparaging ethnic stereotypes in their everyday lives (Frank, Akresh, and Lu 2010; Jiménez 2010; Vasquez 2011; Zhou and Lee 2007). The board members hope that the ALB, its successful members, and its business activities will provide an alternative to the poor and uneducated group-based stereotypes that follow them despite their class. However, women bear an additional ethnic stereotypical burden as Latina professionals and entrepreneurs must also contend with gendered stereotypes that whites hold of Latinas (Marquez 2003; Pessar 1999; Segura 1992). They might be middle class, but their race/ethnicity, combined with their gender, automatically makes them victims of the stereotyped Latino machismo (Villenas 2001). Non-Latinos rely on gendered cultural stereotypes to define what it means to be a middle-class Latina, assuming that Latinas live within a patriarchal ethnic community where early childbearing, motherhood, and a "cultural" desire for large families are valued over education or professional success (Zavella 1997). Scholars have consistently deconstructed these stereotypes. For example, sociologist Gloria González-López (2004) demonstrates that Mexican immigrant fathers want their teenage daughters to postpone sex not because they are controlling but because they understand that teenage pregnancy might mean "not completing high school or attending college, becoming poor, being abandoned, and encountering social stigma and sexism as a single mother." Furthermore, scholars have also dismantled the idea that Latina fertility is out of control by demonstrating that the number of children born per woman converges to that of whites the further removed Latinas are from the immigrant generation and the more income and education they obtain (L. Chavez 2004; Parrado and Morgan 2008).

The vast majority of the women who belong to the ALB do not conform to negative Latina stereotypes. A small minority of the Latinas who belong to the ALB bore children in their teenage years and only a small proportion have gone no further than high school. The majority of the ALB's members were not teenage mothers and most have attained some years of college, completed trade school, or earned college degrees. The members also displayed significant variations in family type and views on marriage and childbearing. Some of the women are single, others are divorced, and some are married with or without children. And a number of the women I spoke with said that they made an explicit decision to postpone marriage or childbearing until they graduated from college or started their careers. One of the most revered members of the organization openly talks about her decision to forgo marriage until her early forties in order to develop her business. Conversely, some of the members are starting businesses now that their children are older or in school. Many of the successful members deal with the challenges of balancing their families and careers, something that women of all racial ethnic backgrounds must manage (Moen 1992; Roehling, Hernandiz Jarvis, and Swope 2005). While the women I studied do not fit the socially constructed Latina stereotype, I frequently overheard the ALB's members discuss instances where their white coworkers are amazed to learn that their fathers or husbands supported their education or career choices or that they are startled to learn that they do not have a brood of children waiting for them at home.

I personally experienced the stereotype that Mexican American women have high fertility rates when I worked at Orange County's Largest Business Mixer. A white woman, dressed in a three-piece suit and heels, approached the table, lured by the promise of free Jell-O. When I recited my spiel on the benefits of joining the organization, she replied, "Good for you Mexicans. Usually people take over countries with wars but you Mexicans are doing it by having lots of babies." Even after I explained that the goal of the ALB is to "empower Latinas through business education, referrals, and networking," the white woman relied on gendered immigrant stereotypes about Mexican women to interpret what it means to be a professional Latina. When I immediately related this conversation to the ALB's members who were also working the mixer, Rosa replied, "Obviously we are not just staying home and having babies. We are Latinas in business! That's why we are here, because we want a career."

While my observations and interviews reveal that one informal purpose of the ALB is to counteract derogatory immigrant and gender stereotypes, my participant observation substantiates the idea that professional Latinas experience a negative social context in Orange County's larger business community where whites continue to conflate class, ethnicity, gender, and generation when interpreting what it means to be a Latina professional. Not only is it difficult for middle-class Mexican Americans to thwart the immigrant shadow; they must also deal with gendered stereotypes resulting from negative perceptions of Mexican immigrant women. Despite these hurdles, middle-class Latinas do not utilize the ALB to formally challenge and systematically deconstruct racial and ethnic hierarchies and class and gender stereotypes. Instead, membership in the ALB is seen as a medium to promote the mobility of Latinas in the community individually, so that successful members can blur rigid ethnic and class boundaries on the merits of their own accomplishments.

Intraclass Conflict and Social Distancing

The ALB believes that success in the business world is twofold. First, Latinos must be educated in financial literacy, negotiating, networking, and building a business from the ground up. Second, Latinos must approximate a normative middle-class image in terms of etiquette, styles of dress, and speech patterns in the larger professional community in order to delegitimize racialized and gendered stereotypes and to partake in corporate rituals, such as golf. This does not entail shedding your ethnic identity or becoming white, but rather, learning the skills that will "shatter" the immigrant stereotypes that Latinos in general are low class and uneducated or that Latinas value family over their careers. The members of the organization do not disparage immigrants directly, especially because they or their parents are immigrants and because many retain ties to poorer coethnics. However, they are keenly aware that immigrant stereotypes affect how they are perceived in the larger business community, making them feel that it is important to demonstrate that Latinos are not a monolithic population in terms of class and education.

The eighteen women who make up the board of directors are the public face of the ALB. They run the various meetings, attend networking events with other minority and white-dominated business associations in the community, and are the first point of contact with the corporate sponsors who underwrite their events and educational programs. Their very visible position within and outside the community leads a number of the board members to believe that the entire board of directors should personify the middle-class Latina image they carefully attempt to craft among their larger membership. Some view those board members who do not exhibit middle-class cultural cues as detrimental to the organization's image because they reify immigrant and gender stereotypes among affluent whites. While the majority hail from less advantaged backgrounds, the board members who have college educations and some of those who are employed in corporate settings actively attempt to distance themselves and the organization from board members with high school or trade school educations or those who were teenage mothers.

This intraethnic conflict became clear when a less polished woman applied for a vacant position on the board of directors. Adriana is a second-generation Mexican American and a real estate broker in her early twenties whose target market is the Latino community. She has completed numerous trade courses and holds specialty brokerage licenses. More important, her inexperience in the business world, unrefined manners, and speech patterns set her apart from the more polished board members. A number of the board members have accents, particularly the 1.5 generation, but the East Los Angeles–like lilt to Adriana's less articulate speech and her out-of-turn outbursts instantly expose her low-income background.

After one meeting where Adriana gave a lengthy presentation, I joined three of the board members for dinner at a local restaurant. Much of the conversation revolved around the ALB's upcoming events and potential sponsors, until the talk turned to Adriana's presentation. In a frustrated tone, Lydia said, "Adriana has no class! Can you imagine her pitching to Mercedes Benz [a potential corporate sponsor]? They won't take us seriously." Laura, who holds an associate's degree and is a successful corporate executive, chided Lydia by saying, "Everyone deserves a chance. She is young but willing to work hard and we can teach her how to be more professional." While the college-educated board members do not dislike Adriana personally, she does not bring middle-class capital to the board of directors. Despite her professional accomplishments, they feel that her demeanor marks her, and potentially the organization, as low class and uneducated, stereotypes they constantly contend with as they negotiate their place in Southern California's professional community. Some board members employed various behind-the-scenes tactics to prevent Adriana from meeting with potential corporate sponsors alone or representing the organization in the larger community. For example, the president elect would often accompany Adriana to meetings, or she was encouraged to join committees that do not require face-to-face contact with sponsors.

More of the board members, and members of the larger organization, distanced themselves from Adriana after she was interviewed for an article published in an Orange County newspaper. The article highlighted the stories of successful Latina entrepreneurs and professionals. Adriana related that her family was more concerned about marrying her off than her career and emphasized that they would not consider her fully successful until she was married with children. The writer, a white woman, maintained that these outdated gender roles and expectations are culturally specific to Latinos and common in the Latino community, thereby hindering Latina mobility. Two of the board members were incensed by the article and furious with Adriana for legitimizing the stereotype that Latino parents privilege domesticity over education and professional success for their daughters. They were also distraught that the article briefly mentioned Adriana's affiliation with the ALB because they feared that readers, and potential sponsors, would view Adriana's personal experiences as representative of all the organization's members, and thus make the organization's business programs less investment worthy.

The board members' fears were warranted, as the article did reinforce the gendered stereotypes that white professionals in Southern California hold of Latinas. Shortly after its release, I attended a cocktail reception with Lydia and Alicia, thrown by a prominent Orange County women's business organization. The cocktail reception was held at a private estate located in an exclusive gated neighborhood of South Orange County. The majority of the women at the reception were white, with a small proportion of African Americans, Asians, and Latinos in attendance. Some men and a number of prominent politicians were also present. I followed Lydia, who is very well connected in the larger business community, as she networked with a range of people in the resort-like backyard where tuxedoed waiters passed hors d'oeuvres and glasses of white and red wine. Both Lydia and Alicia wore metal name tags emblazoned with "The Association of Latinas in Business," their name, and their title. About a half hour after we arrived, Lydia introduced us to Megan, a white woman who owns an established corporate public relations and marketing firm in Orange County. After they chatted for a moment about each other's businesses, Megan said, "It's sad to hear that Latinos still don't support their daughters' careers." For the first time that night, Lydia was speechless. Her face turned red and she sputtered, "Well, that's not really true." After Megan walked away, Lydia, red in the face, exclaimed, "I know she read that article! This is terrible. Everyone here probably read it and thinks that we are all the same, that our parents didn't support us." After relating this incident to a few of the others after the next board meeting, Gwen, another board member, initiated a letter-writing campaign to the newspaper among her successful Latina colleagues in a "damage control" effort for the middle-class Latino community. Gwen, Lydia, and others wanted the public to know that Adriana's comments represented her personal experiences, not the experiences of the majority of professional Latinas, especially those involved with the ALB. They wanted the newspaper to offset the potential damage done to the middle-class Latina population by running a follow-up article spotlighting Latinas whose families support their education and careers. Conversely, most of the board members whose businesses serve the ethnic community did not agree with the campaign to correct the newspaper article. Because those who serve the ethnic community interact primarily with coethnics, rather than the larger white business community, they could not see how Adriana's comments would affect them.

The more class-conscious board members, particularly those who work in white corporate environments or who own businesses outside the ethnic community, also distanced themselves from those who they believe reify the stereotype that Latinas are likely to be teenage mothers. Angelica is a prosperous owner of two small businesses who is vocal about the challenges to mobility she has overcome, such as growing up in the "barrio" and being a teenage mother and high school dropout. Although they openly admire Angelica for overcoming numerous mobility obstacles, the more class-conscious board members were apprehensive about allowing her to represent the organization in the larger business community. They did not want her to bring up that she was a teenage mother when interacting with sponsors for fear that this would reify negative stereotypes of Latinas and mark the larger membership as likely to be teenage mothers and "irresponsible." They constantly scrutinized her actions and attributed any mistake she made, from misplacing a file to showing up late, to her lower level of education.

Adriana's comments in the newspaper and Angelica's background support whites' pejorative stereotypes of Latinas and overshadow the more socially acceptable traditional path to mobility others have followed. The more class-conscious board members did not want Adriana and Angelica's personal experiences to become stock stories for Orange County's upwardly mobile Latinos (Lee 2002). Stock stories can be constructed from a combination of "direct experiences, written word, rumor and media" (Yamamoto 1999: 181). In other words, whites might use stock stories, influenced by media depictions of Latinos combined with personal experiences, to explain socioeconomic inequalities between Latinas and whites. For example, when white professionals meet a middle-class Mexican American woman who was a teenage mother and high school dropout, they might adopt the stock story that Mexicans view early childbearing and having a family as more important than obtaining an education, something that is also reinforced through the media with headlines like "Pregnancy Rates Up for Hispanic Teens, Numbers Decline for Blacks and Whites" ("Pregnancy Rates Up" 2005). The Latina's background reinforces the stock story and "becomes symbolic of the power, class and status distinctions between two ethnically distinct groups" (Lee 2002: 97). Thus, with stock stories, differences between whites and Latinas due to socioeconomic background become erroneously attributed to ethnicity and culture.

The ALB's members and board members do not vilify immigrants or reject their ethnic background. In fact, they celebrate their minority middle-class status. However, they face negative group-based stereotypes as they climb the mobility ladder and enter the mainstream economy outside ethnic communities, as is reflected in Lydia's experience at the golf course, my confrontations at the business mixer, and Alicia and Lydia's conversation with Megan at the cocktail reception. As a result, they feel that they must distance themselves from negative perceptions of immigrants to achieve upward mobility. In her study of working-class and middle-class Latinos, political scientist Lisa García Bedolla (2005: 93) also finds that some middle-class Latinos who experience discrimination attempt to distance themselves from, or change the behavior of coethnics "to make them 'fit in' in the United States" in an attempt to improve their image. In this same vein, one strategy the ALB employs is to cultivate a middle-class presentation of self that contradicts the idea that Mexican

Americans are uneducated or focused only on being wives and mothers. While the board members work hard to instill middle-class cultural cues in their members, they distance themselves, and attempt to distance the organization, from board members who they feel reinforce pejorative stereotypes and stock stories, even though they might be economically successful. In other words, it is acceptable for the general membership to display markers of lower-class status, but the board members are held to a higher standard because they represent the ALB within the larger non-Latino business community in Orange County. Since they interact more frequently in Orange County's business scene outside the ethnic community, the more class-conscious board members feel that not having a college education or being a teenage mother overshadows professional accomplishments for all and that it works against the middle-class image they are trying to create.

Not all of the board members distanced themselves from Adriana and Angelica. Those who easily fit into a white middle-class business world but who lacked a college education were less likely to distance themselves from those whom the college educated sometimes disparaged. For example, Laura, one of the founders of the Orange County chapter, whose highest level of education is an associate's degree but who worked her way up to become vice president of a major corporation, regularly came to the defense of the members who did not have college degrees. I often heard her respond to complaints by saying that professional grooming takes time and that no one should be penalized because of his or her speech or behavior around sponsors. She would often invoke an immigrant narrative of struggle and sacrifice, reminding the women of the barriers they have all overcome to achieve mobility.

Overall, within-group social distancing demonstrates the nuances of class, identity, and gender among middle-class Latinas. Those with college degrees view the opportunities of upwardly mobile Latinas as inextricably bound to the ability to fit into a business sphere dominated by whites, especially in Orange County, where Latinos are constantly "othered" through the media, through the laws, and in their everyday life. Like middle-class blacks, middle-class Latinos, especially those who grew up poor or who are one generation removed from poverty, who move more regularly in white social worlds are more likely to experience discrimination than those who mainly work with coethnics. Outside the ethnic community, their race or ethnicity, class background, and gender frequently become more salient than their class (Feagin 1991; Feagin and Sikes 1994; Lee 2000; Segura 1992). Hence, while they maintain a salient ethnic identity, some members of the ALB erect intragroup boundaries as a strategy to unambiguously define the organization and themselves as nothing less than middle class, and they police those who reinforce pejorative stereotypes. Those who have created the ALB do not advocate becoming white to get ahead; in fact, they enjoy being Latina and middle class. Still, they make a concerted effort to ensure that the organization projects a polished middle-class image as protection against discrimination so they do not lose out on opportunities in Orange County's business community. However, pejorative images are constantly created and reinforced by the mass media and politicians, outside of the group, making it very difficult for Latino ethnic professional organizations to dismantle group-based stereotypes (García Bedolla 2005).

Finally, while middle-class Mexican Americans join these organizations and clubs for the professional benefits, ethnic professional associations offer a reprieve from a white, middle-class world. Similar to middle-class African Americans who participate in black social clubs (Lacy 2004), middle-class Mexican Americans consciously participate in ethnic spaces that provide a social outlet where they can relate to each other. Although official business is conducted in English, middle-class Mexican Americans freely speak Spanish or Spanglish when participating in events sponsored by these organizations, which, as Frank explained in Chapter 5, has no place in corporate America, but in the ethnic community, it is an attribute that helps to maintain a collective identity. They also discuss ethnic tastes, like salsa dancing and Spanish-language movies, and they regularly exchange war stories about their interactions with middle-class whites.

The Limitations of the Minority Culture of Mobility

In addition to cultivating social capital and promoting skills that will allow an individual to excel in business, the members of the ALB, especially those on the board of directors, constantly talk about the necessity of working for the collective good of the greater ethnic community. The idea of giving back to kin and the community is especially salient among members of the Mexican-origin middle class who preserve an "immigrant narrative" and are one generation removed from poverty, as demonstrated in Chapter 4. Laura, the ALB's president, reinforces this idea as she closes each board meeting by saying, "We are here not for ourselves but for the community. . . . You are here because you care, you want to give back, and you want to be a part of it." During one board meeting, the group discussed the opportunity of promoting the ALB's celebration of Hispanic Heritage Month on a daily news show on Univision, a television channel that broadcasts in Spanish. As the board members debated the pros and cons of appearing on the show, one board member questioned whether the show would reach the ALB's target audience of middle-class professionals. The same board member mentioned that she would like to see their membership materials printed in Spanish, so that they could reach a larger segment of the Mexican-origin population, not just those with some economic resources. Laura agreed:

> Spanish language information is really important to me as I want everyone to continually reflect if they are doing everything possible to bring resources to all segments of the Latina population. Speaking Spanish is a trust thing, an acceptance thing, and will allow us to continue bringing resources to help our people.

The board maintains that giving back to poorer and more recently arrived coethnics is a priority, but they have yet to actively reach out to or create programs that directly target these lower-class groups. One reason may be that the ALB recruits the majority of its members through the networks of current members and through other professional associations and business mixers. As a result, the membership is biased toward those who are already upwardly mobile and who have some resources. Another explanation is that the board members, who are all volunteers with careers and families of their own, need to direct the organization's limited financial resources and time toward one slice of the community in order to be the most effective. As one board member countered to Laura's reminder,

> It would be nice to help those who don't speak English, but we can't do everything and there are organizations that help immigrants and the poor. We need to keep our focus on the business people and give back to the community by educating women.

Thus, a minority culture of mobility is directed at socially mobile and more established minorities and does not directly target the low-income population in ethnic communities. Even though the ALB does not directly give back to poorer and more recently arrived coethnics, the role this ethnic organization plays in providing resources to a traditionally marginalized community is extremely important for two reasons. First, the ALB increases social and human capital and fills a resource gap in the larger ethnic community by fostering extensive networks and providing business training for an upwardly mobile segment of the community that has generally lacked ethnic institutions. As Lydia, the president-elect, proudly informed me as we observed the ALB's members networking at an evening mixer held in the courtyard of the Artists' Village in Downtown Santa Ana, "There was a huge void in the Latino community before we came along—a huge void. There was absolutely no organization that supported business education for Latinas." Lydia makes clear that the ALB acts as a resource within the ethnic community for Latino adults, especially women. Second, while the ALB does not officially give back to less advantaged members of the community, most of the organization's members have not severed ties with their poorer counterparts. As I demonstrate in Chapter 4, middle-class Mexican Americans, especially those who grew up poor, offer extensive financial and social support to poorer coethnics. Therefore, we can expect that many of the social and financial resources gained through membership in the ALB will trickle down to less affluent coethnics. In fact, a number of the Mexican Americans (and individuals of other Latin American national-origin groups) who belong to the organization, and who are not a part of the original interview sample, similarly provide financially and socially for kin who have not experienced comparable patterns of mobility. The successful members of the ALB not only help provide financially for poorer coethnics, they also serve as role models in the community, demonstrating to an economically marginalized community what it is possible to achieve.

Conclusion

This chapter shows that Mexican American ethnic communities, and Latino ethnic communities more generally, are not class homogeneous, nor are they lacking in "high-quality resources" in terms of ethnic, social, and human capital. Socially mobile Mexican Americans are civically active and retain an ethos of giving back to the community, and a thriving minority middle-class population in Santa Ana helps to promote the social and economic mobility of co-ethnics as they achieve upward mobility, leave ethnic communities, and enter the American middle class. The growing presence of a distinct Mexican American middle class act as role models and provide institutional and emotional support through their creation of, and participation in, ethnic professional associations. Ultimately, these middle-class ethnic spaces reinforce a class-based minority identity and are indicative of a middle-class minority culture of mobility because they help the minority middle class manage social and structural exclusion. This chapter shows how a larger social context of group disadvantage intersects with race and ethnicity, class, and gender to foster a middle-class ethnic environment where Latinos transmit and draw on "middle-class ethnic capital" to learn valuable business skills and forge coethnic networks and where they share specific strategies to blur the white boundary, all of which they believe will help them get ahead in their careers. Because Mexican Americans start off so far behind other immigrant groups in terms of human and social capital, it takes an extra generation for Mexican American ethnic communities to form professional institutions and establish middle-class interpersonal networks that act as social structures for mobility.

While ethnic professional associations disseminate social and human capital resources to the ethnic community that the upwardly mobile and middle class can draw on, the board members of the ALB also attempt to construct and present a normative middle-class business image among their members so that they can be accepted in Orange County's larger professional milieu where middle-class Mexican Americans must constantly work to distance themselves from pejorative group-based stereotypes about Mexicans. They hope that professionally polished Latinas will counteract immigrant and class-based stereotypes one by one and that a successful Latina business organization will project a more positive image of Mexican Americans in general. Instead of directly challenging America's racial and ethnic hierarchy that privileges whites, proclaiming an educated and professional middle-class persona is part of the minority culture of mobility and is used to negotiate a variety of middle-class white social and professional spaces.

7 Conclusion: The New American Middle Class

A COMMON ASSUMPTION IS THAT Mexican Americans are not achieving social mobility and incorporating into the middle class. Politicians maintain that Mexican immigrants and their descendants drain America's coffers; the public views the second generation as *cholos* and teenage mothers; scholars warn that Mexican Americans pose a threat to America's national identity; and some researchers assert that the second and later generations are perpetually racialized and that they experience a downward or stagnated mobility trajectory. Contrary to these one-dimensional characterizations, Mexican Americans are not predestined for downward mobility. As I have demonstrated in this book, a middle-class Mexican American population has emerged in America. They hold college degrees, work in white-collar occupations, live in white middle-class neighborhoods, and make comfortable incomes. In direct opposition to alarmist arguments, some achieve remarkable rates of intergenerational mobility relative to the parental generation, moving from poor to middle class in a span of just a few years. The classic theory of linear assimilation (Gordon 1964) and the more contemporary framework of segmented assimilation (Portes and Zhou 1993) would expect this slice of the structurally incorporated Mexican American population to cut ties to the ethnic community and to identify as, and be accepted by, whites, the majority group. Some middle-class Mexican Americans are indeed following the canonical model of linear assimilation into the white middle class through traditional mechanisms like education, residential assimilation, and intermarriage (Waters and Jiménez 2005). However, a close examination of middle-class Mexican Americans' experiences demonstrates that incorporating into the white middle class is not the only pathway into the middle class.

This book improves on existing thinking about assimilation and the ways in which immigrants and their descendants incorporate into the middle class. In contrast to earlier theories of assimilation, this research shows that pathways into the middle class, and the experiences of individuals once they enter it, vary *within* ethnic groups. Assimilation into the middle class does not require that individuals become members of the white-majority group (Alba, Kasinitz, and Waters 2011; Jiménez 2010; Vasquez 2011). Moving beyond the conventional group-based models of linear assimilation and segmented assimilation/racialization, this book draws on an underutilized theoretical paradigm, the minority culture of mobility, to illustrate that there is more than one route into the middle class (Neckerman, Carter, and Lee 1999). The minority culture of mobility framework allows us to see the nuances within the Mexican American population in terms of their experiences and pathways into the middle class because this framework focuses on the ways in which class background structures everyday life and mobility pathways. This perspective contends that socially mobile immigrants and their descendants face unique challenges that emerge from their minority and middle-class status. These problems arise from interethnic relationships with middle-class whites who draw rigid class and ethnic boundaries, and interclass contact with poorer kin and coethnics who request financial and social support and who may also resent their ascent into the middle class. A minority culture of mobility becomes salient once socially mobile immigrants and their descendants reach adulthood, leave ethnic communities, move into the mainstream economy, and experience economic success. It emerges from a larger social context of discrimination and provides strategies that help middle-class minorities navigate the dilemmas that accompany minority middle-class status (Neckerman, Carter, and Lee 1999).

This book adds an important layer to studies of immigrant incorporation by using class backgrounds as an analytical comparative tool that yields a nuanced analysis of different trajectories into the middle class and experiences within it. I delve into a cross-section of the middle-class Mexican American population to show that the category includes individuals from a variety of class backgrounds, from 1.5-, second-, and later-generation individuals who were raised in poor inner-city communities or long-established working-class Mexican American *colonias* to those in the second and later generations who are raised in middle-class households and white neighborhoods. Some middle-class Mexican Americans are the first in their families to join the middle class and remain strongly connected to poor kin and communities, while others are far removed from the immigrant struggle for upward mobility. I demonstrate that growing up poor or privileged conditions educational experiences, the strength of ties to poorer coethnics, the retention of family obligations and patterns of giving back, ethnic identification, and civic participation. Class background also largely conditions whether and to what extent middle-class Mexican Americans are able to cross the white boundary, and ultimately whether Mexican Americans follow the traditional linear, or a minority, pathway into the middle class.

As the minority culture of mobility predicts, socially mobile Mexican Americans must cope with burdens that accompany their minority and middle-class status. The first challenge is that the nouveau riche, particularly the 1.5 and second generation with immigrant parents, retain strong connections to poor and working-class kin. Their enduring familiarity with poverty means that they must manage relationships with poor kin who request financial and social support. The freshly minted middle class sometimes provide for the daily survival of poorer kin, they pay younger siblings' private school tuition so they can attend schools outside the inner city, they loan money to fend off home foreclosures or business failures, and some must defer educational goals to become primary breadwinners when their parents, who toil in low-wage jobs, experience financial or medical emergencies. They also spend a significant amount of time acting as language and cultural brokers for kin. Their patterns of giving back often go beyond the nuclear family unit as the socially mobile sometimes feel obligated to give back to uncles and aunts who do not have middle-class children of their own.

Giving back arises out of class background and intersects with the economic context of Mexican migration. More specifically, the collectivism demonstrated by 1.5- and second-generation middle-class respondents is not born out of a shared history of racial discrimination and disadvantage, as is the motivation for their middle-class African American counterparts (Dawson 1994; Hochschild 1995), but rather, emerges from a collective sense of struggle for upward mobility born out of a marginalized immigrant experience and is framed within an immigrant narrative. And while later generations who grew up poor also retain familial obligations, the immigrant narrative frame fades away after the second generation. The socially mobile later generations frame their financial support within a class narrative of growing up poor alone, rather than the immigrant narrative, because they are further removed from the immigrant generation.

In sharp contrast, Mexican Americans who grew up in middle-class households do not give back financially to kin and coethnics (although some perform translating duties for their parents) even though they also maintain class-heterogeneous networks. Instead, they more closely mirror white middle-class families in that the flows of financial and social support are strictly unidirectional from parents to children, something the respondents themselves point out. That those who grew up middle class do not give back financially to poorer coethnics in their networks further demonstrates that giving back is not derived from linked fate, nor is it a practice that is culturally specific to Mexican Americans, who are often portrayed as more "familistic" than other racial/ethnic groups. Giving back is a structural, rather than cultural, response to the economically marginalized position of many Mexican Americans.

Middle-class Mexican Americans are structurally incorporated, and traditional assimilation theorists would expect that such high levels of incorporation will translate into fading patterns of ethnicity and identificational assimilation with the dominant group. While some follow this model, the majority, regardless of class background, espouse an ethnic identification. However, the adoption of an ethnic identity varies in meaning and salience. Ethnic identities are shaped by interactions in different class and ethnic contexts, outsiders' ascription, and how far removed one is from the immigrant generation and the struggle for upward mobility.

The ethnicities of the socially mobile 1.5- and second-generation respondents are the most salient. They primarily identify ethnically as Mexican, although a few claim a Mexican American ethnicity, but the meanings attached to ethnic identities are defined by their interactions in different class and ethnic contexts. As they enter what they perceive to be white professional milieus, they must manage interethnic relationships with middle-class whites who rely on class, immigrant, and ethnic stereotypes to define what it means to be Mexican American. Although they are now middle class, those who grow up poor lack middle-class status cues, such as speech patterns, childhood vacations, white-collar parental occupations, and childhoods embedded in middle-class neighborhoods, which distinguishes them from their white colleagues, resulting in a rigid class boundary. In addition, ethnic boundaries also become firm when socially mobile Mexican Americans overtly display their ethnicity through ethnic cues such as speaking Spanish or Spanglish. While their ethnicity and class background are salient in middle-class institutions, their newfound class status is salient when interacting with poor kin and coethnics. Together, these experiences lead to a class-based minority identity that is reinforced by the institutionalization of a middle-class Mexican American identity by mechanisms such as corporate diversity initiatives and media targeting affluent Latinos.

Despite their middle-class status and distance from the immigrant generation, the socially mobile third and fourth generations do not identify exclusively as American as the linear assimilation model predicts. They also remain embedded in low-income or working-class ethnic communities and experience rigid boundaries with whites stemming from their ethnicity and class background, both of which reinforce an ethnic identity. However, their ethnic identities, and the labels they choose, are the most situational and shift over time and space. While some identify as Mexican American, others are unable to resist the external classification and homogenization of Latin American groups under the Latino category. Overall, the freshly minted middle class feel that they are incorporating as middle-class minorities, rather than as middle-class whites.

The second generation who are raised in middle-class households and neighborhoods identify ethnically as Mexican American, but they are more likely to see themselves "as American as apple pie" and they are viewed as "whitewashed" by poorer coethnics, socially mobile Mexican Americans, and middle-class whites. In fact, many live their everyday lives as middle-class whites. However, growing up middle class does not automatically protect one from discrimination, as those raised in middle-class households are occasionally mistaken for immigrants, especially if they have dark skin, and they must often deal with pejorative stereotypes, yet they do not view these exchanges as racially motivated, nor do they feel that they suffer from institutional discrimination. They assert that "when people get to know you" the ethnic boundary is easily blurred. In other words, established middle-class Mexican Americans might initially be viewed as members of a foreign and culturally distinct group, which makes their ethnicity salient at that moment in time, but they are able to present themselves as a nonminority and closer to whites once they distance themselves from narrow negative group stereotypes and display middle-class cultural conventions (Alba 2009; Bourdieu 1977). That some Mexican Americans can claim they are whitewashed is institutionally supported by the fact that Mexicans are federally defined as an ethnic group and can be of any race, including white.

Later-generation respondents with one white parent emphatically identify as Mexican American, but they convey an ethnicity that is the most optional and symbolic, demonstrating that ethnic boundaries are fading rapidly for multiethnic Latinos (Lee and Bean 2010). They consciously choose to become "more Mexican." They take Spanish family surnames, consume vats of salsa, listen to mariachi, and learn Spanish as adults, and they join ethnic-oriented organizations, such as the Ballet Folklórico, all in an effort to get in touch with their Mexican roots. Finally, as the linear assimilation model forecasts, some later-generation Mexican Americans identify ethnically as American and have nearly disappeared from sight, a pattern different from the black middle class, who can never fully "disappear" into the white population (Feagin and Sikes 1994; Waters 2000).

Overall, the contemporary Mexican American middle class comprises individuals who espouse an array of ethnic identities, from Mexican among the socially mobile 1.5 and second generations to Mexican American to Latino and to simply American among some of the later generation respondents. At first blush, these identity choices seem to follow the canonical model of assimilation evidenced by a linear progression from immigrant to American, and are consistent with recent research demonstrating that exclusively identifying as Mexican decreases in salience over the generations, while identifying as American increases (Alba 2006; Ono 2002; Telles and Ortiz 2008). However, the most common identity choice, regardless of class background, generation, or gender, is Mexican American. It is an identity adopted by those raised in both poor and middle-class households within and across generations, and by those who experience nativism and discrimination and by those who do not. The significance and salience of a Mexican American identity among the middle class should be interpreted with caution, as it holds vastly different meanings in everyday life and does not necessarily connote an ethnic identity that is born out of discrimination. For the established middle-class second generation, it means that their parents were born in Mexico but they are American, or closer to white. For some who are far removed from the immigrant generation, it means that although they see themselves as acculturated Americans, they are viewed by others as Mexican because of their dark skin (Jiménez 2010). A Mexican American identity can also be present among the second and later generations, who are acculturated and structurally assimilated but who retain a cultural attachment to their ethnic ancestry (Vasquez 2011). What is more, a Mexican American identity captures an optional and symbolic ethnicity when it is claimed by later-generation white and Mexican multiethnics (Lee and Bean 2010).

This book demonstrates that some individuals adopt a minority identity yet incorporate into the middle class. The majority of the respondents do not completely opt out of the Mexican category, which suggests that indicators of incorporation like education, occupation, and intermarriage might be better measures of assimilation than self-identification alone (Bean and Stevens 2003). This is not to say that when these indicators of structural incorporation are achieved Mexican ethnicity becomes optional in the same vein as white ethnics, as middle-class Mexican Americans undoubtedly experience more discrimination than their white ethnic counterparts of the same social class and generation (Telles and Ortiz 2008; Jiménez 2010). However, in this book I demonstrate that not all of the Mexican American population is persistently viewed as a racialized ethnic group. Established whites are more willing to accept Mexican Americans who grow up middle class because they exhibit middle-class status cues that mark them as members of their in-group (Weber 1978).

Examining patterns of giving back and racial or ethnic identification by class background elucidates the different ways in which Mexican Americans incorporate into the middle class. Those who grow up in middle-class households are following the traditional linear trajectory and incorporating closer to whites—the majority group—as evidenced by their patterns of individualism measured through giving back, waning ethnic identities, scant civic participation in ethnic professional associations, and their ability to distance themselves from pejorative stereotypes and cross the white boundary. Conversely, the socially mobile face acute challenges as they enter the middle class stemming from their enduring familiarity with poverty, strong financial and social obligations to poor kin, and the rigid class and ethnic boundaries they confront in professional milieus. It is these dilemmas that lead to a middle-class minority identity and a minority pathway into the middle class.

I use the Association of Latinas in Business (ALB) as a strategic research site to study the ways in which race/ethnicity, class, and gender intersect in the ethnic community to produce a minority culture of mobility that helps the minority middle class manage social and structural exclusion. The class context of Mexican ethnic communities is characterized as overwhelmingly poor and working class and lacking robust ethnic institutions and high levels of social and community capital that can promote upward mobility. Having spent a great deal of time in the middle-class Mexican American community, my fieldwork reveals that Mexican, and Latino ethnic communities more generally, are not class homogeneous, nor are they lacking social and human capital resources that promote the mobility of coethnics. Socially mobile Mexican Americans are civically active in ethnic professional associations that promote integration into the middle class yet revolve around, and reinforce, a class-based ethnic identity. Latino ethnic professional organizations arm socially mobile Mexican Americans with the middle-class cultural capital, such as learning how to play golf and business etiquette, that will allow them to blur ethnic and class boundaries in white professional settings so that they may generate social and economic capital (Bourdieu 1991; Coleman 1990; Portes 1998). The end goal is not to become white, or to formally challenge the racial/ethnic hierarchy, but to change the narrative of what it means to be middle class and Mexican American. The middle-class newcomer also welcomes the structural and psychological support that the minority middle-class community provides. These findings suggest that because Mexicans start off further behind other immigrant groups, the ethnic community is a resource to upward mobility for adults one generation later than it is for Asian and black immigrant adolescents.

This research demonstrates that one need not become white to achieve mobility, that incorporating as a minority is not synonymous with downward mobility, and that there are a number of "mainstreams" that today's new immigrants might incorporate into (Alba and Nee 2003; Neckerman, Carter, and Lee 1999). Overall, this book challenges scholars to carefully consider the ways in which class background structures experiences and different pathways into the middle class and to take seriously the notion of a minority middle class as a valid destination for immigrants and their descendants.

Middle-Class Mexican Americans and the Future

What assimilation pathway will the descendants of middle-class Mexican Americans follow? While those who grow up poor follow a minority pathway into the middle class, this research suggests that their children, who will likely grow up in middle-class households and neighborhoods, will exhibit the status cues that will allow them to penetrate the white boundary. Thus, a minority pathway to mobility may be a bump in the road experienced by the socially mobile while their children might incorporate closer to middle-class whites (Gans 1992). As scholars have predicted, and as this book validates, some Mexican Americans undergo a social whitening of their ethnicity as they become further removed from the immigrant generation and live lives entrenched in the middle class (Alba and Islam 2009; Duncan and Trejo 2011; Emeka and

Agius Vallejo 2011; Gans 2005; Lee and Bean 2010; Perlmann 2005). Many of those raised in the middle class are able to cross the ethnic boundary with whites and come to be viewed, and view themselves, as closer to whites than to Mexican immigrants or socially mobile Mexican Americans. While Mexicans as a group are racialized as foreign, and while middle-class status does not completely shield accomplished Mexican Americans from discrimination, Mexican ethnicity does not impede the incorporation of Mexican Americans in the same way that race impedes the incorporation of African Americans, or Afro-Latinos, as some Mexican Americans have the option of choosing a white racial identity.

A trend of linear assimilation into the white middle class could be accelerated if rates of Mexican migration remain at historic lows and by the graying of the white population, which heralds unprecedented opportunities for minorities to enter the middle class as retiring baby boomers leave vacancies in the upper echelons of the labor market (Alba 2009). In the future, the middle and upper classes will reflect much more ethno-racial diversity, which will foster interethnic contact and might lead to the blurring of racial and ethnic boundaries, or a wholesale boundary shift, a pattern that is already emerging with large-scale intermarriage between today's new immigrants (Alba, Kasinitz, and Waters 2011; Lee and Bean 2010; Perlmann and Waters 2007). While it is feasible that the most successful members of the Mexican American population will disappear into the white middle class, there are two reasons why we might see an expansion of the minority middle class. First, the retention of a minority middle-class identity is not necessarily a liability in American society. Accomplished Mexican Americans, regardless of whether they were raised in poor or privileged households, are well positioned to take advantage of the increasing number of programs and institutions developed in post–civil rights America that revolve around a minority identity, such as college and corporate diversity outreach programs and affirmative action, which makes the retention of a minority identification beneficial, and likely for some, even for those who grow up in middle-class privilege. Second, we might also see an expansion of the minority middle-class category if whites continue to view Mexican Americans as a group as belonging on the minority side of the ethnic boundary. If socially mobile Mexican Americans continue to experience rigid class and ethnic boundaries with whites, they will likely develop a minority middle-class identity, engage a minority culture of mobility, and feel that they belong to a minority middle-class community.

I do not mean to be overly optimistic about the prospect of upward mobility and incorporation into the middle class for the Mexican-origin population. Some of my respondents are the first (and only) in their families to enter the middle class, and as I demonstrate, they retain strong ties to low-income or working-class kin. I am not arguing that incorporation into the middle class is inevitable for all, but this book demonstrates that the Mexican American population is not an undifferentiated mass and that there is another reality for Mexican Americans beyond the poor, uneducated, and unassimilable stereotypes. As I show, it is possible for the children of low-wage, poor, unauthorized, and uneducated Mexican labor migrants to move from barrios to burbs. In fact, it is particularly remarkable that some middle-class Mexican Americans are raised in extreme disadvantage and achieve rapid class mobility, considering the socioeconomic standing of their parents and the negative social and political contexts Mexicans face in the United States. While some achieve rapid intergenerational mobility through business ownership, the majority in this study enter the middle class through the occupational advances that follow higher education. The role of educational tracking, outside programs that promote academic achievement, and access to mentors are critical mechanisms that help Mexican Americans from disadvantaged backgrounds achieve high levels of educational attainment.

Finally, I want to emphasize that the Mexican American middle class plays an important role in the social and economic integration of the Mexican-origin population, particularly the socially mobile who remain strongly tied to poorer coethnics and communities. The growing presence of Mexican Americans in the middle and upper classes provides role models, institutional support, and mobility opportunities for immigrants and their descendants. Although family obligations drain their own resources, socially mobile Mexican Americans are an important source of financial and social capital for poorer coethnics. For instance, giving back helps to secure the economic stability of poor kin, and the socially mobile are also important sources of information that help poor kin navigate social institutions, like hospitals and government agencies (e.g., Social Security). Moreover, socially mobile Mexican Americans are a critical source of financial support and knowledge on the educational system for younger siblings and kin. They pay for private school tuition for younger siblings who remain in inner-city communities, assist with homework, and help prepare college applications, all of which foster educational mobility. Equally important is that middle-class Mexican Americans are role models within and outside ethnic communities, demonstrating to a socioeconomically marginalized group what it is possible to achieve. The socially mobile also exhibit an ethos of giving back to the community and create institutions within ethnic communities, like the ALB, that facilitate incorporation by infusing ethnic communities with social and human capital. Ethnic organizations ultimately provide strategies for mobility in the context of group disadvantage. Without question, these individual and collective activities help to advance the educational and occupational mobility of Mexican Americans into the middle class. However, the burden of incorporating the Mexican American population is one that should not rest on the shoulders of the freshly minted or established middle class. Minorities in general, and Mexican Americans in particular, are the future of this nation, and it is critical that we enact public policies that promote upward mobility and facilitate incorporation into the middle class (Hayes-Bautista 2004; Myers 2007; Pastor et al. 2010; Pastor and Ortiz 2009).

Public Policy Recommendations

This research provides key insights to policy makers as they address the pressing issue of Mexican American population growth and how to increase Mexican Americans' ranks in the middle class. I offer three policy recommendations. The first is to dispel the falsehood that Mexican immigrants, their children, and later generations are unassimilable and likely to remain poor for generations to come. The second and third policy recommendations will help support and secure Mexican Americans' advancement into the middle class.

First, we need to dispel the myth among media, politicians, lay Americans, and scholars that the Mexican-origin population is poor, unassimilable, and uniformly headed for downward mobility. Dispelling this myth will lessen the immigrant shadow not only for upwardly mobile Mexican Americans but for all Latinos. Moreover, changing the narrative of what it means to be Mexican American will hasten full inclusion into the middle class for those who experience upward mobility, leave ethnic communities, and enter white professional and social milieus. The media can help dispel the myth that the Mexican-origin population is overwhelmingly poor, and a threat to American ideals by highlighting successful entrepreneurs, business owners, and professionals, both those who grew up poor and are now middle class and those who hail from affluent backgrounds. Equally important is that the media should not portray these cases as exceptional. The media should also give greater attention to research that demonstrates the significant intergenerational mobility the

Mexican-origin population attains in terms of income, education, and occupation relative to their parents, to demonstrate that they are indeed incorporating into the fabric of American society. New media metaphors are important because they will more accurately represent the Mexican American population and the progress that occurs over time, helping to dispel the deep-rooted myth that Mexicans are a threat to American values and our future (L. Chavez 2008).

My second recommendation is that we promote policies that improve the economic stability of low-income Mexicans through targeted efforts to raise their skills and wages so that they do not drain the resources of their more affluent kin (Pastor and Ortiz 2009). Policies that address minority wealth gaps are particularly important at this historical juncture, as a 2011 Pew Hispanic Center report finds that Latino household wealth decreased by 68 percent between 2005 and 2009, a percentage drop that was the largest among all racial and ethnic groups (Kochhar, Fry, and Taylor 2011).

Plunging home values are the primary cause of diminishing wealth levels; however, on a micro level, if Mexicans regularly give back to poorer coethnics, they may be less able to accumulate assets and wealth that are critical buffers in times of financial crises, such as the loss of a home or medical emergencies, consequently impeding their own mobility and hindering their ability to transfer their class status to their children. As my interviews reveal, family obligations prevent some respondents from completing a college education, sending their children to college, or adequately funding their retirement accounts. My data are not longitudinal, so I cannot measure the effects that family obligations have over time. However, one respondent, Paco, made a point of phoning me two years after our initial interview to explain that his financial obligations have increased along with his salary increases, preventing him from building his retirement portfolio and accumulating a financial cushion. While some middle-class Mexicans act as financial safety nets for their families, many are living without safety nets themselves. One solution is to provide access to low-interest microloans that low-income Mexican Americans can draw on in times of economic and medical emergencies so that they do not draw on the financial resources of their low-income kin.

The most critical policy measure that needs to be implemented without delay is a pathway to citizenship for the estimated eleven million unauthorized migrants presently in the United States. Legal status has important implications for the social mobility of the children of immigrants, whose educational and occupational trajectories are tied to parental citizenship (Zhou et al. 2008;

Bean et al. 2007, 2011). This books shows that parental legal status expedites both intragenerational and intergenerational mobility. Legal status obtained through labor visas, the "baby clause," Silva Visas, and the 1986 Immigration Reform and Control Act (IRCA) in the two decades following the 1965 Immigration Act allowed some first-generation parents to acquire greater financial and social resources, which stream down to children. This research also illustrates the importance of obtaining legal status early on in children's life course trajectory, because the financial returns allow for greater investment earlier in the life course and lead to cumulative advantages from better neighborhoods, middle-class schools, and middle-class peer networks that provide access to professional mentors and financial resources for college. Because parental legal status helps secure the status of the first generation, it may also lessen the burden of financial obligations among the 1.5- and second-generation adult children of immigrants, helping to increase their assets and wealth.

My third recommendation is that we promote policies that infuse low-income Mexican American communities with different types of capital. In an era of declining resources and moribund tax bases, capital need not always be financial. This book demonstrates the importance of middle-class mentors in shaping upward mobility trajectories and facilitating entry into the middle class. Mentors are crucial in bridging the social and human capital gaps that are present in poor immigrant families, and they provide those from underprivileged backgrounds with knowledge, information, and connections that those who grew up middle class have access to by virtue of their class status. In short, middle-class mentors not only show low-income youth what can be achieved; they actively help channel aspirations into reality because they fill the gaps in educational resources in families and schools. A national effort should be made to create programs that match minority adolescents with professionals who can help fill the gaps in educational knowledge and professional networks. Moreover, we should closely examine the effects of educational tracking and the ways in which it leads to divergent mobility pathways.

In the same vein, it is important that we provide financial resources to ethnic professional associations promoting business ownership and professional development among the Mexican-origin population. The ALB provides strategies for economic mobility in the context of group disadvantage through its business education and professional development programs. The women of the ALB work diligently to create a minority culture of mobility by disseminating the human and social capital they have attained to the larger community;

however, they barely scrape by on a limited budget and rely on corporate donations to fund the majority of their programs. Corporations invest in these
organizations because they want to tap into the growing Mexican American
middle-class market. Federal and state governments need to invest in these
organizations to advance incorporation into the middle class. Budgets are
tight, and the ALB's board members are volunteers with careers and families
of their own, which means that they are only able to effectively reach a population that already has some resources. Allocating more funds to these organizations could translate into the inclusion of poor and more recently arrived
coethnics within the organization and the greater diffusion of middle-class
capital throughout the community. Overall, highlighting and supporting the
mobility of middle-class Mexican Americans and the ethnic professional institutions they create help contradict the poor, uneducated, and unassimilated
stereotypes. They show another side of the Mexican American population, a
side that powerfully contradicts prevailing images and paints a more promising
portrait of America's future.

Reference Matter

Appendix A: Notes on Fieldwork

WHEN I BEGAN THIS STUDY, I wanted to discover whether middle-class Mexican Americans are incorporating closer to whites, as traditional assimilation theory predicts, or whether they are following a minority pathway into the middle class. I did not originally intend to answer this question by studying an ethnic professional organization. The significance of ethnic organizations emerged from the interview data as it became clear that many socially mobile Mexican Americans were involved in different types of professional organizations that revolved around a profession and an ethnic orientation, such as the Hispanic Bar Association, or their middle-class status, like the Association of Latinas in Business (ALB). The ethnography of the ALB is integral to this study because it elucidates how socially mobile middle-class Mexican Americans muster class and ethnic resources to create a minority culture of mobility.

The fieldwork consisted of the following approaches:

1. *Nonparticipant observation.* I observed at the ALB's monthly breakfast meetings, quarterly networking events, and other events in the Latino professional community. I kept my eyes and ears open in an attempt to learn as much as possible about middle-class Mexican American life.
2. *Informal visiting with the organization's members, board members, and sponsors.* My husband, Johnny (a Latino business owner), and I became friends with members of the ALB and spent time at community and social events, which provided valuable data in informal settings.
3. *Participant observation.* After taking on an official role at the ALB, I helped register new members, organized events, and attended official

events in the Latino community with board members of the organization. I also attended monthly board meetings and special committee meetings. Johnny accompanied me to many public events, showing up early and volunteering his time to help set up fundraisers, galas, and meetings. Johnny became an accomplice in my field research, and I constantly discussed my observations with him. As he became more involved with the ALB, he sometimes pointed out things I failed to see, validated my analyses, and most importantly, questioned my assumptions. While my daily interactions were embedded in the ALB, the participant observation tapped a rich cross-section of the Mexican-origin middle class as I also spoke with politicians, sponsors of the organization, members, and other business leaders. Throughout the study, I collected newspaper articles, flyers, brochures, business cards, photographs, and other supportive data.

Acquiring access to a field research site, especially an organization, can be difficult. However, a serendipitous encounter provided me with relatively easy access to the ALB. While in Mexico City at an academic conference, I asked Johnny to call and confirm my interview with Laura, a founding board member of the ALB, with whom I scheduled a meeting first thing in the morning after my return. When Johnny called Laura on my behalf to confirm the interview, he discovered that he and Laura knew each other professionally. In the years before I began researching the Mexican American middle class, Johnny's family owned well-known Latino grocery stores in Los Angeles and Orange County, and Johnny had frequently fulfilled Laura's requests for large donations of groceries for a Latino community organization she was involved in. During our face-to-face interview, Laura related that she was extremely excited to reconnect with Johnny, whom she said she would never forget because he always contributed to her cause. She also mentioned that she was a founding board member of the ALB and she encouraged me to join the organization. When I later decided to research an ethnic organization, I approached Laura about the possibility of studying the ALB and requested permission to observe at the ALB's events and board meetings. Access was granted that very week after she spoke with the board of directors. Laura became my most important gatekeeper (Becker 1970), as she constantly vouched for me, frequently mentioning to others her long-standing connection to Johnny, his family's ethnic businesses, and his "compassion for the community."

I initially remained relatively passive and tried to "blend into the wood-work" so that the activities that occurred in my presence did not differ signifi-cantly from those that occurred in my absence (Bogden and Biklen 1998; 35); however, it was difficult to remain a passive observer for two reasons. First, the organization's events encourage networking, so it was common for people to approach me, introduce themselves, and ask to exchange business cards. When people asked, "And what do you do?" I would simply reply in a truthful but vague manner that I was conducting a study of middle-class Mexican Ameri-cans. Many people replied with statements like, "It's about time!" "That's great! Our stories need to be told," and "Finally, someone is showing the real side of our community." A few asked why I was concentrating on Mexicans, and not on other Latin American groups. It also proved difficult to blend into the wood-work because the board members were extremely proud that someone from UC Irvine (UCI) was studying their organization. They constantly introduced me to their contacts and boasted that I was a UCI researcher studying Latino pro-fessionals and business owners.

When I attended breakfast meetings, networking events, community events, and board meetings, I typically wrote detailed field notes as events unfolded, unless my note taking was extremely conspicuous, like at a black-tie gala. Dur-ing one such event, where I jotted notes intermittently in a tiny notebook I stashed in my evening bag, a woman at the next table asked if I was a reporter. After this incident, I wrote field notes as soon as I was able to, sometimes on the way home as Johnny drove, and I even wrote field notes or conversational interview notes (after the fact) on my BlackBerry if I did not have access to a notebook at the time. All of the interview and participant observation data were coded into over forty themes of interest, some of which were driven by theory (e.g., segmented assimilation, minority culture of mobility). However, the majority of the codes became salient only after I had been in the field for a significant amount of time, emerging only once I started coding the inter-views and observation data (e.g., whitewashed, gendered stereotypes, immi-grant narrative, intraclass distancing).

As often occurs with researchers who study organizations, I was eventually asked to take on a more formal role within the organization. I was apprehen-sive about becoming officially involved because I feared that it might hinder my research, but after careful thought, I decided to accept an official role, as I knew my more visible participation and insider knowledge gleaned from working closely with the board members would provide a more holistic and nuanced portrait of the organization. I also completed small tasks to assist the executive board. For example, I wrote business letters and created and administered a membership survey. I also co-chaired the annual gala event, the ALB's largest fundraiser.

Another phenomenon that occurs with ethnographic research is that participants under study often forget that you are a researcher, even if you occasionally remind them. However, because they forget, they oftentimes disclose telling information. I always reminded those with whom I had sustained relationships that I was a researcher, but I realized that the ALB's board members came to view me as one of their own after about nine months in the field. I was jotting notes in my little field notebook during a board meeting when one woman reproached me by saying, "Jody, you are always taking notes! That's what we have a secretary for." I reminded her that I was taking notes for my research project, but these sorts of memory lapses were frequent. However, my role as a researcher never faded completely into the background. The board members were excited that I was writing about them and they would ask me questions like, "What will my fake name be? I want to be named Isabella. I've always loved that name!" Others became self-conscious when something they deemed embarrassing occurred. "*Dios mio*! Are you going to put that in the book?" they would ask after the fact. Thus, while the line between researcher and board member was constantly blurred, and sometimes forgotten, there were occasions when my researcher status became salient.

The primary difficulty with this research was that I began to identify with the people I studied. As sociologist Herb Gans describes in his classic study of Italian Americans, *Urban Villagers* (1962: 342–43),

> Every participant observer becomes emotionally involved not only in his study, but also with the people, since it is through their willingness to talk that he is able to do his research. And this involvement does have some advantages: it allows the observer to understand the people with whom he is living, and to look at the world through their eyes. At the same time, it can also blind him to some of their behavior patterns, and thus distort the study. The identification is probably more intense if the people being studied are suffering from deprivation, and if they are a low-status group whose point of view is not being taken notice of in the world outside. In such a situation, the researcher feels a need to do something about the deprivation, and to correct stereotypes about the people. This reaction also befell me . . . this identification can be socially

useful . . . for the sociologist then becomes an informal spokesman for groups who themselves lack the power to voice their demands to larger society.

Identifying with the women of the ALB did not detract from the research, for as Gans also notes in a later passage, I was fully aware of what was happening and I worked hard to maintain analytic distance. However, there was one occasion where I felt compelled to "correct stereotypes" about middle-class Latinas. I wrote a draft of a letter to the editor of the newspaper deconstructing the racialized and gendered stereotypes their article (detailed in Chapter 6) reinforced about Latinas. As I relate in Chapter 6, I saw firsthand through participant observation how the article reinforced negative stereotypes of Latinas, and I felt that I could use my sociological training to provide a structural, rather than cultural, explanation for Latina differences in education and occupational attainment, which would help to "correct" negative Latino stereotypes. I went so far as to craft an email, but eventually decided to hit the delete button as I was still engaged in the research activities and I did not want my letter to influence the data and the ways in which community members viewed me, and reacted to me, if they were to read it.

I stopped researching the setting after nearly three years, when my continual participation failed to yield additional insights and when the data became repetitive, what Glaser and Strauss (1967) call "theoretical saturation." The most difficult part of the research was extricating myself from the field and the subjects' lives. I informed the board members that I was resigning because my research had concluded. I reiterated that my resignation was not personal; however, it was clear that some of the women, who came to view me as a good friend, as I did them, were deeply hurt as I resigned from my post and slowly retreated from the organization and their daily lives.

At the final board meeting I attended, the board members unexpectedly hosted a little going away party for me. Laura gave a tearful speech, saying how proud she and the organization were of my successes, and they thanked me for the work I put into the ALB. The president-elect then presented me with a card, signed by all of the board members, and a handmade Mexican artisan Catrina doll, something they knew I collect. I was humbled and moved by this gesture of kindness and appreciation, and the Catrina doll presently rests on a shelf in my office.

This close identification with the women, and the friendships I developed, made it difficult initially to write about the conflicts that occurred within the organization, such as intraclass distancing. I fretted that I was betraying their trust, I worried that they would be upset with me, and I experienced guilt about whether I was exploiting the relationships I made. However, I was not expecting to encounter the conflicts I observed within the organization. These "trouble cases" emerged from the data, and they are an important part of the story that elucidates the larger nativist social structure within which socially mobile Mexican Americans, and Latinos more generally, negotiate their upward mobility and the conditions under which a minority culture of mobility emerges. Distancing myself from the organization and the research for a short period of time helped me to reconcile these feelings of guilt and anxiety. I have changed the names of my informants and distorted some facts and characteristics in order to maintain their privacy.

A Note on Ethnicity

I am not of Mexican origin, yet I study Mexican Americans. When I was a small child, my father married a socially mobile Mexican American woman, and I was instantly absorbed into a large, primarily working-class, Mexican American family. My sister and I were immediately indoctrinated into Mexican American life including cultural practices (food, Mexican-style weddings, *baptismos*, and music) and travel to Mexico. These experiences laid the early foundation for my interest in the Mexican American population. In junior high I became close friends with Nichol Vallejo, a second-generation Mexican American who was raised in a middle-class household and neighborhood. I traveled frequently with her to South Gate, Lynwood, and La Habra—Latino-concentrated areas of Los Angeles and Orange County where her relatives lived—for more weddings, *quinceañeras, baptismos*, and weekend carne asadas. When we graduated from high school, our senior trip was an excursion to the small pueblo, Jalostotitlan, Mexico, where both of her parents were born. As fate would have it, I ended up marrying Nichol's older brother, Johnny. Thus, my personal history has provided me with "insider" knowledge of the Mexican American population, yet I am unquestionably an outsider. This tension has shaped my work on the Mexican-origin population in several ways.

First, my long history with two class-diverse and multigenerational Mexican American families led me to question the sociological literature on Mexican Americans, which generally portrays Mexican Americans as a monolithic ethnic group in terms of class and assimilation outcomes. At the time this research commenced, scholars generally argued that the class context of the Mexican-origin population was overwhelmingly poor and working class and that the descendants of Mexican immigrants were likely to assimilate in a downward direction. However, I observed consistent intergenerational mobility in terms of education, occupation, and neighborhoods, within both my stepfamily and Nichol and Johnny's family, and very few cases of downward mobility, even among the third generation, leading me to question these assumptions.

Second, when I began the interviews, I hoped that my non-Mexican ethnicity would not create a barrier with my subjects. One of the first things the respondents typically asked me was, "Where in Mexico are you from?" The majority assumed I was of Mexican origin not only because I was studying the group but also because of my perceived "Mexican" or "Spanish" features. At the time I used only my maiden name, and some asked whether I was half Mexican or whether I was intermarried. Others assumed that "Agius," which is Maltese, was Spanish or Basque in origin. Other viewed me as "Anglo" right off the bat and asked how I became interested in studying Mexican Americans.

Regardless of how my subjects ethnically identified me, I always disclosed my ancestry before the interview commenced, but I also typically revealed that my husband was Mexican American. I sometimes included my Mexican American stepfamily in my back story, and a number of the respondents were thrilled that I had frequently traveled "off the beaten path" to Los Altos de Jalisco and other areas of Mexico. My personal experiences seemed to place me a little closer to my respondents' worlds, but ethnic differences were never completely erased. Still, my personal connections, travels, and insider's knowledge gave me a greater level of credibility and trust, allowing me to ask important follow-up questions that a true outsider might have overlooked. My long association with the Mexican American community also seemed to make my respondents feel more at ease discussing sensitive issues like undocumented status and discrimination. At the same time, my outsider status allowed me to play naïve if necessary, a tactic that encouraged my respondents to elaborate on their statements and "teach me" about the unique facets of middle-class Mexican American life (S. Taylor and Bogdan 1998). Despite my long association with two Mexican American families, there were certainly many aspects of Mexican American middle-class life that were completely unfamiliar to me and to which I could not identify, such as the immigrant narrative or parental unauthorized status. I also could not relate to experiences of dealing with white racism, until I started the ethnographic fieldwork. What is telling about the ambiguities of race, ethnicity, and phenotype among the Latino population is that when I was with the ALB as a group, most people identified me as Latina, both Latinos and non-Latinos. However, this effect was particularly salient when we attended events outside the Latino ethnic community in white business and social spaces, where I directly experienced discrimination and white nativism directed at Latinos as a group (as detailed in Chapter 6).

Third, my personal history seemed to put the women of the ALB at ease, as they did not hesitate to offer me a formal position within the organization despite the fact that I am not Mexican American or Latina. In fact, my non-Latino ethnicity did not seem to matter to them whatsoever. During my time in the field, many of the women selectively forgot that I was not Mexican American or Latina, even though I made no bones about disclosing my ethnic background. When I would remind them that I was not Latina, some proclaimed that my marriage to Johnny and my understanding of particular Spanish sayings and Latino cultural practices made me an "honorary Latina." A few constantly pressured to me to take Johnny's last name so that I could finally become "A real Latina." When my parents attended the annual gala event, one board member reacted in surprise when she met my mother, who is "blond and fair," and asked whether I was a "halfer," meaning half Mexican and half white. Another woman met my father, who is "tall and dark" and who was wearing a *gauyabera* (a traditional Cuban shirt), and questioned whether we were Cuban. While the ALB seemed to take pleasure in giving me "honorary Latina status," they also sometimes reacted in surprise if I spoke Spanish or sang along with popular Spanish songs. I want to be clear that ethnic differences were never erased, but they were frequently blurred.

Appendix B: List of In-Depth Interview Respondents

Name	Generation	Age	Occupation	Education	Class Background
Lissette	1.5	25	Financial Planner	BA	Poor
Gabriel	1.5	28	Software Engineer	BA	Poor
Esperanza	1.5	29	Financial Planner	SC	Poor
Inez	1.5	31	Nonprofit Director	BA	Poor
Jose	1.5	31	Architect	BA	Poor
Geena	1.5	32	Lawyer	JD	Poor
Felicitas	1.5	32	Teacher	MA	Poor
Leti	1.5	33	Business Owner	SC	Poor
Leo	1.5	34	Architect	MA	Poor
Linda	1.5	34	Nurse Practitioner	BA	Poor
Brianna	1.5	34	Lawyer	JD	Poor
Gloria	1.5	35	Teacher	MA	Poor
Alejandra	1.5	36	Executive	BA	Poor
Priscilla	1.5	37	Accountant	BA	Poor
Esperanza	1.5	38	School Principal	MA	Poor
Sylvia	1.5	41	Human Resources	BA	Poor
Zeke	1.5	41	Sales Rep	SC	Poor
Alfredo	1.5	42	Business Owner	HS	Poor
Chon	1.5	45	Realtor	SC	Poor
Michael	1.5	51	Business Owner	HS	Poor
Jeff	1.5	29	Teacher	BA	Poor
David	1.5	37	Architect	MA	LMC
Adrian	2	25	Teacher	MA	Poor
Maria	2	25	Business Owner	HS	Poor
Manuel	2	28	Engineer	MA	Poor
Magdalena	2	28	Financial Adviser	BA	Poor
Andrea	2	29	Business Owner	SC	Poor
Letti	2	29	Business Owner	SC	Poor
Martha	2	30	Lawyer	JD	Poor
Carmen	2	31	VP of Sales	SC	Poor
Lupe	2	32	VP of Bank	BA	Poor

(continued)

Name	Generation	Age	Occupation	Education	Class Background
Lorenzo	2	32	Writer	MA	Poor
Frank	2	33	Engineer	BA	Poor
Paco	2	33	Vice President	MBA	Poor
Pablo	2	33	Nurse	BA	Poor
Natalie	2	34	Business Owner	BA	Poor
Brenda	2	35	Lawyer	JD	Poor
Brian	2	40	Insurance Manager	SC	Poor
Lydia	2	44	Salon Owner	AA	Poor
Jazmin	2	44	Business Owner	BA	Poor
Julian	2	44	Business Owner	BA	Poor
Mateo	2	45	Lawyer	JD	Poor
Robert	2	46	X-Ray Technician	Trade School	Poor
Tom	2	31	Financial Analyst	BA	LMC
Lana	2	45	VP of Bank	AA	LMC
Karina	2	29	Human Resources	MA	MC
Yvonne	2	29	Medical Billing	AA	MC
Monica	2	30	Human Resources	BA	MC
Vincent	2	32	Sales Executive	BA	MC
Art	2	32	Financial Adviser	SC	MC
Alia	2	33	Nurse	BA	MC
Deena	2	34	Nurse	BA	MC
Maya	2	34	Corporate Executive	BA	MC
Jenny	2	35	Human Resources	BA	MC
Patty	2	36	Business Owner	SC	MC
Joe	2	38	Psychologist	PhD	MC
Nicole	2	42	Accountant	BA	MC
Nacio	2	45	Dentist	DDS	MC
Jesus	2	45	Project Manager	BA	MC
Isabel	3	32	School Administrator	MA	Poor
Adriana	3	35	Teacher	MA	LMC
Belicia	3	41	Teacher	MA	Poor
Ray	3	42	Parks Manager	BA	Poor
Amy	3	35	Dance Director	AA	MC
John	3	48	Professor	PhD	LMC
Darren	3	32	Business Owner	BA	MC
Jessica	3	33	Writer	MA	MC
Melissa	3	32	Marketing Director	MA	UMC
Elisa	3	34	Social Services	MA	MC
Katie	4	34	Homemaker	BA	LMC
Tim	4	42	Auditor	MA	LMC
Tina	3 and 4	32	Human Resources	BA	MC
Julie	4	36	Corporate Executive	BA	MC
Janie	4	39	Writer	BA	MC
Melissa	3 and 4	43	Parks Manager	BA	MC

Notes

Chapter 1

1. It is important to note that future events, such as recessions, economic booms, and immigration policy, could increase or decrease this projection.

2. A notable exception is García Bedolla's (2005) research on Latino political attitudes and behaviors in working-class and middle-class Latino communities.

3. The median age of Mexican Americans in the United States is 25, compared with 30 for non-Mexican-origin Hispanics, 32 for blacks, 35 for Asians, and 41 for whites. See Passel and Cohn (2011).

4. The Current Population Survey (CPS) is a monthly survey of about 50,000 households conducted by the Bureau of the Census for the Bureau of Labor Statistics. The sample is scientifically selected to represent the civilian noninstitutional population. The sample provides estimates for the nation as a whole and serves as part of model-based estimates for individual states and other geographic areas.

5. African Americans are the least likely of all ethnic groups to own a home in Los Angeles, which is not surprising considering that African Americans have historically suffered from a racially discriminatory housing market. Specific tactics employed in Los Angeles, such as blockbusting, redlining, and racial covenants, have historically prevented African Americans from qualifying for home loans. For a discussion, see Massey and Denton (1993) and Oliver and Johnson (1984).

6. Differences in the total household income and median incomes were negligible. I use total household income because I asked my respondents to specify their total household income.

7. Los Angeles is a mecca for the highly educated, regardless of racial or ethnic origins. Whites, Asians, and blacks in Los Angeles have higher levels of education, occupational status, and incomes than their national counterparts as do 1.5-, second-, third-, and later-generation Mexican Americans (see Tables 1–3).

8. In a 1996 report, Gregory Rodriguez details the emergence of Los Angeles' Latino middle class. He finds that about 25 percent of the Latino population are middle class. See Gregory Rodriguez (1996).

9. This may seem high considering that the 2008 median income for the United States is $61,000. However, the majority of the respondents are married to similarly employed professionals, which subsequently increases their household income.

10. "The Association of Latinas in Business" is a pseudonym.

Chapter 2

1. In the early twentieth century, racial covenants, which are a contractual agreement between a seller and a buyer of real estate to not sell to minorities, were a mechanism by which neighborhoods ensured that "undesirables," which included African Americans and Latinos, would remain segregated and would not be able to purchase homes in white neighborhoods. The Federal Housing Administration supported these covenants and engaged in redlining, which is the practice of denying home loans in minority-dominated areas. Racial covenants and redlining were in full effect in Southern California during the first half of the twentieth century (see Bender 2010).

2. For a thorough history of the Mexican Revolution, see Gonzales (2002).

3. Cynthia Feliciano (2005) demonstrates that immigrants are selected upon particular attributes, such as education or high- or low-skilled work, before they even arrive in the United States. She shows that immigrant selectivity slots immigrants into different starting positions upon arrival resulting in different mobility outcomes.

4. These data are derived from a phone interview with Terry Feiertag, January 4, 2011, and subsequent email correspondence.

5. In December 2005, a sharply divided House of Representatives approved H.R. 4437, the Sensenbrenner Immigration Bill, which criminalized unauthorized status in the United States as a felony, added 700 miles of fence along the border, and increased penalties for employers who hire unauthorized migrants. Republicans framed the issue as a matter of "national security," calling the bill "antiterrorism" legislation, while some Democrats felt the bill was too harsh and would criminalize "millions of hard-working people." The bill moved into the Senate for debate, provoking numerous public protests culminating in the famed 2006 May Day Boycott, where immigrants and their supporters—some of whom were second-, third-, and later-generation middle-class Mexican Americans and not all of whom were Mexican—boycotted industry, skipped work, and walked out of schools in over 200 cities nationwide. A million people flooded downtown Los Angeles, and demonstrations occurred in cities like Nashville, Chicago, Dallas, and San Diego. Demonstrators demanded an overhaul of H.R. 4437 and advocated that a path to citizenship be included for those living with unauthorized status. Backlash against Mexican immigrants ensued. Some commentators labeled the protestors "Anti-American," membership in the Minuteman Project quadrupled, Latino day-

laborer sites across the country were shut down, and Mexican flags were burned by anti-immigrant protestors at the Mexican consulate in Arizona. Soon after the protests, Congress approved the Comprehensive Immigration Reform and Control Act (CIRCA), but the bill was dead by the time Congress adjourned for the summer. Republicans and Democrats were back at the bargaining table in 2007, attempting to craft a bill that would garner enough support from both parties to officially reform existing law. Despite the attempt to compromise, the bill drew its last breath in the Senate.

Chapter 3

1. California's GATE program "applies the state-adopted approach of Depth and Complexity to enhance and make the core curriculum different. Depth and Complexity is used to differentiate learning opportunities that stress the complexity of subject matter, develop greater depth in thinking and reasoning skills, and provide for the creation of new ideas and new products. GATE instruction emphasizes the use of multiple resources and research. Students create unique products that apply higher level critical thinking skills and involve purposeful communication" (Santa Ana Unified School District GATE Brochure, http://www.sausd.us/14431028114956613/site/default .asp).

2. *Straight edge* typically refers to a subculture of the hardcore punk movement and is a term coined by the 1980s hardcore punk band Minor Threat in their song "Straight Edge." However, it has become a common term, and is used by Brenda here, to refer to those who abstain from using tobacco, alcohol, or drugs (see Haenfler 2006).

3. Some conservative politicians and nativists perpetuate the myth that unauthorized Mexican immigrant parents purposefully have children in the United States to obtain citizenship and welfare benefits for themselves. *Anchor baby* is a derogatory term referring to children born to unauthorized parents in the United States, and is used in debates about whether to change the Fourteenth Amendment of the U.S. Constitution to deny American citizenship to children born to unauthorized immigrants.

4. This study does not rigorously measure gender differences in educational tracking within families. However, studies have shown that different processes are at work within families and the educational system that lead to gendered mobility patterns. For example, Rob Smith (2002) demonstrates that Mexican American boys are racialized in educational institutions, which hinders their progress. Other studies have shown that girls have more responsibilities and less free time and are therefore likely to spend more time on homework, which results in higher grades and greater teacher investment. In contrast, boys have autonomy and free time to get involved in activities outside the home, which detracts from studying and can even lead to gang involvement (see Kasinitz, Waters, and Mollenkopf 2009; R. Smith 2002).

Chapter 4

Portions of this chapter are related to a previously published article: Jody Agius Vallejo and Jennifer Lee (2009), "Brown Picket Fences: The Immigrant Narrative and 'Giving Back' Among the Mexican Origin Middle-Class," *Ethnicities* 9 (1): 5–23.

Chapter 5

1. Despite their official classification as an ethnic group, some Mexican Americans reject the government's definition of their ancestry as an ethnicity, often defining their ethnicity as a race. For example, the majority of those who checked the box "Some other race" in the 2000 Census were Latino (Hirschman, Alba, and Farley 2000; Rumbaut 2009).

2. This growth in Latino college enrollment is not attributable solely to population increases, as the Hispanic 18- to 24-year-old population increased by only 7 percent from 2009 to 2010. As of 2010, 32 percent of young Latinos were enrolled in college (Fry 2011).

3. Estimates from the Mexican Migration Project, codirected by Doug Massey and Jorge Durand, indicate that net unauthorized migration fell to zero in 2008 (Massey 2011). Researchers at the Pew Hispanic Center also estimate that flows of unauthorized migration decreased by two thirds between March 2007 and March 2009 (Passel and Cohn 2010).

4. People of Latino origin intermarry at much higher rates than do African Americans. For example, in 2008, white-Latino couples accounted for about 41 percent of all new interracial or interethnic marriages, whereas white-black couples made up just 11 percent of such marriages (Passel, Wang, and Taylor 2010).

5. Studies and journalistic accounts of socially mobile white ethnics have found that upwardly mobile whites experience similar feelings of alienation and displacement in middle-class settings (Lubrano 2005). However, their experiences as socially mobile Americans are much different than the experiences of those of Mexican origin. Their race grants them the privileges associated with whiteness, and they do not have to blur an ethnic boundary and deflect negative stereotypes attached to their race or ethnicity.

6. The primary diversity categories are race and ethnicity; however, corporations also use gender, age, religion, and sexual orientation as measures of diversity.

7. See "Leading with Diversity" (2005) a special advertising feature included in the *New York Times*. http://www.nytimes.com/marketing/jobmarket/diversity/index .html.

8. See "Workplace Diversity Practices" (2010). The survey sample is composed of 402 randomly selected human resources professionals who are members of the Society for Human Resource Management. The corporations are headquartered across the United States and are engaged in different industries including health care, service,

manufacturing, retail and wholesale trade, arts and entertainment, insurance, and government. The respondents also represent different sectors including nonprofit organizations, privately owned firms, publicly owned firms, and the government sector.

9. In their study of multiracial adults, Jennifer Lee and Frank Bean (2010) find that most Asian and Latino multiracial adults regularly capitalize on the minority group benefits associated with their multiracial backgrounds, even if their minority identity is not instrumental in their everyday lives.

Chapter 6

Portions of this chapter are related to a previously published article: Jody Agius Vallejo (2009), "Latina Spaces: Middle-Class Ethnic Capital and Professional Associations in the Latino Community, *City & Community* (8) 2: 129–54.

1. Although 22 percent of the organization's members are male, this research focuses on Latinas because all of the board members are female, the majority of the members are female, and the ALB's outreach efforts and educational programs are specifically geared to Latinas.

2. In December 2005, the House of Representatives approved H.R. 4437, the Sensenbrenner Immigration Bill, which criminalized unauthorized status in the United States as a felony, added 700 miles of fence along the border, and increased penalties for employers who hire unauthorized migrants. The bill moved into the Senate for debate (but never passed), provoking numerous public protests culminating in the famed 2006 May Day Boycott.

3. The Society of Mexican Business Women is a pseudonym.

References

"Affluent Marketplace Brief: Hispanic Affluents." 2011 Ipsos Mendelsohn Affluent Survey. New York: Ipsos.

Agius Vallejo, Jody. 2009. "Latina Spaces: Middle-Class Ethnic Capital and Professional Associations in the Latino Community." *City & Community* (8) 2: 129–54.

Agius Vallejo, Jody, and Jennifer Lee. 2009. "Brown Picket Fences: The Immigrant Narrative and 'Giving Back' Among the Mexican Origin Middle-Class." *Ethnicities* 9 (1): 5–23.

Agius Vallejo, Jody, Jennifer Lee, and Min Zhou. 2011. "Family Ties That Bind." Unpublished manuscript.

Alba, Richard. 1990. *Ethnic Identity: The Transformation of White America.* Cambridge, MA: Harvard University Press.

———. 1999. "Immigration and the American Realities of Assimilation and Multiculturalism." *Sociological Forum* 14: 3–29.

———. 2005. "Bright vs. Blurred Boundaries." *Ethnic and Racial Studies* 28: 20–49.

———. 2006. "Mexican Americans and the American Dream." *Perspectives on Politics* 4 (2): 289–96.

———. 2009. *Blurring the Color Line: The New Chance for a More Integrated America.* Cambridge, MA: Harvard University Press.

Alba, Richard, and Tariq Islam. 2009. "The Case of the Disappearing Mexican Americans: An Ethnic-Identity Mystery." *Population Research and Policy Review* 28 (2): 109–21.

Alba, Richard, Philip Kasinitz, and Mary C. Waters. 2011. "Commentary: The Kids Are (Mostly) Alright: Second Generation Assimilation: Comments on Haller, Portes and Lynch." *Social Forces.* 89 (3): 763–73.

Alba, Richard, and Victor Nee. 2003. *Remaking the American Mainstream: Assimilation and Contemporary Immigration.* Cambridge, MA: Harvard University Press.

Arellano, Gustavo. 2006. "O.C. Can You Say . . . Anti-Mexican." *Los Angeles Times*, May 8.

———. 2008. *Orange County: A Personal History.* New York: Scribner.

Arriola, Chris. 1997. "*Mendez v. Westminster* (1947) Children of Mexican Heritage Were Segregated Until a Federal Court Order Was Won Against Orange County, California Schools, in the 9th Circuit Court of Appeals." *Los Angeles Times*, April 15.

Baca Zinn, Maxine. 1982. "Familism Among Chicanos: A Theoretical Review." *Humboldt Journal of Social Relations* 10: 224–38.

Baca Zinn, Maxine, and Barbara Wells. 2001. "Diversity Within Latino Families: New Lessons for Family Social Science." In *Handbook of Family Diversity*, edited by David H. Demo, Katherine R. Allen, and Mark A. Fine, 252–73. New York: Oxford University Press.

Barth, Fredrik. 1969. "Introduction." In *Ethnic Groups and Boundaries: The Social Organization of Culture Difference*, edited by Fredrik Barth, 9–38. Boston: Little, Brown.

Bean, Frank D., Susan K. Brown, Mark Leach, and James Bachmeier. 2007. "Becoming U.S. Stakeholders: Legalization and Integration Among Mexican Immigrants and Their Descendants." Irvine, CA: Merage Foundation for the American Dream.

Bean, Frank D., Susan K. Brown, and Rubén Rumbaut. 2006. "Mexican Immigrant Political and Economic Incorporation." *Perspectives on Politics* 4 (2): 309–13.

Bean, Frank D., Mark Leach, Susan K. Brown, James Bachmeier, and John Hipp. 2011. "The Educational Legacy of Unauthorized Migration." *International Migration Review* 45: 348–85.

Bean, Frank D., and Gillian Stevens. 2003. *America's Newcomers and the Dynamics of Diversity.* New York: Russell Sage Foundation.

Becker, Howard. 1970. *Sociological Work: Method and Substance.* Chicago: Aldine.

Bender, Steven W. 2003. *Greasers and Gringos: Latinos, Law, and the American Imagination.* New York: New York University Press.

———. 2010. *Tierra y Libertad: Land, Liberty, and Latino Housing.* New York: New York University Press.

Bettie, Julie. 2003. *Women Without Class: Girls, Race, and Identity.* Berkeley: University of California Press.

Bianchi, Suzanne M., V. Joseph Hotz, Kathleen McGarry, and Judith A. Seltzer. 2008. "Intergenerational Ties: Theories, Trends and Challenges." In *Intergenerational Caregiving*, edited by Alan Booth, Ann C. Crouter, Suzanne M. Bianchi, and Judith A. Seltzer, 3–34. Washington, DC: Urban Institute Press.

Billingsley, Andrew. 1992. *Climbing Jacob's Ladder: The Enduring Legacies of African-American Families.* New York: Simon and Schuster.

Blau, Peter, and Otis Dudley Duncan. 1967. *The American Occupational Structure.* New York: Wiley.

Bogden, Robert, and Sari Knopp Biklen. 1998. *Qualitative Research for Education: An Introduction to Theories and Methods*. Boston: Allyn & Bacon.

Bonilla-Silva, Eduardo. 2003. *Racism Without Racists: Color-Blind Racism and the Persistence of Racial Inequality in the United States*. Lanham, MD: Rowman & Littlefield.

Borjas, George. 2001. "Welfare Reform and Immigration." In *The New World of Welfare*, edited by Rebecca Blank and Ron Haskins, 369–90. Washington DC: Brookings Institution Press.

Bourdieu, Pierre. 1977. *Outline of a Theory of Practice*, translated by Richard Nice. Cambridge: Cambridge University Press.

———. 1991. "Sport and Social Class." In *Rethinking Popular Culture: Contemporary Perspectives in Cultural Studies*, edited by Chandra Mukerji and Michael Schudson, 357–73. Berkeley: University of California Press.

Bourdieu, Pierre, and Jean-Claude Passerson. 1977. *Reproduction in Education, Society and Culture*. London: Sage Publications.

Bowles, Samuel, and Herbert Gintis. 1977. *Schooling in Capitalist America: Educational Reform and the Contradictions of Economic Life*. New York: Basic Books.

Bridenball, Blaine, and Paul Jeselow. 2005. "Weeding Criminals or Planting Fear." *Criminal Justice Review* 30: 1–22.

Brown, Susan. 2007. "Delayed Spatial Assimilation: Multi-Generational Incorporation of the Mexican-Origin Population in Los Angeles." *City & Community* 6 (3): 193–209.

Burdman, Pamela. 2000. "Extra Credit, Extra Criticism." *Black Issues in Higher Education* 17 (18): 28–33.

Burgess, E. W. 1926. *The Urban Community: Selected Papers from the Proceedings of the American Sociological Society*. Chicago: University of Chicago Press.

Carter, Prudence. 2005. *Keepin' It Real: School Success Beyond Black and White*. New York: Oxford University Press.

Charles, Camille Zubrinsky. 2003. "The Dynamics of Residential Racial Segregation." *Annual Review of Sociology* 29: 167–207.

Chavez, Leo. 2001. *Covering Immigration: Population Images and the Politics of the Nation*. Berkeley: University of California Press.

———. 2004. "A Glass Half Empty: Latina Reproduction and Public Discourse."*Human Organization* 63 (2): 173–88.

———. 2008. *The Latino Threat: Constructing Immigrants, Citizens, and the Nation*. Stanford, CA: Stanford University Press.

Chávez, Maria. 2011. *Everyday Injustice: Latino Professionals and Racism*. Lanham, MD: Rowman & Littlefield.

Chiswick, Barry. 2008. *Immigration: Trends, Consequences, and Prospects for the United States*. Oxford: Elsevier.

Clark, William A. V. 2003. *Immigrants and the American Dream: Remaking the Middle Class*. New York: Guilford Press.

Cole, Elizabeth, and Safiya Omari. 2003. "Race, Class, and the Dilemmas of Upward Mobility for African Americans." *Journal of Social Issues* 59: 785–802.

Coleman, James. 1990. *Foundations of Social Theory*. Cambridge, MA: Harvard University Press.

Coleman, James, E. Q. Campbell, C. J. Hobson, J. McPartland, A. M. Mood, F. D. Weinfeld, and R. L. York. 1966. *Equality of Educational Opportunity*. Washington, DC: U.S. Department of Health, Education and Welfare, Office of Education (OE-38001 and supp.).

Conley, Dalton. 1999. *Being Black, Living in the Red: Race, Wealth, and Social Policy in America*. Berkeley: University of California Press.

Cornelius, Wayne. 2001. "Death at the Border: Efficacy and Unintended Consequences of U.S. Immigration Control Policy." *Population and Development Review* 27: 661–85.

Current Population Survey. 2008. *Annual Social and Economic Supplement*. Washington, DC: Bureau of the Census.

Dauber, Susan, Karl L. Alexander, and Doris R. Entwisle. 1996. "Tracking and Transitions Through the Middle Grades: Channeling Educational Trajectories." *Sociology of Education* 69: 290–307.

Davis, F. James. 1991. *Who Is Black? One Nation's Definition*. Philadelphia: Pennsylvania State University Press.

Dawson, Michael C. 1994. *Behind the Mule: Race and Class in African American Politics*. Princeton, NJ: Princeton University Press.

Deal, Terry, and Allan Kennedy. 2000. *Corporate Cultures: The Rites and Rituals of Corporate Life*. New York: Basic Books.

Decker, Cathleen. 2010. "Latino Power Comes Full Circle in L.A." *Los Angeles Times*, April 11.

Deverell, William. 2005. *Whitewashed Adobe: The Rise of Los Angeles and the Remaking of Its Mexican Past*. Berkeley: University of California Press.

DiMaggio, Paul. 1982. "Cultural Capital and School Success." *American Sociological Review* 47: 189–201.

Dockterman, Daniel, and Gabriel Velasco. 2010. *Statistical Portrait of the Foreign-Born Population in the United States, 2008*. Washington, DC: Pew Hispanic Center.

Dohan, Daniel. 2003. *The Price of Poverty: Money, Work, and Culture in the Mexican-American Barrio*. Berkeley: University of California Press.

Du Bois, W. E. B. 1903. "The Talented Tenth." In *The Negro Problem: A Series of Articles by Representative Negroes of Today*, edited by Booker T. Washington, 33–75. New York: J. Pott & Company.

Duncan, Brian, and Steven J. Trejo. 2007. "Ethnic Identification, Intermarriage and Unmeasured Progress by Mexican Americans." In *Mexican Immigration to the United States,* edited by George J. Borjas, 229–68. Chicago: University of Chicago Press.

——. 2011. "Who Remains Mexican? Selective Ethnic Attrition and the Intergenerational Progress of Mexican Americans." In *Latinos and the Economy: Integration and Impact in Schools, Labor Markets, and Beyond,* edited by David L. Leal and Stephen J. Trejo, 285–320. New York: Springer Science.

Durand, Jorge, and Douglass Massey. 2003. "The Costs of Contradiction: U.S. Immigration Policy 1986–1996." *Latino Studies* 1: 233–52.

Emeka, Amon, and Jody Agius Vallejo. 2011. "Non-Latino Identities Among the Latin American Descended Population." *Social Science Research,* 40: 1547–63.

Escobar, Edward. 1999. *Race, Police, and the Making of a Political Identity.* Berkeley: University of California Press.

Estrada, Emir, and Pierrette Hondagneu-Sotelo. 2011. "Intersectional Dignities: Latino Immigrant Street Vendor Youth in Los Angeles." *Journal of Contemporary Ethnography* 40 (1): 102–31.

Farlie, R., and C. Woodruff. 2008. "Mexican-American Entrepreneurship." Institute for the Study of Labor Working Paper.

Feagin, Joe, R. 1991. "The Continuing Significance of Race: Antiblack Discrimination in Public Places." *American Sociological Review* 56: 101–17.

Feagin, Joe R., and José A. Cobas. 2008. "Latinos/as and White Racial Frame: The Procrustean Bed of Assimilation." *Sociological Inquiry* 78: 39–53.

Feagin, Joe, R., and Melvin Sikes. 1994. *Living with Racism: The Black Middle Class Experience.* Boston: Beacon Press.

Feliciano, Cynthia. 2005. "Does Selective Migration Matter? Explaining Ethnic Disparities in Educational Attainment Among Immigrants' Children." *International Migration Review* 39 (4): 841–71.

Feliciano, Cynthia, and Rubén Rumbaut. 2005. "Gendered Paths: Educational and Occupational Expectations and Outcomes Among Adult Children of Immigrants." *Ethnic and Racial Studies* 28 (6): 1087–1118.

Fernández-Kelly, Patricia. 2008. "The Back Pocket Map: Social Class and Cultural Capital as Transferable Assets in the Advancement of Second-Generation Immigrants." *Annals of the American Academy of Political and Social Science* 620: 36–61.

Flores, Glenda. 2011. "Racialized Tokens: Latina Teachers Negotiating, Surviving and Thriving in a White Woman's Profession." *Qualitative Sociology* 34: 313–35.

Foley, Neil. 1997. "Becoming Hispanic: Mexican Americans and the Faustian Pact with Whiteness." In *Reflexiones 1997: New Directions in Mexican American Studies,* edited by Neil Foley, 53–57. Austin, TX: CMAS Books.

Foner, Nancy. 2000. *From Ellis Island to JFK: New York's Two Great Waves of Immigration.* New Haven, CT: Yale University Press; and New York: Russell Sage Foundation.

———. 2005. *In a New Land: A Comparative View of Immigration.* New York: New York University Press.

Ford, Donna. 1998. "The Underrepresentation of Minority Students in Gifted Education: Problems and Promises in Recruitment and Retention." *Journal of Special Education* 32 (1): 4–14.

Fordham, Signithia, and John Obgu. 1986. "Black Students' School Success: Coping With the Burden of 'Acting White.'" *Urban Review* 18 (3): 176–206.

Frank, Reanne, Ilana Redstone Akresh, and Bo Lu. 2010. "Latino Immigrants and the U.S. Racial Order: How and Where Do They Fit In?" *American Sociological Review* 75 (2): 378–401.

Fry, Richard. 2002. "Latinos in Higher Education: Many Enroll, Too Few Graduate." Washington, DC: Pew Hispanic Center.

———. 2011. "Hispanic College Enrollment Spikes, Narrowing Gaps with Other Groups." Washington, DC: Pew Hispanic Center.

Fuligni, Andrew J., and Sarah Pederson. 2002. "Family Obligation and the Transition to Adulthood." *Developmental Psychology* 38: 856–68.

Fuligni, Andrew J., Vivian Tseng, and May Lam. 1999. "Attitudes Toward Family Obligations Among American Adolescents with Asian, Latin American, and European Backgrounds." *Child Development* 70: 1030–44.

Gandara, Patricia. 1995. *Over the Ivy Walls: The Educational Mobility of Low-Income Chicanos.* Albany: State University of New York Press.

Gans, Herbert J. 1962. *Urban Villagers: Group and Class in the Life of Italian-Americans.* New York: The Free Press.

———. 1979. "Symbolic Ethnicity: The Future of Ethnic Groups and Cultures in America." *Ethnic and Racial Studies* 2: 1–20.

———. 1992a. "Comment: Ethnic Invention and Acculturation: A Bumpy-Line Approach." *Journal of American Ethnic History* 11 (1, Fall): 42–52.

———. 1992b. "Second-Generation Decline: Scenarios for the Economic and Ethnic Futures of the Post–1965 American Immigrants." *Ethnic and Racial Studies* 15: 173–93.

———. 2005. "Race as Class." *Contexts* 4: 17–21.

Garcia, Richard. 1991. *Rise of the Mexican American Middle Class: San Antonio, 1929–1941.* College Station: Texas A&M University Press.

García Bedolla, Lisa. 2005. *Fluid Borders: Latino Power, Identity, and Politics in Los Angeles.* Los Angeles: University of California Press.

Gibson, Margaret A. 1988. *Accommodation without Assimilation: Sikh Immigrants in an American High School.* Ithaca, NY: Cornell University Press.

Gittelshon, John. 2008. "Where OC's Poorest Dwell." *Orange County Register*, January 1.

Glaser, Barney, and Anselm Strauss. 1967. *The Discovery of Grounded Theory: Strategies for Qualitative Research*. Chicago: Aldine Publishing Company.

Glazer, Nathan, and Daniel P. Moynihan. 1963. *Beyond the Melting Pot: The Negroes, Puerto Ricans, Jews, Italians, and Irish of New York City*. Oxford, UK: MIT Press.

Golash-Boza, Tanya, and William Darity. 2008. "Latino Racial Choices: The Effects of Skin Colour and Discrimination on Latinos' and Latinas' Racial Self-Identifications." *Ethnic and Racial Studies* 31 (5): 899–934.

Goldsheider, Calvin, Eva Berhnhardt, and Frances Goldsheider. 2004. "What Integrates the Second Generation? Factors Affecting Family Transitions to Adulthood in Sweden." In *International Migration in Europe: New Trends and New Methods of Analysis*, edited by Corrado Bonifazi, Marek Okolski, Jeannette Schoorl, and Patrick Simon, 225–46. Amsterdam: Amsterdam University Press.

Gonzales, Michael J. 2002. *The Mexican Revolution: 1910–1940*. Albuquerque: University of New Mexico Press.

Gonzalez, Arturo. 2007. "Day Labor in the Golden State." San Francisco: Public Policy Institute of California.

González, Gilbert. 1994. *Labor and Community: Mexican Citrus Worker Villages in a Southern California County, 1900–1950*. Champaign: University of Illinois Press.

Gonzalez, Juan. 2000. *Harvest of Empire: A History of Latinos in America*. New York: Penguin.

González-López, Gloria. 2004. "Fathering Latina Sexualities: Mexican Men and the Virginity of Their Daughters." *Journal of Marriage and Family* 66: 1118–30.

Gordon, Milton S. 1964. *Assimilation in American Life: The Role of Race, Religion, and National Origins*. New York: Oxford University Press.

Grasmuck, Sherri, and Patricia Pressar. 1991. *Between Two Islands: Dominican International Migration*. Berkeley: University of California Press.

Grebler, Leo, Joan W. Moore, and Ralph C. Guzman. 1970. *The Mexican American People, the Nation's Second Largest Minority*. New York: The Free Press.

Griswold del Castillo, Richard G. 1983. *La Familia: Chicano Families in the Urban Southwest, 1848 to the Present*. Notre Dame, IN: University of Notre Dame Press.

———. 1990. *The Treaty of Guadalupe Hidalgo: A Legacy of Conflict*. Norman: University of Oklahoma Press.

Grogger, Jeffrey, and Steven Trejo. 2000. *Falling Behind or Moving Up? The Intergenerational Progress of Mexican Americans*. San Francisco: Public Policy Institute of California.

Grunert, Jeanne. 2009. "Target the Affluent Hispanic Market: Tips to Creating Effective Latino Marketing Campaigns." Marketing and PR @ Suite 101. http://jeanne-grunert.suite101.com/target-the-affluent-hispanic-market-a94265.

Gutierrez, David. 1995. *Walls and Mirrors: Mexican Americans, Mexican Immigrants, and the Politics of Ethnicity*. Berkeley: University of California Press.

Haenfler, Ross. 2006. *Straight Edge: Clean-Living Youth, Hardcore Punk, and Social Change*. Piscataway, NJ: Rutgers University Press.

Hagan, Jacqueline. 1998. "Social Networks, Gender, and Immigrant Incorporation: Resources and Constraints." *American Sociological Review* 63: 55–67.

Halle, David. 1984. *America's Working Man*. Chicago: University of Chicago Press.

Haney-López, Ian. 1996. *White by Law: The Legal Construction of Race*. New York: New York University Press.

———. 2003. *Racism on Trial: The Chicano Fight for Justice*. Cambridge, MA: Harvard University Press.

Hansen, Marcus, L. 1938. "The Problem of the Third Generation Immigrant." Rock Island, IL: Augustina Historical Society, July.

Hayes-Bautista, David. 2004. *La Nueva California: Latinos in the Golden State*. Berkeley: University of California Press.

Heath, Shirley Brice. 1983. *Ways with Words: Language, Life and Work in Communities and Classrooms*. New York: Cambridge University Press.

Heer, David, M. 1990. *Undocumented Mexicans in the United States*. New York: Cambridge University Press.

Heflin, Colleen, and Mary Pattillo. 2006. "Poverty in the Family: Race, Siblings and Socioeconomic Heterogeneity." *Social Science Research* 35 (4): 804–22.

Hernández-León, Rubén. 2008. *Metropolitan Migrants: The Migration of Urban Mexicans to the United States*. Berkeley: University of California Press.

Higginbotham, Elizabeth, and Lynn Weber. 1992. "Moving Up with Kin and Community: Upward Social Mobility for Black and White Women." *Gender and Society* 3: 416–40.

Hirschman, Charles, Richard Alba, and Reynolds Farley. 2000. "The Meaning and Measurement of Race in the U.S. Census: Glimpses into the Future." *Demography* 37: 381–93.

Hochschild, Jennifer L. 1995. *Facing Up to the American Dream: Race, Class, and the Soul of the Nation*. Princeton, NJ: Princeton University Press.

Hoffman, Abraham. 1974. *Unwanted Mexican Americans in the Great Depression: Repatriation Pressures, 1929–1939*. Tucson: University of Arizona Press.

Hogan, Dennis P., David J. Eggebeen, and Clifford C. Clogg. 1993. "The Structure of Intergenerational Exchanges in American Families." *American Journal of Sociology* 98: 1428–68.

Hondagneu-Sotelo, Pierrette. 1994. *Gendered Transitions: Mexican Experiences of Migration*. Berkeley: University of California Press.

———. 2001. *Domestica: Immigrant Workers Cleaning and Caring in the Shadows of Affluence*. Berkeley: University of California Press.

Horan, Patrick. 1978. "Is Status Attainment Research Atheoretical?" *American Sociological Review* 43: 534–41.

Hout, Michael. 2008. "How Class Works: Objective and Subjective Aspects of Class Since the 1970s." In *Social Class: How Does It Work?* edited by Annette Lareau and Dalton Conley, 25–64. New York: Russell Sage.

Hout, Michael, and Emily Beller. 2006 . "Intergenerational Social Mobility in Comparative Perspective." *The Future of Children* 16: 19–36.

Huber, Lindsey Perez, Corina Benivades Lopez, Maria C. Malagon, Veronica Velez, and Daniel G. Solorzano. 2008. "Getting Beyond the 'Symptom,' Acknowledging the 'Disease': Theorizing Racist Nativism." *Contemporary Justice Review* 11: 39–51.

Huntington, Samuel, P. 2004. "The Hispanic Challenge." *Foreign Policy,* March/April, 30–42

Ignatiev, Noel. 1995. *How the Irish Became White*. New York: Routledge.

Jacobson, Robin Dale. 2008. *The New Nativism: Proposition 187 and the Debate over Immigration*. Minneapolis: University of Minnesota Press.

Jiménez, Tomas. 2004. "Multiethnic Mexican Americans and Ethnic Identity in the United States." *Ethnicities* 4: 75–97.

———. 2010. *Replenished Ethnicity: Mexican Americans, Immigration and Identity*. Berkeley: University of California Press.

Jones-Correa, Michael. 1998. "Different Paths: Immigration, Gender, and Political Participation." *International Migration Review* 32 (2): 326–49.

Kao, Grace, and Marta Tienda. 1995. "Optimism and Achievement: The Educational Performance of Immigrant Youth. *Social Science Quarterly* 76 (1): 1–19.

Kasinitz, Philip, John. H. Mollenkopf, and Mary C. Waters. 2006. *Becoming New Yorkers: Ethnographies of the Second Generation*. New York: Russell Sage Foundation.

Kasinitz, Philip, Mary Waters, John Mollenkopf, and Jennifer Holdaway. 2009. *Inheriting the City: The Children of Immigrants Come of Age*. New York: Russell Sage Foundation.

Keefe, Susan, and Amado Padilla. 1987. *Chicano Ethnicity*. Albuquerque: University of New Mexico Press.

Kershaw, Terry. 1992. "The Effects of Educational Tracking on the Social Mobility of African Americans." *Journal of Black Studies* 23: 152–69.

Kingston, Paul W. 2000. *The Classless Society*. Stanford, CA: Stanford University Press.

Kochhar, Rakesh, Richard Fry, and Paul Taylor. 2011. "Wealth Gaps Rise to Record Highs Between Whites, Blacks, Hispanics." Washington, DC: Pew Hispanic Center.

Lacy, Karyn R. 2004. "Black Spaces, Black Places." *Ethnic and Racial Studies* 27 (6): 908–30.

————. 2007. *Blue-Chip Black: Race, Class, and Status in the New Black Middle Class.* Berkeley: University of California Press.

Lamont, Michèle. 2000. *The Dignity of Working Men: Morality and the Boundaries of Race, Class, and Immigration.* New York: Russell Sage Foundation.

Lamont, Michèle, and Annette Lareau. 1988. "Cultural Capital: Allusions, Gaps and Glissandos in Recent Theoretical Developments." *Sociological Theory* 6: 153–68.

Lareau, Annette. 2003. *Unequal Childhoods: Class, Race, and Family Life.* Berkeley: University of California Press.

"Leading with Diversity. 2005. " *New York Times*, special advertising feature. http://www.nytimes.com/marketing/jobmarket/diversity/index.html.

Lee, Jennifer. 2000. "The Salience of Race in Everyday Life: Black Customers' Shopping Experiences in Black and White Neighborhoods." *Work and Occupations* 27: 353–76.

————. 2002. *Civility in the City: Blacks, Jews, and Koreans in Urban America.* Cambridge, MA: Harvard University Press.

Lee, Jennifer, and Frank D. Bean. 2007. "Reinventing the Color Line: Immigration and America's New Racial/Ethnic Divide." *Social Forces* 86 (2): 561–86.

————. 2010. *The Diversity Paradox: Immigration and the Color Line in 21st Century America.* New York: Russell Sage Foundation.

Levine, Arthur, and Jana Nidiffer. 1996. *Beating the Odds: How the Poor Get to College.* San Francisco: Jossey-Bass.

Levy, Frank. 1998. *The New Dollars and Dreams: American Incomes and Economic Change.* New York: Russell Sage Foundation.

Light, Ivan, and Steven J. Gold. 2000. *Ethnic Economies.* San Diego: Academic Press.

Lipset, Seymour Martin. 1997. *American Exceptionalism: A Double-Edged Sword.* New York: W. W. Norton.

Loewen, James. 1974. *The Mississippi Chinese: Between Black and White*, 2nd edition. Long Grove, IL: Waveland Press.

Lofland, John, and Lyn Lofland. 1984. *Analyzing Social Settings.* Belmont, CA: Wadsworth Publishing Company.

Lopez, David, and Ricardo Stanton-Salazar. 2001. "Mexican Americans: A Second Generation at Risk." In *Ethnicities: Children of Immigrants in America*, edited by Rubén G. Rumbaut and Alejandro Portes, 57–90. Berkeley: University of California Press.

Lopez, Mark Hugo, Rich Morin, and Paul Taylor. 2010. "Illegal Immigration Backlash Worries, Divides Latinos." Washington, DC: Pew Hispanic Center.

Lopez, Nancy. 2002. *Hopeful Girls, Troubled Boys: Race and Gender Disparity in Urban Education.* New York: Routledge.

Lubrano, Alfred. 2005. *Limbo: Blue Collar Roots, White Collar Dreams*. New York: Wiley.

Mabry, J. Beth, Roseann Giarrusso, and Vern Bengston. 2004. "Generations, the Life Course, and Family Change." In *The Blackwell Companion to Sociology of Families*, edited by Jaqueline Scott, Judy Treas, and Martin P. Richards, 87–108. Malden, MA: Blackwell Publishing.

Macedo, Stephen. 2005. *Democracy at Risk: How Political Choices Undermine Citizen Participation, and What We Can Do About It*. Washington, DC: Brookings Institution Press.

Marin, Gerardo. 1993. "Influence of Acculturation on Familism and Self-Identification Among Hispanics. In *Ethnic Identity: Formation and Transmission Among Hispanics and Other Minorities*, edited by Martha E. Bernal and George P. Knight, 181–96. Albany: State University of New York Press.

Marquez, Benjamin. 2003. *Choosing Issues, Taking Sides: Constructing Identities in Mexican American Political Organizations*. Austin: University of Texas Press.

Marrow, Helen B. 2011. *New Destination Dreaming: Immigration, Race, and Legal Status in the Rural American South*. Stanford, CA: Stanford University Press.

Massey, Douglass. 2009. "Racial Formation in Theory and Practice: The Case of Mexicans in the United States." *Race and Social Problems* 1 (1): 12–26.

———. 2011. "It's Time for Immigration Reform." CNN.com, July 7. http://globalpublic square.blogs.cnn.com/2011/07/07/its-time-for-immigration-reform/.

Massey, Douglass, and Nancy Denton. 1987. "Trends in Residential Segregation of Blacks, Hispanics, and Asians 1970–1980." *American Sociological Review* 52: 802–25.

———. 1993. *American Apartheid: Segregation and the Making of the Underclass*. Cambridge, MA: Harvard University Press.

Massey, Douglass, Jorge Durand, and Nolan Malone. 2003. *Beyond Smoke and Mirrors: Mexican Immigration in an Era of Economic Integration*. New York: Russell Sage Foundation.

Matute-Bianchi, Maria E. 1986. "Ethnic Identities and Patterns of School Success and Failure Among Mexican-Descent and Japanese-American Students in a California High School: An Ethnographic Analysis." *American Journal of Education* 95: 223–25.

Menchaca, Martha. 2002. *Recovering History, Constructing Race: The Indian, Black, and White Roots of Mexican Americans*. Austin: University of Texas Press.

Menjívar, Cecilia. 2000. *Fragmented Ties: Salvadoran Immigrant Networks in America*. Berkeley: University of California Press.

Messner, Michael. 2009. *It's All for the Kids: Gender, Families, and Youth Sports*. Berkeley: University of California Press.

Mindel, Charles H. 1980. "Extended Familism Among Urban Mexican Americans, Anglos, and Blacks." *Hispanic Journal of Behavioral Sciences* 2: 21–34.

Moen, Phyllis. 1992. *Women's Two Roles: A Contemporary Dilemma*. Westport, CT: Auburn House.

Monroy, Douglass. 1999. *Rebirth: Mexican Los Angeles from the Great Migration to the Great Depression*. Berkeley: University of California Press.

Montini, E. J. 2010. "What Part of Distortion Doesn't Brewer Understand?" *Arizona Republic*, June 24.

Morrill, Calvin. 1995. *The Executive Way: Conflict Management in Corporations*. Chicago: University of Chicago Press.

Moss, Philip, and Charles Tilly. 2001. *Stories Employers Tell: Race, Skill, and Hiring in America*. New York: Russell Sage Foundation.

Murguia, Edward, and Edward Telles. 1996. "Phenotype and Schooling Among Mexican Americans." *Sociology of Education* 69: 276–89.

Myers, Dowell. 2007. *Immigrants and Boomers: Forging a New Social Contract for the Future of America*. New York: Russell Sage Foundation.

Nagel, Joanne. 1994. "Constructing Ethnicity: Creating and Recreating Ethnic Identity and Culture." *Social Problems* 41 (1): 152–71.

Naples, Nancy. 1991. "Just What Needed to Be Done: The Political Practice of Women Community Workers in Low-Income Neighborhoods." *Gender and Society* 5 (4): 478–94.

Neckerman, Kathryn, Prudence Carter, and Jennifer Lee. 1999. "Segmented Assimilation and Minority Cultures of Mobility." *Ethnic and Racial Studies* 22 (6): 945–65.

Newman, Katherine S. 1988. *Falling from Grace: Downward Mobility in the Age of Affluence*. New York: Vintage.

———. 2000. *No Shame in My Game: The Working Poor in the Inner City*. New York: Russell Sage Foundation.

Ngai, Mai. 2005. *Impossible Subjects: Illegal Aliens and the Making of Modern America*. Princeton, NJ: Princeton University Press.

Oakes, Jeannie. 1986. *Keeping Track: How Schools Structure Inequality*. New Haven, CT: Yale University Press.

Obregón Pagán, Eduardo. 2006. *Murder at the Sleepy Lagoon: Zoot Suits, Race, and Riot in Wartime L.A.* Chapel Hill: University of North Carolina Press.

Ochoa, Gilda. 2004. *Becoming Neighbors in a Mexican American Community*. Austin: University of Texas Press.

Oliver, Melvin, and James Johnson. 1984. "Interethnic Conflict in an Urban Ghetto: The Case of Blacks and Latinos in Los Angeles." *Research in Social Movements, Conflict, and Change* 6: 57–94.

Oliver, Melvin, and Thomas M. Shapiro. 1995. *Black Wealth, White Wealth: A New Perspective on Racial Inequality*. New York: Routledge.

Omi, Michael, and Howard Winant. 1994. *Racial Formation in the United States: From the 1960s to the 1990s*, 2nd edition. New York: Routledge.

Ong, Paul. 1999. *Impacts of Affirmative Action: Policies and Consequences in California*. Walnut Creek, CA: AltaMira Press.

Ong, Paul, and Veronica Terriquez. 2008. "Can Multiple Pathways Offset Inequalities in the Urban Spatial Structure?" In *Beyond Tracking: Multiple Pathways to College, Career, and Civic Participation*, edited by Jeannie Oakes and Marisa Saunders, 131–52. Cambridge, MA: Harvard Education Press.

Ono, Hiromi. 2002. "Assimilation, Ethnic Competition, and Ethnic Identities of U.S.-Born Persons of Mexican Origin." *International Migration Review* 36 (3): 726–45.

Orellana, Marjorie, Lisa Dorner, and Lucila Pulido. 2003. "Accessing Assets, Immigrant Youth as Family Interpreters." *Social Problems* 50: 505–24.

Orozco, Cynthia E. 2009. *No Mexicans, Women, or Dogs Allowed: The Rise of the Mexican American Civil Rights Movement*. Austin: University of Texas Press.

Ortiz, Vilma. 1996. "The Mexican-Origin Population: Permanent Working Class or Emerging Middle Class?" In *Ethnic Los Angeles*, edited by Roger Waldinger and Mehdi Bozorghmehr, 247–78. New York: Russell Sage Foundation.

Pachon, Harry, and Louis DeSipio. 1994. *New Americans by Choice: Political Perspectives of Latino Immigrants*. Boulder, CO: Westview Press.

Park, Lisa Sun Hee. 2005. *Consuming Citizenship: Children of Asian Immigrant Entrepreneurs*. Stanford, CA: Stanford University Press.

Park, Robert E. 1950. *Race and Culture.*. Glencoe, IL: The Free Press.

Park, Robert, E., Ernest W. Burgess, and Roderick McKenzie. 1925. *The City*. Chicago: University of Chicago Press.

Parrado, Emily, and S. Philip Morgan. 2008. "Intergenerational Fertility Among Hispanic Women: New Evidence of Immigrant Assimilation." *Demography* 45 (3): 651–71.

Passel, Jeffrey, and D'Vera Cohn. 2008. "U.S. Population Projections: 2005–2050." Washington, DC: Pew Hispanic Center.

———. 2009a. "Mexican Immigrants: How Many Come? How Many Leave?" Washington, DC: Pew Hispanic Center, July.

———. 2009b. "A Portrait of Unauthorized Immigrants in the United States." Washington, DC: Pew Hispanic Center.

———. 2010. "U.S. Unauthorized Immigration Flows Are Down Sharply Since Mid-Decade." Washington, DC: Pew Hispanic Center, September 1.

———. 2011. "Unauthorized Immigrant Population: National and State Trends, 2010." Washington, DC: Pew Hispanic Center, February.

Passel, Jeffrey S., Wendy Wang, and Paul Taylor. 2010. "Marrying Out: One-in-Seven New U.S. Marriages is Interracial or Interethnic." Washington DC: Pew Research Center, June 4.

Pastor, Manuel, and Ronda Ortiz. 2009. "Immigrant Integration in Los Angeles: Strategic Directions for Funders." University of Southern California, Center for the Study of Immigrant Integration.

Pastor, Manuel, Justin Scoggins, Jennifer Tran, and Rhonda Ortiz. 2010. "Economic Benefits of Immigrant Authorization in California." University of Southern California, Center for the Study of Immigrant Integration. http://csii.usc.edu/economic _benefits.html.

Pattillo-McCoy, Mary. 2000. *Black Picket Fences: Privilege and Peril Among the Black Middle Class.* Chicago: University of Chicago Press.

Perlmann, Joel. 2005. *Italians Then, Mexicans Now: Immigrant Origins and Second-Generation Progress, 1890–2000.* New York: Russell Sage Foundation.

Perlmann, Joel, and Roger Waldinger. 1997. "Second Generation Decline? Children of Immigrants, Past and Present: A Reconsideration." *International Migration Review* 31 (4): 893–922.

Perlmann, Joel, and Mary Waters. 2007. "Intermarriage and Multiple Identities." In *The New Americans: A Guide to Immigration Since 1965,* edited by Mary C. Wagers and Reed Udea, 110–23. Cambridge, MA: Harvard University Press.

Pessar, Patricia. 1999. "The Role of Gender, Households, and Social Networks in the Migration Process: A Review and Appraisal." In *The Handbook of International Migration,* edited by Charles Hirschman, Philip Kasinitz, and Josh DeWind, 53–70. New York: Russell Sage Foundation.

Pew Forum on Religion and Public Life. 2010. "Religion and the Issues: Results from the 2010 Annual Religion and Public Life Survey." Washington DC: Pew Research Center.

Pew Hispanic Center. 2011. "The Mexican-American Boom: Births Overtake Immigration." Washington DC: Pew Hispanic Center, July.

Phelan, Patricia, Ann Locke Davidson, and Hanh Cao Yu. 1991. "Students' Multiple Worlds: Navigating the Borders of Family, Peer, and School Cultures." In *Cultural Diversity: Implications for Education,* edited by Patricia Phelan and Ann L. Davidson, 52–88. New York: Teachers College Press.

Phelps, Edmunds. 1972. "The Statistical Theory of Racism and Sexism." *American Economic Review* 62 (4): 659–61.

Pitt, Leonard. 1999. *Decline of the Californios: A Social History of the Spanish-Speaking Californias, 1846–1890.* Berkeley: University of California Press.

Portes, Alejandro. 1998. "Social Capital: Its Origins and Applications in Modern Sociology." *Annual Review of Sociology* 24: 1–24.

Portes, Alejandro, Patricia Fernández-Kelly, and William Haller. 2005. "Segmented Assimilation on the Ground: The New Second Generation in Early Adulthood." *Ethnic and Racial Studies* 28: 1000–40.

———. 2009. "The Adaptation of the Immigrant Second Generation in America: A Theoretical Overview and Recent Evidence." *Journal of Ethnic and Migration Studies* 35: 1077–1104.

Portes, Alejandro, and Rubén G. Rumbaut. 2001. *Legacies: The Story of the Immigrant Second Generation*. Berkeley: University of California Press.

Portes, Alejandro, and Min Zhou. 1993. "The New Second Generation: Segmented Assimilation and Its Variants." *Annals of the American Academy of Political and Social Science* 530: 74–96.

"Pregnancy Rates Up for Hispanic Teens, Numbers Decline for Blacks and Whites." 2005. *Atlanta Journal-Constitution*, May 21.

Raijman, Rebecca, and Marta Tienda. 1999. "Immigrants' Socioeconomic Progress Post-1965: Forging Mobility or Survival?" In *The Handbook of International Migration: The American Experience*, edited by Charles Hirchman, Philip Kasinitz, and J. DeWind, 239–56. New York: Russell Sage.

———. 2003. "Ethnic Foundations of Economic Transactions: Mexican and Korean Immigrant Entrepreneurs in Chicago." *Ethnic and Racial Studies* 26 (5): 783–801.

Reed, Deborah, Laura E. Hill, Christopher Jepson, and Hans P. Johnson. 2005. "Educational Progress Across Immigrant Generations in California." San Francisco: Public Policy Institute of California.

Reimers, David, M. 1985. *Still the Golden Door: The Third World Comes to America*. New York: Columbia University Press.

Rist, Ray. 1970. "Student Social Class and Teacher Expectations: The Self-Fulfilling Prophecy in Ghetto Education." *Harvard Educational Review* 40: 411–51.

Rivas-Rodriguez, Maggie. 2005. *Mexican Americans and World War II*. Austin: University of Texas Press.

Rodriguez, Gregory. 1996. "The Emerging Latino Middle Class." Pepperdine, CA: Pepperdine Institute for Public Policy.

———. 2008. *Mongrels, Bastards, Orphans, and Vagabonds: Mexican Immigration and the Future of Race in America*. New York: Pantheon.

Roediger, David. 2005. *Working Toward Whiteness: How America's Immigrants Became White*. New York: Basic Books.

Roehling, Patricia, Lorna Hernandez Jarvis, and Heather Swope. 2005. "Variations in Negative Work-Family Spillover Among White, Black, and Hispanic American Men and Women: Does Ethnicity Matter?" *Journal of Family Issues* 26 (6): 840–65.

Romero, Mary. 2000. *Maid in the USA*. New York: Routledge.

Romo, Richard. 1983. *East Los Angeles: History of a Barrio*. Austin: University of Texas Press.

Roschelle, Anne, N. 1997. *No More Kin: Exploring Race, Class, and Gender in Family Networks*. Thousand Oaks, CA: Sage Publications.

Roscigno, Vincent. 1998. "Race and the Reproduction of Educational Disadvantage." *Social Forces* 76: 1033–60.

Roscigno, Vincent, and J. W. Ainsworth-Darnell. 1999. "Race, Cultural Capital, and Educational Resources: Persistent Inequalities and Achievement Returns." *Sociology of Education* 72 (3): 157–78.

Rowan, Brian, and Andrew Miracle Jr. 1983. "Systems of Ability Grouping and the Stratification of Achievement in Elementary Schools." *Sociology of Education* 56: 133–44.

Rumbaut, Rubén. 2009. "Pigments of Our Imagination." In *How the U.S. Racializes Latinos: White Hegemony and Its Consequences,* edited by José A. Cobas, Jorge Duany, and Joe R. Feagin, 15–36. Boulder, CO: Paradigm Publishers.

Rumbaut, Rubén, and Goldie Komaie. 2009. "Immigration and Adult Transitions." *Transition to Adulthood* 20 (1): 43–66.

Rumbaut, Rubén, Douglass Massey, and Frank Bean. 2006. "Linguistic Life Expectancies: Immigrant Language Retention in Southern California." *Population and Development Review* 32: 447–60.

Sabah, Georges, and Mehdi Bozorgmehr. 2001. "Population Change: Immigrant and Ethnic Transformation." In *Strangers at the Gates: New Immigrants in Urban America,* edited by Roger Waldinger, 79–108. Berkeley: University of California Press.

Sanchez, George. 1995. *Becoming Mexican American: Ethnicity, Culture, and Identity in Chicano Los Angeles, 1900–1945.* New York: Oxford University Press.

Sanders, J., and Victor Nee. 1996. "Immigrant Self-Employment: The Family as Social Capital and the Value of Human Capital." *American Sociological Review* 61: 231–49.

Santa Ana, Otto. 2002. *Brown Tide Rising: Metaphors of Latinos in Contemporary American Public Discourse.* Austin: University of Texas Press.

Santibañez, Lucrecia, Georges Vernez, and Paula Razquin. 2005. *Education in Mexico: Challenges and Opportunities.* Santa Monica, CA: Rand Corporation.

Sarkisian, Natalia, Mariana Gerena, and Naomi Gerstel. 2007. "Extended Family Integration Among Euro and Mexican Americans: Ethnicity, Gender and Class. *Journal of Marriage and Family* 69: 40–54.

Schleef, Deborah, and H. B. Calvacanti. 2009. *Latinos in Dixie: Class and Assimilation in Richmond, Virginia.* Albany: State University of New York Press.

Segura, Denise. 1992. "Chicanas in White Collar Jobs: 'You Have to Prove Yourself More.'" *Sociological Perspectives* 35: 163–82.

Shapiro, Tom. 2004. *The Hidden Cost of Being African American: How Wealth Perpetuates Inequality.* New York: Oxford University Press.

Shelton, Jason, and Wilson, George. 2006. "Socioeconomic Status and Racial Group Interests Among Black Americans." *Sociological Spectrum* 26: 183–204.

Silverstein, Merril, and Vern Bengston. 1997. "Intergenerational Solidarity and the Structure of Adult Child–Parent Relationships in American Families." *American Journal of Sociology* 103: 429–60.

Simmel, Georg. 1950. *The Sociology of Georg Simmel*. Translated by Kurt Wolff, 402–8. New York: Free Press.

Singer, Audrey. 2008. "Twenty-First-Century Gateways." In *21st Century Gateways: Immigrant Incorporation in Suburban America*, edited by Audrey Singer, Susan W. Hardwick, and Caroline B. Brettell, 3–37. Washington, DC: Brookings Institution Press.

Skocpol, Theda, and Morris P. Fiorina. 1999. "Making Sense of the Civic Engagement Debate." In *Civic Engagement in American Democracy*, edited by Theda Skocpol and Morris P. Fiorina, 1–23. Washington, DC: Brookings Institution Press.

Skrentny, John D. 2002. *The Minority Rights Revolution*. Cambridge, MA: Belknap Press of Harvard University Press.

Skrentny, John D., and Micah Bell-Redman. 2011. "Comprehensive Immigration Reform and the Dynamics of Statutory Enforcement." *Yale Law Journal Online* 120: 325–45.

Smith, James P. 2003. "Assimilation Across Latino Generations." *American Economic Review* 93 (2): 315–19.

———. 2006. "Immigrants in the Labor Market." *Journal of Labor Economics* 24: 203–33.

Smith, Robert Courtney. 2002. "Race, Ethnicity and Gender in the School Outcomes of Second Generation Mexican Americans in New York." In *Latinos in the 21st Century*, edited by Marcelo Suarez-Orozco and Mariela Paez, 110–25. Berkeley: University of California Press.

———. 2005. *Mexican New York: Transnational Lives of New Immigrants*. Berkeley: University of California Press.

———. 2008. "Horatio Alger Lives in Brooklyn: Extra-Family Support, Intra-Family Dynamics, and Socially Neutral Operating Identities in Exceptional Mobility Among Children of Mexican Immigrants." *Annals of the American Academy of Political and Social Science* 620: 37–61.

Snow, David. 2001. "Collective Identity and Expressive Forms." In *International Encyclopedia of the Social and Behavioral Sciences*, edited by Neil Smelser and Paul D. Bates, 2212–19. Oxford: Pergamon Press.

Stack, Carol, B. 1974. *All Our Kin: Strategies for Survival in a Black Community*. New York: Harper and Row.

Stein, Mark L., Mark Berends, Douglass Fuchs, Kristen McMaster, Laura Saenz, et al. 2008. "Scaling Up an Early Reading Program." *Educational Evaluation and Policy Analysis* 30: 368–88.

Sullivan, Dennis, and Andrea Ziegert. 2008. "Hispanic Immigrant Poverty." *Population Research and Policy Review* 27 (6): 667–87.

Suro, Roberto. 1998. *Strangers Among Us: Latino Lives in a Changing America*. New York: Vintage Books.

Suro, Roberto, and Jeffrey Passel. 2003. "The Rise of the Second Generation." Washington, DC: Pew Hispanic Center.

Takaki, Ronald. 1993. *A Different Mirror: A History of Multicultural America*. Boston: Little, Brown.

Taylor, Paul, Cary Funk, and Courtney Kennedy. 2005. "Baby Boomers Approach Age 60: From the Age of Aquarius to the Age of Responsibility." Washington, DC: Pew Research Center.

Taylor, Steven, and Robert Bogdan. 1998. *Introduction to Qualitative Research Methods*. New York: Wiley.

Telles, Eddie, and Vilma Ortiz. 2008. *Generations of Exclusion: Mexican Americans, Assimilation, and Race*. New York: Russell Sage Foundation.

Tienda, Marta, and Faith Mitchell, eds. 2006. *Multiple Origins, Uncertain Destinies*. Washington, DC: National Academy Press.

Tovar, Jessica, and Cynthia Feliciano. 2009. "'Not Mexican-American, but Mexican'" *Latino Studies* 7 (2): 197–221.

U.S. Bureau of the Census. 1972. "1970 Census of Population and Housing. Census tracts. Anaheim-Santa Ana-Garden Grove, Calif. Standard Metropolitan Statistical Area." Washington, DC: U.S. Bureau of the Census.

———. 2000. "American FactFinder: Summary Files 1, 2, and 3." Washington DC: U.S. Bureau of the Census. www.factfinder.census.gov.

———. 2008. "Social, Economic, and Housing Statistics Division: Poverty." Washington DC: U.S. Bureau of the Census. http://www.census.gov/hhes/www/poverty/data/threshld/thresho8.html.

———. 2010. "State and County QuickFacts for Cudahy City." http://quickfacts.census.gov/qfd/states/06/0617498.html.

Valdez, Zulema. 2011. *The New Entrepreneurs: How Race, Class, and Gender Shape American Enterprise*. Stanford, CA: Stanford University Press.

Valenzuela, Abel. 1999. "Gender Role and Settlement Activities Among Children and Their Immigrant Families." *American Behavioral Scientist* 42 (4): 720–42.

Vasquez, Jessica. 2011. *Mexican Americans Across Generations: Immigrant Families, Racial Realities*. New York: New York University Press.

Vega, William. 1995. "The Study of Latino Families." In *Understanding Latino Families: Scholarship, Policy and Practice*, edited by Ruth E. Zembrana, 3–17. Thousand Oaks, CA: Sage.

Venkatesh, Sudhir. 2006. *Off the Books: The Underground Economy of the Urban Poor*. Cambridge, MA: Harvard University Press.

Villenas, Sofia. 2001. Latina Mothers and Small-Town Racisms. *Anthropology and Education Quarterly* 32 (1): 3–28.

Waldinger, Roger, and Cynthia Feliciano. 2004. "Will the Second Generation Experience 'Downward Assimilation'?" *Ethnic and Racial Studies* 27 (3): 376–402.

Waldinger, Roger, and Jennifer Lee. 2001. "New Immigrants in Urban America." In *Strangers at the Gates,* edited by Roger Waldinger, 30–79. Berkeley: University of California Press.

Waldinger, Roger, and Michael Lichter. 2003. *How the Other Half Works.* Berkeley: University of California Press.

Warner, R. Stephen. 2007. "The Role of Religion in the Process of Segmented Assimilation." *Annals of the American Academy of Political and Social Science* 612 (1): 100–115.

Warner, W. Lloyd, and Leo Srole. 1945. *The Social Systems of American Ethnic Groups.* New Haven, CT: Yale University Press.

Waters, Mary C. 1990. *Ethnic Options: Choosing Identities in America.* Berkeley: University of California Press.

———. 1999. *Black Identities: West Indian Immigrant Dreams and American Realities.* New York: Russell Sage Foundation.

Waters, Mary C., and Tomás R. Jiménez. 2005. "Assessing Immigrant Assimilation: New Empirical and Theoretical Challenges." *Annual Review of Sociology* 31: 105–25.

Weber, Max. 1978. *Economy and Society.* Berkeley: University of California Press.

Wirth, Louis. 1928. *The Ghetto.* Chicago: University of Chicago Press.

"Workplace Diversity Practices: How Has Diversity and Inclusion Changed over Time? A Comparative Examination: 2010 and 2005." 2010. Alexandria, VA: Society for Human Resource Management (SHRM), October 12.

Yamamoto, Eric. 1999. *Interracial Justice: Conflict and Reconciliation in Post–Civil Rights America.* New York: New York University Press.

Yancey, George. 2003. *Who Is White? Latinos, Asians, and the New Black/Nonblack Divide.* Boulder, CO: Lynne Rienner Publishers.

Zamora, Emilio. 1993. *The World of Mexican Workers in Texas.* College Station: Texas A&M University Press.

Zavella, Patricia. 1997. "Reflection on Diversity Among Chicanas." In *Challenging Fronteras: Structuring Latina and Latino Lives in the United States,* edited by Mary Romero, Pierrette Hondagneu-Sotelo, and Vilma Ortiz, 187–94. New York: Routledge.

Zhou, Min, and Carl Bankston III. 1998. *Growing Up American: How Vietnamese Children Adapt to Life in the United States.* New York: Russell Sage Foundation.

Zhou, Min, and Susan Kim. 2006. "Community Forces, Social Capital, and Educational Achievement." *Harvard Educational Review* 76 (1): 1–29.

Zhou, Min, and Jennifer Lee. 2007. "Becoming Ethnic or Becoming American? Reflecting on the Divergent Pathways to Social Mobility and Assimilation Among the New Second Generation." *Du Bois Review* 4 (1): 189–205.

Zhou, Min, Jennifer Lee, Jody Agius Vallejo, Rosie Tafoya-Estrada, and Yang Sao Xion. 2008. "Success Attained, Deterred, and Denied." *Annals of American Academy of Political and Social Science* 620: 37–61.

Zolberg, Aristide R. 2006. *A Nation by Design: Immigration Policy in the Fashioning of America*. Cambridge, MA: Harvard University Press.

Zolberg, Aristide, and Litt Woon Long. 1999. "Why Islam Is Like Spanish: Cultural Incorporation in Europe and the United States." *Politics & Society* 27: 5–38.

Index

agriculture: Bracero Program and, 30–31; and first wave of Mexican migration, 28–29

ALB (Association of Latinas in Business). *See* Association of Latinas in Business (ALB)

Alba, Richard, 17, 108

Americanization. *See* assimilation

AP classes, 60–62, 68–69

Asian immigrants, 28–29

assimilation: anti-immigration sentiments and, 40–41; assumptions on Mexican Americans, 174, 184–85; boundary-oriented perspective on, 17–18; in business practices, 157–59; education and, 7–8; ethnic identity and, 104–10, 139–40, 180; future of Mexican Americans, 181–84; identificational, 106–7, 127, 141; and interclass relations, 117–20; of middle-class Mexican Americans, 124–27, 175; perspectives on, 2–3; and socioeconomic background, 70, 175–76, 181; study of, 2–3; theories on, 12–18; white ethnic, 14, 17

Association of Latinas in Business (ALB): combating stereotypes through, 160–64; community context of, 150–53; and creation of minority culture of mobility, 156–59; establishment and purpose of, 153–56; and intraclass conflict, 164–70; and limitations of minority culture of mobility, 170–72; overview of, 23, 147–53; social capital and, 186–87

attrition, ethnic, 131

baby clause, citizenship through native-born, 35–36, 55

Baca Zinn, Maxine, 144

Ballet Folklórico, 134–35, 136

Bean, Frank, 139

Beason-Hammon Alabama Taxpayer and Citizen Protection Act (2011), 40

Bettie, Julie, 121

blurred boundaries, 105–6, 141, 157–59

boundary crossing, 105, 141

boundary-oriented perspective on assimilation, 17–18

Bracero era, 30–32

business associations. *See* professional associations

business ownership, 54–55, 57, 149

business practices, 116, 157–59, 164, 181

Carter, Prudence, 16

census, racial classification in, 107–8

Chavez, Leo, 40

Chávez, Maria, 116

Chicano movement, 33, 129

childbearing, stereotypes on, 163–64, 168

children: citizenship through native-born, 35–36, 55; employment of Mexican Americans, 53–54

"Chuppies," 125

citizenship: through native-born children, 35–36, 55; policy recommendations for, 185–86. *See also* legal status

civic participation, 22–23, 144–56. *See also* professional associations